THE WOLF
OF THE
KREMLIN

Also by Stuart Kahan
The Expectant Fathers Survival Kit
For Divorced Fathers Only
Do I Really Need a Lawyer?
Photography: What's the Law?
The Business of Photography
The Stock Handbook
Professional Business Practices

THE WOLF
OF THE
KREMLIN

Stuart Kahan

WILLIAM MORROW AND COMPANY, INC.
New York

Library of Congress Cataloging-in-Publication Data

Kahan, Stuart.
The wolf of the Kremlin.
Bibliography: p.
1. Kaganovich, L. M. (Lazaŕ Moiseevich), 1893–
2. Police—Soviet Union—Biography. 3. Secret service—
Soviet Union—Biography. I. Title.
HV7911. K24K24   1987   363.2'83'0924   87-13900
ISBN 0-688-07529-0

PRINTED IN THE UNITED STATES OF AMERICA

FIRST EDITION

1 2 3 4 5 6 7 8 9 10

BOOK DESIGN BY JAY ADDANTE

to my mother and father

Preface

Some of my own family will not like what they read here. That's unfortunate but realistic. When most people set out in search of their "roots," they look for relatives who were members of a royal family, or perhaps a physician who discovered a cure for a dread disease, or a great statesman who kept the peace. In my own family, I found a number of these "good" people, including honest tradesmen and laborers. But the leader of the clan, the one relative who towered above them all, was, to put it mildly, a devil. That relative exuded evil, an evil that put millions of people to death, an evil that turned against his own people.

The purpose of this book is to detail what this man did and how he did it, how he survived, and how far he went. But, more important are the reasons behind the actions. Here is the prime example of the species known to my fellow landsmen as "the self-hating Jew."

The subject is L. M. Kaganovich, who was known as the "Apparatus of Terror" under Stalin in the Soviet Union.

There have been no books on this man whatsoever. There are no monographs on him or memoirs by him. Not even the *samizdat* ("underground") has published any extensive material on him, and his country's own press has not mentioned him in three decades. Thus, what makes this book so important—a first, if you will—is that the bulk of the source material comes from the subject himself, Uncle Lazar Moiseyevich Kaganovich.

I hope that this book will put to rest some of the conflicting material previously written about Lazar Kaganovich, and at the same time I trust it will give others a basis for additional analysis of the years of his power.

Except for the subject, who at this writing is still alive and living in Moscow, I have had to respect the anonymity of many of my sources. A law that is still in existence forbids Soviet citizens from "furnishing information" to a foreigner, so that any story, even one told in confidence, becomes a crime. The crime of this story, in my judgment, must be told.

AFFIDAVIT

State of New York :
                    : ss.:
County of New York:

    JACK D. KAHAN, being duly sworn, deposes and says:

    1) I am the father of STUART KAHAN, author of the book presently entitled "The Wolf of the Kremlin."

    2) Most of the material included in the above-mentioned book is a result of conversations with two primary sources: LAZAR MOISEYEVICH KAGANOVICH, about whom the book is written, and MORRIS LEVICK KAGANOVICH, Lazar's first cousin, closest boyhood friend, and my father.

    3) The information from MORRIS KAGANOVICH was obtained in personal conversations during the years 1958-76. Such conversations took place in New York City, Philadelphia, Pa., and Cape May, New Jersey. They were all in English.

    4) The information from LAZAR KAGANOVICH was obtained in a personal conversation in Moscow, USSR, on September 23, 1981 at Lazar's apartment on the Frunzenskaya. No photographs or tape recordings were permitted. The conversation was in Yiddish.

    5) I had accompanied my son, STUART KAHAN, to Moscow for the purpose of meeting LAZAR KAGANOVICH and our trip was reported in the Philadelphia Bulletin and the Jewish Exponent.

JACK D. KAHAN

Sworn to before me this

⌐/ day of July, 1983

ROBERT M. CAVALLO
Notary Public, State of New York
No. 31-4500009
Qualified in New York County
Commission Expires March 1, 1985

This affidavit, signed by my father, attests to our trip to the Soviet Union and identifies the sources of the material in this book.

По сведениям адресного бюро

Проживает с «   »,   19   г.

в Москве, дом № _50_ , квартира № _384_

по улице _Фрунзенская наб_

_107_ отделение милиции

в области _____

район, город, поселок, село, деревня, улица

Справку наводил _____

_22/IX_   198_ г.

ПО «Вымпел» УИМ, 1978 г. з 2893 —100'000

Парк культуры ТРАМ

Current address of Lazar Kaganovich,
as given to me by the Soviet government

Цена 3 коп.

С П Р А В К А
Московского адресного бюро

Фамилия _Каганович_

Имя _Лазарь_   Отчество _Моисеевич_

Год рождения _1893_   Место рождения: город г. _Киев_

область _____ район _____

село, деревня _____

Род занятий _____

Предполагаемое местожительство _____

Acknowledgments

This book has been in the making for more years than I care to remember. The information contained within these pages has been culled from so many sources that it would be totally unfair to cite just a few people. Obviously, much of the credit must go to those that have spoken to me and who have supplied the bulk of the material. But, it would also be unfair not to mention certain individuals who had so much to do with seeing that these words reach the printed page.

First and foremost is my father, Jack D. Kahan, who accompanied me to the Soviet Union despite countless warnings against such a trip and who was the one person who supported everything I wanted to do. His encouragement was constant and unswerving . . . and thank God for his command of Yiddish. He, like me, did not have the words *can't do* in his vocabulary.

Second, I must thank Harrison E. Salisbury for his superb and objective guidance. He was the one who said, "Go ahead and write the book. Don't just do an outline. Write what needs to be written. It's a story that must be told. There will be someone out there who will understand what this is all about and will believe in its importance."

ACKNOWLEDGMENTS

He was right, which brings me to Bruce Lee, the editor at William Morrow who saw that importance. To him, I owe my admiration and respect. This is an editor graced with enthusiasm and professionalism.

Then, there is Grace D. Polk, who I acknowledge for her relentless research. In her quest for information, she poured over countless newspaper clippings and books in a multitude of languages (she is proficient in many) to supply much of the background material.

And, of course, there is my lovely wife, Rosie, my own jewel from the Nile, who watched me pound away at the typewriter while she tripped over papers, boxes, and books that were strewn from one end of our house to another. But, she never said quit.

I am indebted to all these people . . . and to my own persistence. As far as I am concerned, these are the elements that make a book truly fly.

Contents

Introduction

Even when the sun is out, Moscow is a gray-and-tan mass. The huge, stone buildings, devoid of any subtlety, appear to soak up the sun's rays like giant sponges.

I have never really understood this city. It is one of the cleanest, most orderly, and best-run cities I have ever seen, and I have lived in a number of them, all over the world. But this one is an enigma, a sprawling blob of concrete containing 8 million people. In comparison, New York City is known to be in constant motion; it is said that even the garbage moves. In Rome, there is gaiety, laughter, and the ability of its citizens to pretend that nothing serious ever happens. In Tokyo, 11 million people think and act as one.

Moscow, though, is different. The city's surface is calm, cool, aloof, stoic, but underneath, it is poised ominously, ready to explode at any given moment.

I stare out the hotel window and watch the Muscovites troop toward the subway. The rush hour is on. It is time for me to start. After five years of planning, this is now the moment to show what I have learned and how well I have learned it.

I double-check the address for the last time. It has been memorized for the past year, ever since I secured it. Five years it had taken to locate someone, and I had succeeded only because I had slipped enough rubles—*a nalevo*— under the table. A city without phone books always presents a problem, and a city that doesn't want to relinquish a particular address or phone number presents an even greater challenge.

I tear the paper into small pieces and flush them down the toilet. I give myself a final search. No camera, no tape recorder, no guidebook. Only a simple English-Russian/Russian-English dictionary with a pronunciation key. That will be enough. It has to be enough.

I head toward the Metro, one of the joys of Moscow, a sparkling-clean subway system that is an underground museum with stainless-steel columns, granite walls, stained-glass windows, mosaic ceiling tiles, statues galore—and it is efficiently run, cheap, and readily available.

I step onto the high-speed escalator, which plunges two hundred yards in fewer than sixty seconds, and I think back over what has transpired from the time I found that article in the newspaper some five years ago. It said that he was still alive. I chuckled inwardly. That old bastard will outlive everybody. He must be well into his nineties by now, and I had heard about him for most of my forty-seven years. I remember how, too. It was always in whispers, always around the kitchen table, never in public, and never in front of nonfamily. It was as if we were trying to minimize who he was and treat him like a figment of our imagination, good for a dinnertime conversation but not to be believed after you left the table.

And yet I couldn't simply close my eyes and will him to go away. From the moment my surname was changed, my interest—an obsession—with this side of the family grew and grew. After all, how many people have an uncle who remained in power in the world's largest country for over forty years? How many people have an uncle who was the right-hand man of the most hated dictator the country ever had? How many people have an aunt who was this dictator's wife and another uncle who was this dictator's commissar of aviation?

Although Rosa and Mikhail were important, it was Lazar who controlled the center stage. Lazar Moiseyevich Kaganovich, Stalin's closest confidant, the chairman of the Soviet Presidium, the man who set up the amalgamation of the state security forces that later became the infamous KGB, the man who personally supervised the purges that ran rampant through Russia in the thirties and forties, the man who instituted more restrictions and quotas on the Jews than anyone else, the man who urged and orchestrated the deaths of 20 million people, the man who brought Khrushchev to power, the man who was in charge of building this fantastic subway system—which bore his name for over twenty years—the ultimate Jew-hater himself, and the only Jew in the hierarchy. That is who I am on my way to see.

"Uncle Lazar," as he was reverently called by the entire family (mostly out of fear), is now a half-hour away as I step onto the first car of the Kaluzhsko (orange) line.

I am fully aware that most people research their family trees looking for royalty, seeking the princes and princesses, the kings and queens, the great peacemakers. But, here I am en route to meet the most "ruthless man" (as Khrushchev termed him) ever to sit in the Kremlin, with the purpose of writing about him, exposing him.

However, I need to know more than just the "whats" and "whens." I need to understand the "whys." Why a man would do the things he has done against his own people, his own religion. He had turned his back on everything he had ever learned. That was what I was after to make the story complete: the Rosebud.

I had spent practically a lifetime following his exploits and those of his sister and brothers. I had read extensively and attended lectures by wise political scientists at one college after another. I had taken a smattering of information from one source, a smattering from another. One prominent author said Lazar was this, another thought he was that. But nobody, nowhere, seemed to have pinned down exactly what had happened during the tumultuous years after Lenin's death, when this enormous nation moved grudgingly and belatedly into the Industrial Revolution, emerging as the superpower it is today.

I had the source material. I had the inside track on that romantic and somewhat glorious period of Russian history, and the time was ripe to expose it.

My mind quickly refocuses. I must get it back to the plan. I can't wander too far, at least not now. I know how things are done in this land. They are not done as we read in spy books. I used to laugh hysterically at the books that flooded the market on the Soviet secret police, the KGB. Most of them were completely removed from reality. I became convinced that the only person who can understand a Russian is another Russian.

I know I am not being followed. I can feel it. There is even a way to find out, by doing the illogical. This is the source of Russian logic, the illogical. I am simply taking a subway ride, not looking around, not fidgeting, not checking notes in my pocket, not intensely studying the map on the wall, not pretending to be someone else. Instead, I am sleeping.

As the train rumbles on, I count the stops. At every one, I lift my head to see the people coming in and to make mental notes of who is around me. Back to sleep. After all, no one on a "spy search" would be sleeping.

My memory keeps a visual record of the people on the train. At each stop, it subtracts and adds. Now, *I* am the person doing the watching.

At the Kirovskaya station I push my way off along with the silent crowd and edge toward the red-line train. Again, I make mental notes of who is in front of me. I look back when I reach the bottom of the escalator, pretending to check my footing. Only two persons seem familiar: a short, fat woman with a large pimple on the end of her nose and a man in a black-and-white checkered hat. She is obviously going shopping, from the string bag she carries already filled with food items, while he looks like a cement worker, from the dried, white blotches on his overalls. Certainly not the trenchcoat types that the movies depict.

I board the red-line train for the seven-stop ride to the Frunzenskaya station. Coming out of the Metro, I turn and walk into a small park opposite the Moscow River. This is a quiet part of the city, with shade trees along the riverbank fronting large, cream-colored apartment houses that remind me of the beauties lining Riverside Drive in New York City.

I sit down on a bench and look at the water. Anyone following me will now have to either walk by or stop, too. I casually glance to my right and then to my left. No one around. Nothing of importance is happening.

I wait ten minutes and then leave the bench for the building with the number 50 etched into its side. The next semihurdle will be the *dezhurnaya*. These are older women who are hired by the state to sit in building foyers and watch the comings and goings. I know I have to move quickly if she is there. Any hesitation on my part will lead to questions.

An old woman in a baggy sweater is sitting at the desk looking

16

down at a magazine. As I open the door, she looks up. I nod, utter *Dobraye ootra*—"good morning"— and immediately head for the stairs in front of me.

An elevator is to the left, but I can't afford to use it. If there is the slightest uncertainty as to how it works, I will be considered suspicious and bombarded with queries as to who I am and where I am going.

Slowly, I start up the stairs. I can't rush and I can't look back. It must appear that I know where I am going. When I reach the first landing, I drop my eyes. I catch a glimpse of the *dezhurnaya*. Her head is buried in the magazine.

I walk up five more flights, and then I see it. I can feel my heart starting and stopping. Number 384 is looking back at me, and it seems to cover the entire apartment door.

I look around. I must think this out.

A ring on the doorbell can bring an inquisitive person from a neighboring apartment. Yet, a soft knock on the door may not be heard by such an old man. The hell with it. I decide to ring the bell. A short, quick burst. At ten on a Wednesday morning, who can be home? Men and women are away working, and children are in school. Only the old and infirm will be here, and history has shown that they will be of no threat.

There is silence. I wait and count to ten. Again, I ring. I hear footsteps, heavy ones, as if they belong to the feet of someone twenty years of age. Can it be? Was I given a wrong number?

Somebody is coming to the door. I take a deep breath, and then I hear it, a strong, aggressive voice.

O chom?—"What is it?"

It takes me a second or two to realize what is being said. I quickly answer with part of my prepared statement.

"*Ya plemyannik, Amerikanets.*—'I am your nephew. American. Your nephew from America.' "

The voice again. "*U menya nyet rodstvennikov*—'I have no relatives.' "

I answer, "*Nyet, nyet, nyet. Ya plemyannik. Ya plemyannik.*"

There is silence once more. I hold my breath. *Open the door, please,* I murmur to myself. *Open, please.*

The voice. "*Vos zogt ir?*"

The language has changed. He is—he is speaking—damn, it is Yiddish. It has to be him. Who else would—? Immediately, I respond.

17

"Ikh bet dikh. Ofn . . . ofn . . . of.—"Open, please." *"Ikh bet dikh."*

Another deep breath. I hear clicking sounds. The locks are being turned. I count. *One, two, three, four.* That sly old bastard still knows how to protect himself. The door swings slightly ajar. A massive chain keeps it open to about two inches. There is darkness. He can see me, but I can't see him. No wonder he stayed in control for as long as he did. The voice again.

"Vos zogt ir?—'What are you saying?' "

I try the best Russian I can muster, throwing in some Yiddish wherever possible. "I am from America. I am Morris's family. Please let me in. Please, please."

I stare at the black spot.

The door closes. He is shutting me out. Words tumble from my mouth. "Stop . . . stop, I am the only relative you have left who will talk to you. Why abandon me like you did the rest of the family all these years? Even Morris and Uncle Levick. Goddammit, why even me? Why pick on me?"

I can feel the tears forming. It is quiet.

Then metal slides against metal. He is removing the chain. My eyes close. I can feel the knob on the door being turned. A lifetime of stories, years of research, and all the answers are on the other side of seven inches of wood.

The door is opening. I sense it. There is a slight change of light, a rush of air. I seem to have stopped breathing altogether. Slowly, I open my eyes. I begin to focus. I see a massive face in front of me on a man of my height, a shock of gray hair on the sides of his head, a heavy gray mustache, dark brown eyes set wide apart. He is my little brother at ninety years of age. Larry, it is you sixty years from now. The man stares back at me.

"Uncle Lazar . . ." I mutter.

He nods.

I am face to face with the Wolf himself.

The door opens wide, and the large figure steps to the side. He says nothing. The invitation has been extended. I walk straight ahead. It is a short walk to the living room. There is a small pullman kitchen to the left that I catch sight of out of the corner of my eye.

The room is dark but I see a window in the far wall that looks out onto a park below in the back of the building. The top branches of a tree peek just under the window frame. I glance around quickly, aware that he is still standing in the hallway watching me.

The furniture is old and of a dark wood. It looks heavy. There is one couch covered with a green-print slipcover and two brown wing chairs crammed one next to the other. All have doilies on their arms and headrests, a woman's touch, no doubt. I point to them.

"That's Maya," he says. "She visits me once a week. She cleans the apartment and brings some groceries. She is a good person, and I genuinely like her."

Maya is his daughter.

There is a small shelf on the near wall. It is jammed with many photographs in gold-leaf frames depicting different stages in Uncle Lazar's life, including photographs of his associates. Prominent is Stalin. If I hadn't known better, I would have thought that this was Stalin's apartment. One photograph, however, catches my eye. It is Uncle Levick and Morris standing outside Morris's tailor shop in Philadelphia. It must have been taken some fifty years ago. I start to touch it and then hear a no. I back off.

I reach into my coat pocket and pull out an envelope. I hand it to him without saying a word. By now he has come into the room and stands just a few feet from me. His presence is overbearing. The room is small, and he is no longer as big and as powerful, yet he seems to fill the room and to control it.

He takes the envelope and goes to the window, where there is better light. He wears no glasses. He studies the contents intently. I had taken the precaution of bringing photographs of the family to Russia. Many included me. They would be my identification. One, in fact, was similar to the photograph of Uncle Levick and Morris that was now on the shelf.

After a while, he nods and then sits in one of the large, brown wing chairs. He still has not asked me to sit.

From my other pocket, I extract a small bag that contains a raisin pound cake I had bought in the Berioska store at the hotel. His eyebrows shoot up, and now he motions me to sit. He scrutinizes me from the top of my head to my shoes. He looks again at the pictures and then to me until he is completely satisfied.

Minutes go by, and I become aware of a clock on a sidetable. It seems to have the loudest tick I had ever heard. It is unrelenting. Then,

19

too, the excitement I originally felt simply in finding this man is now being replaced by impatience and anxiety. If that was what he was hoping to achieve, it was working. I could feel the tiny apartment begin to close in on me. It is warm, and my mouth is drying.

I am searching for something to say but nothing seems appropriate. The harsh voice speaks again, and what I hear doesn't help.

"Why?" it says.

Only one word. He waits.

In America, my response would have been "Why not?" But I knew that would be foolhardy. I had to give him a good reason, and I emphasize the word *good*. If I told him I was here to write a book, I would find myself back on the street in seconds and perhaps with the KGB at my side. No, I had to be careful. I had thought about this for the past year and still had not decided on what I would finally say.

"I am here because of these," I say, pointing to the photographs now resting on his lap. "I have heard so much all my life. I wanted to meet you and learn more about my grandfather and my great grandfather. I am proud of my family. I want to meet them. I read the papers about you. I had to see you."

My mouth had totally parched.

"There is more," he says. It is not a question; it is a statement of fact.

"Yes, there is more," I answer. "I want to visit Kabany. I want to see the family birthplace. I want to know—" And then I stop and smile. "Uncle Lazar, I even want to know how Bubbah made that great chung," referring to a dish I remembered from my childhood.

Uncle Lazar threw back his head and smiled. It was as if a gate in his memory had been opened. The old bastard had been touched by something as simple as a harsh-tasting stew. But I could also sense that he wanted to talk. What other opportunities did he have? If Maya came here once a week, who else did he talk with at other times? Maybe it was simply a case of being in the right place at the right time. Maybe it was all luck, or fate, as I would have liked to believe. If he would just begin, I felt I could lead him somewhere. If he would just begin.

"The secret of making chung," he says, "is indeed a secret. I don't know. For me, I still like a good, strong cup of *chai*. You are interested to go with this nice-looking cake?"

I quickly rise. He waves me down. He will take care of it.

He comes to his feet and starts toward the pullman kitchen still watching me.

"We will have the *chai* and the cake first. That's important. Then you will tell me who everybody is in the photographs. Agreed?"

He stops and looks at me.

"Yes, sir," I answer.

"Good. First things first."

He turns away from me. I close my eyes and feel the back of the chair against my head. I don't dare to look at my watch. We had made a start. And, from the photographs, his entire life would be seen.

I no longer feel warm. Now a chill comes over me. I need the hot tea. I also know I would be drinking lots of tea before I leave. I look at the pictures. How far back will we go? I put them in some order. I wait for the tea and cake. I am ready.

Prologue

March 5, 1953

Moscow's busiest street is Arbat, a name taken from the Arabic and meaning "district." It runs from Arbatskaya Square, the beginning of the fashionable Kalinin Prospekt clear down to Smolenskaya Square and to the Moscow River. Arbat is considered Moscow's primary commercial artery, a thoroughfare some 260 feet wide on which shops, movie theaters, restaurants, and an endless parade of people appear. Every few blocks, a giant red M can be seen denoting a stop on the famed Metro. Banners, slogans, and signs are everywhere: GLORY TO THE COMMUNIST PARTY OF THE SOVIET UNION is constantly in view.

The huge throngs of people jostle one another, courtesy an unknown quantity, as they push and shove along the street. Yet, it is quiet. There is little in the way of noise. Men dress in overalls with black jackets, and women in somber dresses. Everyone carries a string bag that serves to cart home whatever is available in whatever stores feature the long queues outside.

The routine is the same, day in and day out, except when the signal is heard from the other side of Arbatskaya Square. A strange signal.

It is a peep sound, almost inaudible, which a Russian becomes accustomed to hearing but a foreigner never hears. It is almost like the high pitch that only dogs can hear. And with that sound, the Arbat changes instantly.

All traffic lights switch. One by one they turn to a solid red, clear through to the Mozhaisk. Simultaneously, shops begin closing, doors slamming against their frames. Apartment windows snap shut as though the inhabitants don't want to be a witness to what is about to take place.

People quickly dart into whatever shops remain open, into foyers of buildings, into alleyways, anyplace where they cannot be seen.

They are replaced immediately by what seem like thousands of police who appear seemingly out of the cracks in the sidewalks. They move into position, blocking the side streets into and out of the Arbat. Others take up positions along the curb, some facing the buildings, some facing the street. There is an order to all this, everyone knowing his place. The Arbat comes to a sudden halt. Silence prevails, an almost eerie quality.

First they can be heard. The roar of engines. And then they can be seen.

They come one at a time from the Spassky Gate of the Kremlin, within inches of one another, five, huge, black Chaika limousines. They pick up speed as they race down the Arbat, their headlights blinding anyone foolish enough to look. But these are not the white lights of the typical Russian cars. Instead, they are large, yellow beams that sweep the road in front. Horns wail as the drivers press down on the accelerators.

The cars all have bulletproof glass with steel-plated bodies, the same as used for tanks. They are identical even down to the lack of a license plate. You cannot tell one from the other.

As they roar down the street, they begin to play a game, a planned one, exchanging positions, passing and repassing one another. Five cars playing the child's game of tag on what was minutes before the busiest part of the entire city.

The route they travel is a twelve-mile one from the Kremlin to the dacha at Kuntsevo. Four thousand special agents of the Ministry of State Security (MGB) line the way from one seat of power to the other. They try to catch a glimpse of the man who has ruled their country now for nearly thirty years, the man known only as Stalin. There is little to be seen.

Curtains hide all the backseats. In one car and one car only, there is a passenger, but it is not Stalin. He is a stocky man slumped in his seat, his hair balding, his large mustache showing tinges of gray, his fingers twirling a string of beads. He stares straight ahead. He knows exactly what is happening. He knew it as soon as the telephone rang in his third-floor office just after 8:00 P.M.

The same phone call had already been made to the homes of Malenkov, Beria, Bulganin, and Khrushchev. Calls to these people at this time of the night were not uncommon. Stalin had the habit of ringing his closest associates at any time of the day or night. He had no compunction about that. Other things, yes, but in calling people, he would simply pick up the phone and surprise them with his voice. It immediately put the receiving party on the defensive, something in which Stalin delighted.

But now calls had come from Aleksandr Poskrebyshev, Stalin's secretary. Something was wrong. All five men were told to come immediately.

They had rushed from their homes, driving at breakneck speed over a road that was known as the "governmental route," a section that a Russian not connected with the government would never venture near. People were put to death for violating this sacred parcel of land, and that meant simply not traveling on it.

The yellow headlights of the Chaikas blended with the white of the snow, yielding a strange orange color that seemed ominous. Along the sides of the road stood thousands and thousands of pines, firs and white birches still bare of any foliage from the long winter.

The man in the backseat did not see the trees passing by. He knew that he would have to be at his best when he reached the dacha. He had no time to observe anything around him. He also knew that confusion would greet him. After all, Stalin had not rung for his dinner that evening—already a break with the regular scheme. His bodyguards, his security people, had waited for that summons for hours, not daring to enter their master's sacred chamber, never even thinking about questioning what had not taken place. They knew it would be difficult to enter anyway. Stalin had taken extreme precautions against all possibilities of assassination. Paranoia had already become a part of his daily routine, as integral a part of him as breathing.

The guards knew that the armored doors, the gated windows, the solitary confinement in which he had placed himself would eventually prove to his detriment. Yes, the man in the backseat understood all of this, too, just as he knew all the tricks, all the charades, all the maneuvers, knew them as only the man who had been closest to Stalin for the past four decades could know them.

He also knew that Stalin would now be lying there on the rug, fully clothed, with only his boots off. He would lie in a deep sleep, his final one.

He settled back in the soft cushion of the gray seat and fingered the beads, winding them slowly around one finger and then another, ponderously, cautiously.

Years from now, there would be doubts as to what happened and why. Historians would argue and debate as to what went on during this period, this particular day, and the four days preceding. He smiled. Doubt for them, no question about it. Great waves of it for them.

He put a hand to the curtains and parted them slightly. He peered outside as the car came to a halt in front of the wooden gate that led to the main driveway of the dacha. Of the five cars, his was now the lead one. For sixty years, going back to Kabany, he had known he would eventually be the first one.

His smile turned to a frown. *Uncertainty? Doubts? For them, perhaps, but not for me. Never for me. Not for sixty years . . .*

"Terror is the rule of people who themselves are terrorized."

—*Friedrich Engels*

THE WOLF
OF THE
KREMLIN

1

Kabany is one of the few villages that rarely changed its name, at least not until 1935, and then it changed it for only a short period of time to honor one of its own. Most of the other communities took other names with practically every generation. Not Kabany. It remained what it always was, a small village located on a latitude of 51° 17′ North and a longitude of 29° 41′ East, just slightly east of the Pripet Marshes, a few miles north of the town of Martynowicze, and approximately seventy-five miles northeast of Kiev.

Today, it is known as Novokashirsk and lies in the military grid of 32001, and if asked, the Committee of State Security (KGB) will tell you that it's a restricted area, meaning no foreigners are allowed there. Back in 1893, the only restriction was in trying to keep the people from leaving.

At that time, the town had a population of some 2,600 people. It was split rather unevenly between those of the Jewish persuasion, those of the Christian faith—meaning Russian Orthodox Church—and those who walked a fine line between the two, depending on the latest politics.

Most of the Christians worked in the fields. They were farmers, or "agriculturists," as they called themselves, but they were heavily in the minority. Almost 70 percent of the people were Jewish. They didn't go to the fields. Instead, they worked primarily indoors, making goods. Hemp was a major industry in that area, and garments were made from it: clothing and leather goods, shoes in particular.

The system of survival was relatively simple, grounded in the age-old tradition of barter. The farmers sold some of their crops to people who supplied them with clothing, and vice versa. There was little money to be exchanged. That was a luxury. Food and clothing were necessities, things that many in Kabany couldn't buy.

Kabany, stuck between the Ukraine and Byelorussia, had little else to occupy its inhabitants' time and energy. The basics of life were there: food, clothing, and shelter, the last supplied by the 5 percent of the population who were atheists or, rather, showed allegiance to whatever belief was espoused by the person occupying the throne in St. Petersburg. They provided shelter. For a few potatoes or a pair of shoes, they would render services, constructing the tiniest outhouse or an entire home, the largest of which was nothing more than a three-room cottage sitting on a plot of land twenty-five feet by twenty-five feet. They were pasted together with stones, sticks, moss, and mud. But here the family could ramble about its rooms and could work the small garden that occupied every inch of earth left on the plot.

The inhabitants did more than simply exist. They tried to live. They kept the houses as neat and as clean as they could, desperately fighting the onslaught of winter and the accompanying rainy season, which seemed to be three quarters of the year, and the mud in which boots sunk clear to the knees. Much of their toil was just trying to keep the mud away.

The only other rain came not from the God in the sky, but from the "god" who sat on a velvet throne in the city far to the north. At least once every two to three months, "he" would let them descend, fifty to sixty at a time, on draft horses that looked as though they had been bred specially, each horse some twenty hands high and weighing 2,200 pounds, some brown, some spotted, some black. They would storm in from the north with the leader, atop a white horse, clutching a wilted, yellowed paper in his hand, waving it all around and demanding whatever it wanted.

"In the name of the czar . . ."

The people could sense their coming, especially those that did not work in the fields, the Jews. It was for them.

By 1893, the Russification of minorities had become particularly oppressive, and leading the list were the Jews, whose communities had to withstand pogroms conducted by what were then known as the Black Hundred gangs, which were tolerated by the czarist government. *Tolerated* was not the precise word. They were encouraged to extract some measure of obedience to the throne.

The words *anti-Semite* and *Judophobe* were serious words then. There was a marked difference between the Jewish people and those referred to as "Yids." The Jewish people were known to have had a great culture, with lots of suffering—Christ and Karl Marx were just two prominently mentioned. But, as was said frequently among the Jews, "Those people you see milling around at the bazaar, dealing in the black market, bantering with the soldiers of the czar, they're not Jews. They're Yids."

To the Gentile world, though, they were all thought of as the same. No matter what you perceived yourself as, your passport was stamped in large black letters "Yevrei" ("Jew").

From the south in Kishinev through Kiev and to the north in Minsk, and even beyond, the Jews had settled in an area known as the Pale of Residence. Jews actually were confined there by law. Of Russia's 5 million Jews, only 300,000 managed to live outside, most illegally.

Within this area, they moved about freely, bartering, buying, selling, and, most importantly, being constantly thrust into the public eye. They were seen easily enough. They were middlemen, not hidden from public view but in full vision of all, of the peasants from whom they bought, of the wealthy to whom they sold.

Jews had already been identified in the eyes of the Russian people with everything that was considered decadent: This decadence consisted of their aspiration to personal and social rights. Moreover, they were seen as exploiters, even dangerous revolutionaries, and, thus, contrary to the very nature of Russia and its traditions.

The czar had already handed down the edict: "Jews never sleep and never allow you to sleep." Not one element in Russian society would stand up for them. They were accused of everything, even of using the blood of Christian children to mix with their Passover matzoh.

Therefore, a wave of pogroms swept over the Jews, especially after the murder of Alexander II (thought to be by a Jew) in 1881. The government embarked on a nasty and open anti-Jewish policy that covered the spectrum of activities. It closed the civil service to Jews, forbade them to take academic posts, and made it difficult, if not impossible, for them to enter the professional ranks (doctors, lawyers, scientists). And it unleashed pogroms directed at crushing and destroying the spirit and will of these people.

The czar's main enforcers were the Cossacks. The word *cossack* is derived from the Turkish *quzzak*, meaning "adventurer." Fierce fighters and superb horsemen, the Cossacks had been the last line of defense for the czars of Russia for many centuries. Originally serfs during the sixteenth century, they had organized themselves into fighting bands and sold their services to whomever paid the highest price.

Because of their allegiance to the czars, they were granted many special privileges over the centuries, including local self-government. Traditionally, each Cossack village was ruled by a democractically chosen counsel, and the land was held communally for the use of all. Cossacks were required to enter military service at the age of eighteen, and that service lasted twenty years. They provided their own horses while the government supplied the equipment. They enjoyed a favored status in return for rendering military service.

By 1893, there were 4 million Cossacks in Russia, scattered primarily in the Ukraine (which means "borderland") and other frontier outposts where their prowess made them invaluable front-line guards. The Ukrainian Cossacks were chiefly Russians and Poles and included many runaway serfs.

Feeling themselves a very special group in Russia, pampered by the czars for hundreds of years, they were ready to defend the crown at any confrontation with the people.

This was especially true in 1893, the year that saw not only the death of Peter Ilych Tchaikovsky but, on November 10 in the old-style calendar and November 22 in the new, the birth of an entirely different personality.

Each person leaves his or her own imprint on the world, and this new arrival would indeed make himself felt. He was the third son born to Sasha and Moisev Kaganovich and they named him Lazar Moiseyevich.

Like most children of the time, he was born in the tiny house of his mother and father. There were no hospitals within a seventy-five mile radius and the only faint resemblance to any medical attention was supplied by Guita Lichtenthal, a large woman of Prussian descent from the nearby town of Martynowicze who served the two communities as both baker and midwife. It was she who literally sat on the middle of Sasha Kaganovich to propel the husky baby from the mother's body.

Lazar Moiseyevich was given his grandfather's first name and was welcomed into the household on the eve of another Cossack onslaught. This would be but one of many more he would endure.

The boy had two brothers, both older, who tended to disregard him. Mikhail, the eldest, now four, would spend his days watching his father work while the second child, Yuri, age two, would trail after the mother.

In the morning hours, Sasha tended her small garden, which encircled the house, vainly trying to grow something eatable. Mostly, this consisted of potatoes and beets, which were grown underground. The harsh winter made it difficult, if not impossible, to grow fruits.

In the afternoon, she would concentrate on cleaning, cooking, and bartering with the farmers for what she would eventually put on the dinner table. By and large, this consisted of borscht, either beet or schav (a green vegetable resembling a small lettuce leaf) or cabbage. To this she would add potatoes, some bread, and fish or pieces of meat if available. In effect, anything that was filling.

The house itself, though small, was always kept neat and clean. There were only three rooms: a kitchen-dining-living area and two bedrooms. The bathroom was out back in a small shed over a deep hole in the ground.

The children all slept in one bedroom on straw mattresses that lined the room. The youngest slept with the parents. There was little furniture, most of it of wood that seemed like it would last forever: a large rectangular table to eat on, a massive wooden couch with thin pillows to sit on, side chairs of equally thick wood, again with thin pillows, and a few small tables on which rested an occasional vase or candles or small wooden boxes that held matches.

On one wall was a crocheted tapestry depicting a unicorn, a lion, and two maidens, one offering the other a golden platter. It was a mélange of red, blue, yellow and green, the only bright colors visible in the house.

On another wall a small mirror, the only one in the house, was hung toward the floor so that the children could amuse themselves. Lazar was particularly fond of looking at himself.

With three children to occupy her time and a fourth en route, Sasha had little opportunity to reflect on anything other than what she knew she had to do.

She was a small woman in comparison with the others in the village. She couldn't have stood more than five feet, if that. She wore a white scarf tied around her head at all times. Most of the other women wore black, keeping with tradition, but Sasha, whose parents had migrated from the sunny south of Russia near Moldavia, refused to acknowledge the dark color. "Too morbid," she would say.

Rumor had it that her real name was Sarah but that she had been given the primarily male name Sasha by her father, who hadn't wanted to recognize a fifth daughter. It had little effect on her.

The children were everything. They constituted her life and her reason for living. She devoted herself to them and to a lesser extent to her husband. She didn't have to expend more than what was absolutely minimal on him. He didn't require any more. And so, the house was her domain, and she ran it with unceasing energy and with an iron fist.

The townspeople already heard what her husband would say about her behind her back. "She should be married to the czar. She's a regular czarina."

Moisev could say this. He had no fear of her retribution because he knew that she liked the compliment. She felt flattered by it. Yes, perhaps she should be a czarina with her white scarf.

But as domineering as she was, Moisev loved it and he loved her. In fact, he loved practically everyone and was known as the sweetest man in the community. He was tall in stature, with a full beard and bright, alert eyes that could stare for what seemed like hours without blinking.

He was a *schneider*, a tailor, and although he refused to wear glasses because of vanity, his eyes were the weakest part of his body, long since tired and aching from the countless hours hunched over a needle and thread. He would work extraordinary hours, from the crack of dawn to the last rays of sunlight. He enjoyed what he did, and his patience was unlimited. He never raised his voice and would concentrate on the work in front of him, his long thin fingers moving easily over the fabric, while he softly hummed songs from his youth, old Yiddish tunes for which he could never remember the words, only the melodies. His father had been a cantor, and music was an integral part of his being. Nothing bothered him, and he went about his business quietly, almost sheepishly, while his wife and children bustled around him.

Neither of the parents felt the need for undue discipline of their offspring. Everyone knew what he was required to do, no matter what the age. Even the smallest, like Lazar, had a job. At age two, his was to feed the three chickens that hustled and pecked about in the small pen in the backyard.

This was the atmosphere in which Lazar developed in the little house with its tiny plot of land.

The town itself was also tiny, consisting of a bakery, a cobbler, a grocer, a railway station, a militia house, and a bookshop, the latter not really a store but a pushcart set on the side of the road. The people who owned the books also owned the grocery store, and the cobbler served also as the train dispatcher. That was a relatively easy job because very few trains stopped at Kabany.

The militia house held a constable, as he was called, who was technically the czar's representative in the area, and his deputy, a rather dim-witted lad who walked around the village constantly as if to reinforce where he was—and, perhaps, who he was.

Lazar's early years were relatively uneventful. The Kaganovich clan was huge: cousins, aunts, uncles, brothers, a sister. So large was the family that at times it seemed like half of the village's few thousand people were all related.

Passover dinners saw table pushed against table until the dining room stretched from one end of the house clear to the road outside, some fifty feet. It was easy, and even welcomed, for a passerby to simply sit down, or bring his own table, in order to listen and take part in the five-and-one-half hour service on each of the two Passover seders. Everybody contributed to the meals, although many of the dishes, with potatoes as the staple, seemed to resemble one another.

Lazar's closest friend, Morris Kaganovich, lived in the small house next door. He seemed to have a similar set of circumstances: two older brothers, a father who also hunched over a needle and thread all day, and a mother who thought of herself as a czarina, too. He remembers his father proclaiming: "That wife of mine. She spends more money than I give her. And I give her none."

Although some seven years older than Lazar, Morris found his younger cousin more stimulating than any other relative. The two would take long walks in the fields, squatting down and relieving themselves and talking about people and things, from their fathers and their jobs to their mothers and their jobs to the people who worked in those fields to those who used Kabany simply as a way station to somewhere more important.

They would spend hours on just one game of drawing an outline of someone's head on the bark of a tree with a rock, making sure that the nose was the largest part, and then throwing rocks at the nose to see how long it would take to obliterate the image completely. Sometimes they would pretend it was the czar or the terrible Rasputin or even their own fathers.

One thing Lazar noticed by checking the mirror every day was that people had large noses. He would study his nose and his face at great length and then try and duplicate it on the tree. It never worked.

"An artist you're not," said Morris. "Try something else."

He would, too.

Morris found Lazar almost an equal. The boy, though so much younger, could understand, and he could talk, almost incessantly at times, and although much could be dismissed as idle chatter, there was much that seemed to belie the boy's tender years. Even at five years of age, school, to Lazar, seemed a waste of time and energy. He would rather be out throwing rocks at trees or making faces in the mirror.

The one thing the village did have and was permitted to have even by the czar was a Yeshiva, a Jewish school for religious and secular studies. Unlike other similar schools in eastern Europe at that time girls attended as well as boys. The Jewish people in Kabany saw to it that all their children were educated no matter what the Sephardic rabbi from Martynowicze thought.

"Only boys should go. It is written."

"Feh," was Sasha's reply as she took her newest, Rosa, to the classroom. "You are a *zarta*!" She used her little knowledge of Arabic especially to offend and keep others at a distance. *Zarta* meant "fart."

The Gentile children went to no school at all. None was available. They were put into the fields at the earliest age and remained there for most of their lives. But the farmers were particularly kind to the Jewish families, even helping them when the Cossacks rode into town by hiding their chickens and provisions for them. The Jewish community reciprocated by allowing the small blonde-haired children to sit by the window of the Yeshiva and listen to the wisdom expounded by the local rabbis.

It was this aspect and only this one that Lazar found the most influential. It represented a sharing of ideas, of wealth, of interest. Everyone was entitled, although some more than others. To Morris, school was important in another way. He was already deep into the Five Books of Moses, a task that eventually would enable him to learn practically the entire study by heart and at a rather early age. Knowledge, to him, was the reason for existing.

Lazar, though, had no time for simple knowledge. He had no time, either, for the people in his community and less for even his own father, who seemed a weak, ineffectual individual. He considered his mother a victim who didn't seem to understand the first thing about living. Survival, yes, but living?

It seemed almost inconceivable that people would live here all their lives and allow themselves to die here. That was insanity. He would not let that happen to him. Until he was old enough and strong enough to do something more with his life, he would focus his attention on the people around him. He would observe with limitless patience. He watched his father, scrutinizing what he did, learning everything he could about the job.

He concentrated on others as well. His uncle Levick, Morris's father, was working then in leather goods, particularly making lasts of shoes. He was a small man with a small goatee. He wore tiny, rimless glasses that made his eyes seem larger than they were. Lazar wondered if he even needed those because most of the time they were propped on his forehead like headlights.

Uncle Levick was a machine, turning out lasts at an incredible rate. He was also a good businessman. His modus operandi was simple. He would stock up on his materials, spending months putting the lasts together in different sizes, and then he would go from town to town selling the lasts to shoemakers. Or, when the time and money were right, he would actually make the shoes himself and sell them.

He would also travel outside Kabany. He was one of the few who did. Not Lazar's father, though. He would never think of venturing anywhere but within one hundred yards of his little house.

But his uncle would buy more leather, more goods, returning to Kabany after three months on the road and then settling in for a similar period to whip the goods into shape, lasts in some instances, whole shoes in others. And then the procedure would start all over again.

As he grew older and stronger, Lazar would accompany his uncle to some of the surrounding towns. Lazar was taller than either of his older brothers. He was also broader in the shoulders, and while Mikhail and Yuri both seemed to resemble Sasha and Moisev in stature, and even in disposition, Lazar was looked upon by those in the village as a hybrid.

"I think it's Guita's fault," one would say, referring to the huge midwife. "She must have got some of her Prussian blood into Sasha's body. That boy is not all Russian. He is too sour."

Lazar would spend hours each week in front of the mirror, perfecting the "sour" expression. He would arch one eyebrow, close an eye, lower a lip—any gesture that seemed to indicate indifference. To Sasha, it seemed to be a boy's game; to Lazar, it reflected what he felt.

Levick liked to have Lazar accompany him. He was a good worker, was intelligent, and wasn't as concerned with books as was Morris, his own son. So he didn't have a good sense of humor. "He's young. He still has time to develop one. He'll need it in this world."

They would hitch the one droshky to a horse the family shared and set out on their journey. Most of the trips lasted only a few days, but that was good enough for Levick. At ten years of age, Lazar was already considered a better-than-average helper. He would cart leather goods, making sure he had the right lasts for each particular merchant in each particular town. He took an interest in what he was doing, more so than in school, which to him seemed wasteful. He would go to school when he had to. He had no choice. Sasha insisted upon that. But at the first opportunity, he would head for Uncle Levick's departing droshky. Who objected? His father? He objected to nothing and to no one. His mother? She was too busy with Rosa, the newest, to realize fully what was happening. His two brothers? School to them was safe. They relished in it. It also meant no work. His cousin Morris? He was too much the scholar. Besides, he wore glasses. Who, Lazar reasoned, needed a helper who wore glasses? A boss like Uncle Levick could wear glasses, but not important helpers.

No, nobody really cared. And, anyway, who could complain when there was now one fewer mouth to feed? There was just so much the family could occupy its time with before the Cossacks descended once more, torturing the people, torturing the crops. Without him around, there would be one fewer person to torture.

Lazar saw firsthand how it happened. He saw it not only in Kabany but in all the other towns he visted. It came on slowly. Someone from the next village would send a message, simple and concise. "Thursday." That was all. One word and everyone understood its meaning.

Moisev would hide Sasha and Rosa as best he could. There were few hiding places that hadn't already been discovered by the Cossacks. The house was too small, so he would bring them to the woods to lie in ditches far off the main road just in front of a group of trees to protect them from horses hooves. They would lie still in these earth coffins, and Moisev would cover them with dirt, branches of trees, leaves, even manure, anything that would serve as protection.

Whatever food they could save was also put in those ditches, but they knew it was important to leave enough to satisfy the Cossacks, if that were possible, even for a short period of time. They would be back. They always were. It was on days like these that Lazar realized Russia was not a Jewish country and never had been. It had always been anti-Semitic, from its very beginning.

He would watch as the Cossacks came. The sound was ear-splitting. They would descend, soldiers in gray-blue coats and gray fur caps, some with helmets like melon-halves and notched crests on top like those worn by the French militia. These were massive red-faced men with yellow twirled moustaches and big broad stripes down the pants. They thundered into the village, took what they wanted, and thundered away.

He had seen the procedure enough times to know what would happen. He had been present when a Cossack "General" (they decided among themselves who would have what title) entered his own house. A perfunctory knock might be made at the door, but they usually walked in whenever they pleased, no matter what time of day or night. It was like a scavenger hunt, looking constantly for whatever they could take, items that could easily be carried and would be worth something, either in money or in their bellies.

Lazar would watch as his father gave them four of the five potatoes on the shelf, five of the six loaves of bread, three of the four heads of cabbage. It should have been enough to please them until the next time, but his father never stopped there. He would give them all five potatoes, all six loaves of bread, all four heads of cabbage as if that gesture in itself would be enough to satiate the hunger. It never was. Now they would expect more the next time.

And then they would go, leaving the family with nothing except whatever had been hidden in the ditches in the woods.

41

Lazar would watch his father exhale deeply. "They are gone. We have survived them again. See, Lazar? *Du schneider's sund* has learned something even more valuable than making leather. Give them. Give them what they want. Give them what they want, and they will not bother you. Treat them like children, but children who you fear. It is the only way to survive. The only way."

Give them? Lazar thought to himself. *Treat them like children?* He was a child. At only ten years of age he was told to relinquish whatever he had learned, whatever he had made by the sweat of his brow, the calluses on his hands, the soreness of his feet. If someone wants, then let them take. No argument. Take!

He could not even shed a tear for his father, for his family, for himself. For a reason he could not then understand, he felt no sorrow, no pity, no compassion, just an anger that was deep, a feeling that this was not right. It wasn't the Cossacks. They were right. If people will give, they will take. But his father and the others in the village, they were not right. They couldn't be.

His mother would return from wherever she and his sister had been sent, and she would not have to be told the news. She would see it on the cupboard. What was once there was no longer there. And she would simply sigh and put her hands together in a prayer, bending slightly at the waist, giving her thanks that no one was hurt, that her house was still standing. She would look over to her husband. He had not uttered a word but would continue hunched over the material with his needle and thread humming softly to himself, content that he had done the right and proper thing.

She would finish her praying and then just as quickly adjust the white shawl and set out for the farmland to see if she could barter something for a few potatoes, even one. Dinner was still to be made.

Lazar knew that it was simply a matter of time before his village would suffer more than the lack of a few potatoes. In Kishinev to the south, there had been an actual massacre of Jews. People were put to death in about as fast as his father had relinquished the family's dinner. Men were beheaded by the swift-riding Cossacks, women were raped (whether pregnant or not), children were used as target practice, sliced from their groins to their throats by riders storming through the town. Everyone understood that this new way of dealing with the Jews— violence—was traveling all over the Pale of Residence. It was useless to escape, and even if one could, where would one go?

42

Besides, there was something else going on. In 1904, Russia went to war against Japan. Angered by czarist attempts to infiltrate Korea and create a "yellow Russia" in Manchuria, Japan stormed Port Arthur, the Manchurian base of Russia's Pacific navy. In 1905, retreating czarist troops, numbering 300,000, lost 120,000 men in a battle near the capital of Mukden. Arriving in the North Pacific after a trip halfway around the world, Russia's Baltic fleet was cut to pieces by Japanese torpedo boats while trying to reach Vladivostock by sneaking through the narrow Tsushima Straits between Korea and Japan. Of the twenty Baltic warships, seventeen were sunk. The remaining three escaped by fleeing to neutral Chinese ports.

The Russian army was failing miserably against the Japanese, and obviously someone would have to pay for it. Most of the people were not interested in the war that had engulfed the country. They thought it was another of the land-grab ideas of the czar, but other than mutiny in battle, they were unable to do much about it.

The whole political structure was beginning to tremble, and the government then sought to win public favor by its militant anti-Jewish propaganda. After all, as the czar put it, the idea was to attack the "not too attractive character of the Jews." Who would possibly want to protect people who were intelligent, inventive, and aggressive?

Everyone realized what would happen next. The czar was already forcing the Jews to become soldiers at the earliest ages possible, and he was putting them on the front lines. His intention was crystal clear: if he could not get rid of them in one way, he would find another means.

Mikhail had been drafted and was already en route to Kiev. Morris had received his orders, and Yuri was next. Lazar still had some time. Youth was on his side.

Many Jews tried various tactics to stay out of the army. Some submitted to baptism, converting to the Church in order to delay military duty or, if not that, at least to be assigned to a nondangerous post. Others bribed officers with anything they could get their hands on to get out of military service, but even that wasn't a guarantee. Many officers would take the money under a promise to "do something" and then turn right around and draft the individual anyway.

All means were used to avoid serving "time," which also meant shortening your life. Lazar's cousin Herman shot off the big toe on his right foot. That was not enough. He shot off the big toe on his left foot. Still not enough. He was conscripted anyway and could have saved himself the agony of two fewer toes, for he was killed three months later in Manchuria.

Finally, with both sides exhausted (Russia, physically and emotionally; Japan, financially), a peace treaty was signed by which Russia evacuated Manchuria and ceded the southern half of Sakhalin Island.

Meanwhile, European Russia erupted in a spontaneous revolution. The distant war for outside territories had never been popular, and defeat only arose worker discontent. Widespread strikes now started among urban workers, the most dangerous being a nationwide walkout by railwaymen. In many rural districts, peasants too began to seize and divide the nobles' estates.

Russia was thrown into shambles by the defeat at the hands of the Japanese. Peasants burned manor houses in the countryside while workers struck factories in the cities. Posters calling for action among the working class appeared, as if by magic, on the walls of towns, villages, and cities. Into the streets came the masses, determined to win their rights from the autocracy.

The Russo-Japanese War led to a large number of revolutionary outbreaks. The army was called to quell unrest more than ever: Underground reports showed what was happening over the years in the number of outbreaks alone: 1893—19 times; 1899—50 times; 1900 —133 times; 1901 —271 times; 1902—522 times; 1903—1,427 times.

But in 1905, something also was happening in the country's capital: the formation of the Petersburg Soviet of Workers. Here was the first appearance of true democracy in modern Russian history. There was, according to the rumors filtering down, the emergence of real democratic power, with the voters' right to recall their deputies at any moment. Throughout Russia, the word *soviet* (which means "council") began to appear. There were soviets of factories, soviets of shops, soviets of workers. They vied for power with the czar's government.

This movement became increasingly violent in response to the increasing violence of the czarist autocracy. Yet, in the beginning of that year, an attempt was made at a nonviolent means of protest. Some 200,000 workers and their families made their way in dignified procession to the Winter Palace in St. Petersburg. They carried icons as well as portraits of the czar and they even sang "God Save the Czar."

They believed their leader might grant their request for an eight-hour day, a minimum wage of one ruble a day, no overtime, and the calling together of a constituent assembly to draft a constitution for Russia. They would try to reach him peaceably. Maybe he would listen. He had to.

As soon as they came into view, the officers of the palace called upon them to disperse. But 200,000 people cannot be disbanded that quickly. They milled about, anxious but determined to have their say. The guards panicked before this immense throng, and suddenly someone opened fire, shooting into the dense mass of men, women, and children from a distance of about fifteen yards. More soldiers followed suit. They kept firing until the snow turned red. Five hundred people were killed and untold thousands were wounded among the screaming, helpless and unarmed crowd. This became known throughout Russia as "bloody Sunday," and it probably did more than all the underground revolutionaries to give the people a lesson in what autocracy really meant.

A number of different revolutionary organizations were being formed, but according to what Lazar heard, the premier one was the Social Democrats, who were controlled by a young agitator named Vladimir Ilych Ulyanov. He was the younger brother of the Ulyanov who had been executed years before by Alexander III. Information, though, was sparse and infrequent. It would filter down to the small villages by word of mouth. It was the only way. The Ukrainians were not allowed a single newspaper in their own language.

In 1907, Lazar was working practically full time in the town of Mozyr, fifty miles to the north of Kabany. He was toiling in a shoe factory doing what his uncle had taught him, making lasts. Although fourteen years of age, he refused to be bar mitzvahed, unlike his two older brothers and Morris. It was useless to force him. Too much time and effort was expended in just trying to keep the family afloat.

Sasha continued with her bartering, and Moisev continued giving the household supplies away. Mikhail and Yuri had returned home from military service and worked as metalworkers in the nearby town of Gomel. The family was beginning to scatter as more and more relatives left and never returned. Who had time for religious rituals? Lazar could never understand all the praying. If the Jews were such chosen people, why did they have the Cossacks on their backs all the time? If there was a God and he was even listening to all this praying, then why didn't or wouldn't he do something about the suffering?

From the earliest Lazar could remember, he never saw the family not needing something. It seemed that the primary effort was in just keeping alive. Who had time for books and praying?

Lazar felt that work and his job were best for him. "This is good work," he would say to Sasha. "Shoes need lasts and people need shoes. You can never go hungry." Moisev only grumbled, his head deep in a prayer book.

But Lazar could also hear the contradictory rumblings from the north. A man named Lev Davidovich Bronstein, a Jew no less, was making himself heard in the great city of St. Petersburg. Everyone in Kabany knew of Lev Davidovich, who was the son of a well-to-do Jewish farmer in Yanovka, a village in the southern province of Kherson. They also knew that on the southern steppe of Russia, Jewish farmers were treated somewhat equally with non-Jews, not too dissimilar from the original circumstances in Kabany except for the roving bands of Cossacks that altered the acceptable living patterns.

Lev Davidovich, like other men rising in power and influence at that time, had taken another name. He had given himself a false one in case he was caught and questioned—anything to confuse the police. He chose the first name that entered his head when he was arrested: Trotsky, the name of a prison guard in Odessa.

Also filtering down throughout Russia were the results of the Second Congress of the Russian Social Democratic Labor party held in London in 1903. The congress was actually a bitter meeting that split the new party into two factions: the Bolsheviks (majorityites), led by Vladimir Ulyanov, who now called himself Lenin, after the Lena River of Siberia, and the Mensheviks (minorityites), led by a man named Yuri Martov.

The wrangling centered over the organization of the party, with Lenin claiming that "an underground party that wants to overthrow the czarist state must be strictly centralized" while Martov argued that "ours isn't a party of professional revolutionaries but one opened to anyone who believes in its program."

The Jews of Kabany had already taken their sides. Although Lenin had a Jewish grandfather, he himself was not considered a practicing Jew. Rumor circulated that he was nothing more than a Tatar, and "if one simply scratched his body, the Tatar blood would flow," Moisev repeated.

So the support went to the one Jew they knew, Trotsky. He supported the Mensheviks, but the other rumor floating around the towns was that he did so primarily out of anger and because he couldn't understand Lenin's ruthless behavior.

"You see," Moisev would say. "Once a Tatar, always a Tatar."

With the Cossacks trampling everything in sight, it was only natural for the Jews to throw themselves enthusiastically into revolutionary work. After all, what did they have to lose? A number of organizations, including the Black Hundred gangs, supplied with funds by the secret police, openly incited mob action against the revolutionaries. Most successful was the Union of the Russian People, which concentrated its attention on the Jews. Jews had seemingly the most reason publicly to celebrate the grant of civil liberties. They were, however, also the easiest target against which to direct the violence of street mobs only too eager and anxious for blood . . . especially Jewish blood.

In self-defense against the Black Hundred gangs, Jewish workers united in a socialist society called the Bund, which at times even cooperated with the Bolsheviks. Mikhail, as quiet and unassuming as his father, joined. Again, the idea was to survive.

Lazar would sit at the feet of the elders and listen as they discussed and thrashed about what was happening in the country. To some, it meant more problems.

"Leave well enough alone," they would argue. "The czar is bad, but these revolutionaries are even worse."

To others, it was the coming of a new era. They could sense it. It would eventually engulf them and give them a new start for a new way of living. "There is a future beyond merely existing." It was as if the Messiah were coming, right to Kabany.

Uncle Levick was fearful. The czar was a known quantity; the revolutionaries were not. Morris felt the same. In fact, they even went so far as to make plans for the day that people like Lenin or Trotsky came to real power—if that were at all possible.

Lazar absorbed everything he heard. Apparently, this Trotsky was an excitable fellow, but he seemed to know what he was talking about. There were, of course, dissenting views. "Trotsky will never free himself. He cannot separate ideas from men."

To many of the elders, they were all too ready and willing to quote what they had just heard in a speech from St. Petersburg, supposedly attributable to Trotsky: "Lenin's methods lead to this: the party organization at first substitutes itself for the party as a whole; then the central committee substitutes itself for the organization; and finally a single 'dictator' substitutes himself for the central committee.''

It was the czar all over again. But is it better to be on his side or not? Lazar knew he had much more to learn and much more to see before he could ever make such a decision.

He had already heard that many of the revolutionaries had been jailed and even executed. But they would learn a lot from the uprisings during these years. They would come to understand what they had to do to win control of the government.

Fortunately for them, Nicholas II learned almost nothing from the protests. His faith in his autocracy remained unshaken, and instead of realizing what these pockets of resistance—as small as they might be—meant, he moved to reclaim any meager concessions he had been forced to make. The masses and the czar had met face to face, and in the end the people were forced to grovel. Even then, in 1907, the ruling classes did not recognize that the events of two years ago were simply a dress rehearsal for the more decisive struggle which lay just ahead.

A few years later, the curtain went up on what was to be the first scene of the last act. The prime minister, Pyotr Stolypin, proposed that the government sell state-owned land to individual peasants in order to produce a class of peasant landowners who would not be in favor of these revolutionary ideas. Therefore, he reasoned, no revolutionary movement could succeed. The plan was a brilliant one. Unfortunately, Nicholas II was not able to tolerate a man of even the slightest ability for very long. He was supported by the czarina, who detested Stolypin because he opposed the promotion of her favorite friends.

On September 14, 1911, at an opera in Kiev that Stolypin was attending with the czar, a pistol shot rang out during the second act intermission. Stolypin rose with a perplexed look on his face and blood on his uniform. He made the sign of the cross and fell over. He was dead. The czar appeared to be genuinely horrified by the event although he probably welcomed it.

The assassin, Dmitri Bogrov, was said to be a terrorist; however, later it was discovered that he was really a police agent. Word traveled fast. People knew that everything had been planned by the czar because the secret police agents spied on everyone, from peasants to revolutionaries to nobility to the highest members in government.

Kiev was also the scene of another kind of drama that was unfolding in Russia at the time, and Lazar saw it all from the front row. A special meeting was being talked up throughout the area surrounding Kiev. It was one that people said would have "profound effects on your lives. You must attend."

His Uncle Levick and a few others from Kabany planned to go. Lazar decided to accompany them, even though Moisev tried to persuade him otherwise. "You can only find trouble there. And once you find it, you will have it following you forever."

Mikhail had already been arrested just for being a member of the Bolshevik party. He was kept in jail for only two days, but the thought of any of his sons being the target of an executioner's bullet frightened Moisev more than anything else. But again, Moisev backed down. This time the excuse was Lazar's age.

"He is eighteen. A man. What can you tell an eighteen year old? They know everything. When I was eighteen, I was married. I had responsibilities, obligations. I had no time for foolish ideas like meetings."

Sasha, too, offered no resistance. She hid herself once more in whatever child was available. Rosa was far and away the best student of all the children, and each day she would come home with more and more questions and more and more studies. Sasha had her hands full just trying to find answers to her queries.

While the others in the family looked on in partial disbelief and partial disapproval, Levick and Lazar set out for the great city to the south. It was Lazar's first trip to Kiev, and for days prior to his departure he queried anyone he could on its background. His main source was the family's resident scholar, Morris.

"Lazar, listen carefully now. Archaeologists established the city's age at fifteen hundred years. The first written record that has come down was *Povest Vremennykh Let* (The Tale of Bygone Years), compiled by Nestor, a monk at the Kiev-Pecherskaya monastery in the eleventh century; he gave a chronological account of the history of Kiev as the capital of Kiev Rus from the year 862. But Nestor also wanted to know the origins of the Russian land and the name of the first Kievan prince. That was how the folk legend about the three brothers, Kiy, Shchek, and Khoriv and their sister, Lybed, found its way into the chronicle. It says that the three founded a town on the land of Polyane, an East Slav tribe, and called it Kiev in honor of the eldest brother. Today, it is the capital of the Ukraine holding the honorary title of 'Mother of Russian Cities.' It was also called the 'Gem of the East' and rivaled Constantinople in its beauty.''

As the droshky carrying Uncle Levick and Lazar approached the outskirts of the city, Lazar could hear Morris's voice describing what he would see. He had mapped the route, including commentary.

"See the golden dome of the churches sparkling in the sunshine. St. Sophia's Cathedral, the main church, was dedicated in the year 1037. Kiev is an old city rich in archaeological and historic monuments.

"The city itself has over a thousand streets and was built on seven hills with a view of the Dnieper River. Guarding it stands the statue of Prince Vladimir, who brought Christianity to Kiev.''

Now Uncle Levick spoke up. He remembered the words of Gogol. "How beautiful is the Dnieper in calm weather.'' He explained how it was typical Gogol sarcasm for he knew how frigid and sluggish it could be much of the year. But now it was spring, and lilac blossoms welcomed them to Kreshatnik Street, the main thoroughfare. Huge chestnut trees lined both sides.

They passed Kiev University with its red-washed walls. Nicholas II had ordered 180 students to be expelled for revolutionary activities and had sent them into the army. He then had directed that the walls of the university be painted red so that they could "blush for them.''

They passed the St. Vladimir Cathedral and the tomb of Askold and turned into a small street that bore no name. They stopped in front of a building that had no number.

The meeting was being held in a small room in one of these side streets; the room also served as a synagogue. At least two hundred men packed into an area designed to hold no more than half that many. Those who couldn't crowd inside were told to return in an hour, when a second meeting would be had. There were no women present.

Lazar wormed his way toward the front. On the platform sat only a wooden desk. There was no chair, no posters, no flyers, nothing but a wooden desk.

The room buzzed with excitement but instantly quieted down when a small man with pince-nez glasses sitting on a rather large, hook nose entered from the side and strode onto the platform. A visor cap was squashed down on his head, and spindly legs stuck out of his boots. A pack of scruffy men with faces that seemed idiotic to Lazar grouped themselves behind the man they called Trotsky.

He seemed smaller than Lazar had expected. Lazar had always

50

thought that leaders, or certainly would-be leaders, should be tall. Someone said that Lenin was close to seven feet. Could that be true? But this man, this man was short. He did seem a little bit taller when he took off his cap and a bushy head of black hair popped out. The hairs looked like they never saw the teeth of a comb or the bristles of a brush. He also had a matching goatee and mustache. He reminded Lazar somewhat of his father. That was who. He looked just like his father, and Lazar wondered whether he would also sound like him. As soon as Trotsky opened his mouth, Lazar realized that there was a major difference.

Trotsky's voice reached a crescendo within seconds and stayed there throughout his speech. No, the mild-mannered, sweet, and ineffectual disposition of Moisev Kaganovich could not be found in the man before him, who was quick-tempered, arrogant, and stubborn.

"I will answer your question before you ask it," he said. No good evening, no hello, not even a smile. Just right to the heart—to the point.

"The soviet we have formed is an embryo of a revolutionary government. It organizes a free press. It organizes street patrols to secure the safety of the citizens. It takes over the post office, the railroads, everything. But it is for you. You are the soviet. The first wave of the next revolution will lead to the creation of soviets all over the country. You are the soviets. Petersburg has five hundred thousand strong in the workers population. Of these, our new soviet represents half. These are the factory and plant workers. And it represents all their interests."

Trotsky paused. He looked over the audience.

A man to the side with a long, gray beard and with a book clutched under his arm rose. A crooked finger pointed in the air.

"I have studied Marx. I know that no social order ever disappears until new material conditions—new forces of production—develop sufficiently to replace the old ones. Therefore, all backward societies, of which we are one . . ."

A rumble went through the crowd. This they did not like to hear. They were embarrassed enough by their conditions. They didn't need to hear it echoed in public.

". . . that all backward societies must go through the same stages of development as the advanced Western countries and that the next stage of development must be capitalism with a bourgeois revolution."

The men buzzed. Some understood what was being said. Most

51

simply grimaced. What was this all about? Does this put food on tables? Does this stop the pogroms? Wasn't this the main reason they were here?

Lazar watched the man with the goatee and bushy hair. He was unmoved. Then his eyes flashed, and his hand shot out in front of him.

"Why do we have to follow the same path? Who will make the revolution? Not the bourgeoisie. Workers and peasants will, and it will be despite and even against the bourgeoisie."

Another murmur from the crowd. Lazar heard a man from the back.

"What the hell goes on here? I thought this guy was supposed to be following Marx. Jews don't stick together anymore?"

Lazar heard it once and he heard it again. "Jews don't stick together anymore." Should they? Why should they?

Trotsky ignored the outburst.

"Workers and peasants do not have the same social or historical weight. Numerically, the peasants are the overwhelming majority. But they are scattered, they have no common outlook, and they have accepted subordination to an urban class. The choice will confront them: to stay under the czar or to fight alongside us, the workers."

More murmuring.

"We, the working class, are the only social class capable of liberating Russia, of organizing. But why should the workers fight if they are only going to hand over power to their enemy? They won't! Workers are not going to be satisfied just to pull the bourgeoisie into power. The democratic revolution will spill over immediately into a socialist one . . . and thereby become a permanent revolution."

The man with the long beard stood again. His question comprised only three words, and he practically shouted them.

"A socialist revolution?"

Trotsky turned and smiled. For the first time, his voice dropped. It was no longer at fever pitch. One had to lean forward to hear the almost whispered response.

"Yes, but in a backward country like Russia, it cannot be completed within national limits. Suppose the proletariat gains power as a result of the democratic revolution? What will be the fate of socialism? Can it develop? Yes, but it will not depend finally on Russia's productive forces, but upon the development of international socialist revolutions."

Trotsky finished, turned, and walked off the platform. No good-byes, no *do svidaniya*, no acknowledgment. He had said what he wanted to and he left.

The crowd began filing out, chattering to one another, some shaking their heads, some smiling, but the majority with a blank expression. It was real yet it was unreal. It was believable yet it was unbelievable.

Lazar returned to the street. The air was crisp and invigorating. He sought out his uncle who was engaged in discussion with a group of men. They talked in low tones, excitable conversations but kept down, a rarity for Russians, who are known to have tremendous highs and lows of passion.

Lazar understood yet he didn't. The workers would control the revolution. That much he got. Not students, not *schneiders* giving food away to the Cossacks, not farmers, whom Trotsky said were peasants, but workers. Those who worked with and among others. Organized. The cobwebs were beginning to clear. He knew that he was on the right track. The path was being defined better. He would continue what he was doing. He would become a real worker, and he would organize.

The trip back to Kabany was a reflective one. Lazar did little talking. His uncle seemed uneasy about what he had seen and heard. He was obviously trying to put it all in focus. Trotsky had indeed an interesting way of viewing things, but did it mean that it would be the right thing for him, for his family, for the people of Kabany, to support? The czar was a known quantity. They knew the evil they had. Trotsky and Lenin and Martov were unknown.

"I don't know," he said, staring at the road ahead of him as the droshky began to climb the small incline. "I don't know."

He began to chuckle. *Sidet' mezhdu dvukh stul'yev.* "To sit between two chairs." He turned to Lazar. "To run with the hare and hunt with the hounds."

Lazar looked over at his uncle, a man he respected and actually loved more than his own father. He studied the small, gray goatee and the tiny, twinkling eyes. Uncle Levick was a short man, but just like Trotsky there seemed to be power, energy, verve in that slight frame. Perhaps there had been a mixup. Maybe this was his real father, and Morris belonged to Moisev. It all seemed so confusing. He liked things simple, but there were too many people, too many relatives to contend with. He could do without most of them.

Uncle Levick began to laugh, small chuckles at first giving way to hearty guffaws. Lazar was not one to laugh easily. He was usually too serious, and people questioned his apparent lack of a sense of humor. He didn't think there was much to laugh about. Life certainly wasn't funny.

Yet, within a short period of time, he, too, joined in. He had no idea what his uncle was laughing at, but laughter was so infrequent it was best to take whatever you could whenever you could.

His uncle watched him. "Lazar, *du schneider's sund*. It has just come to me like a bolt of lightning, like a thundercloud. Trotsky, Lenin, Martov, the czar, the czarina . . . Who cares? Who really cares? I think I look at it one way and one way only. And you, my nephew, will have to look between the lines. I say. I say . . ."

He gazed up at the stars in the clear, crystal night.

"I say . . . whatever is good for the Jews. That's what I say."

He looked behind him to see if there were any other travelers on the road. He began to laugh again. "Who cares? Who cares? Whatever is good for the Jews . . ."

By the time they reached Kabany, dawn was beginning to appear over the mountains. The clip-clop of the horse pulling the droshky and the cool air had taken their toll. Lazar's eyes opened slowly. He saw that his uncle was asleep. The horse had simply followed the road. It knew as all people in the Ukraine knew. This was a special place. It was economically advanced, the agricultural heart of the nation, and it offered ambitious people, especially workers, considerable room in which to develop their talents. Lazar could still find a niche for himself somewhere in this area, somewhere in this country, somewhere in this world.

Lazar's mind played back what he had heard that evening, from both the small man in the squashed-down cap and the smaller man with the gray goatee sitting next to him. He knew that they both would be good for him. They would hold the banner under which he would march. One had confirmed the other. They were good for him. "Good for the Jews."

He kept close to his uncle from that time on, watching what he did and listening carefully to what he said. Others in the village had mixed feelings about what the Jews should do and who they should support. His father offered no opinion whatsoever, his ambivalency running deep. Communication with his brothers was not there. They were off working somewhere. Sasha busied herself with Rosa. She knew at least that one of her children would not have to be bothered by politics. Girls were exempt from any such participation, and perhaps this was best.

Morris had already decided that when the time came he would leave. He would head north toward Minsk, cross into Poland, and go on toward the Baltic Sea at Riga or Liepaja. There, he would find a boat that would take him across the Atlantic to America. Many other Jews planned to leave Russia, and eventually 2 million would go to the United States, while 200,000 would venture into the United Kingdom, and 60,000 would make the trip to Palestine. America seemed the only logical place for Morris. He found nothing for him inside Russia even though he still did not know what he wanted to do with his life. He knew only that Russia was not the place in which to do it.

Whether Uncle Levick and the rest of the family would also go became the primary subject at practically every dinner table. Lazar hoped that Uncle Levick wouldn't leave, but he also realized that all the talk was simply a prelude to what would really happen. It always seemed to go in that direction: Constant harping on one topic was superfluous. The decisions had already been made somewhere deep down within the person, and the endless discussions were simply ways in which to delay the actual departure date. It was just a matter of time.

Lazar continued working in and around Kabany at whatever jobs he could find. Sometimes he would work as an apprentice to a clothing maker, sewing buttons on coats; other times he would cart bales of goods from the supplier to the buyer.

When he wasn't working, he sought out all the meetings of the various revolutionary groups he could find, seeking them out like a bird dog, listening to all the speeches, weighing who said what and why and when. He traveled to Kiev whenever he could, for that was the center—the hotbed—of activity. He would even walk the 150 miles round trip if he knew someone important was there to speak. But he also knew that the man he had to watch more than any other was the first one he had seen, Trotsky.

He was the one who understood the makings of propaganda. He could put an end to the pogroms. He could handle the Cossacks. He even seemed to have an answer for the czar.

55

He remembered the second time he had seen Trotsky. It was again in Kiev, this time in the basement of a warehouse a few hundred yards from a militia post. Lazar marveled at Trotsky's complete lack of fear. Defiance was ingrained within him, a part of his very being.

On this occasion he had displayed hundreds of beans on a table. He put one by itself in the center.

"Look at these beans," he said. "That one in the middle represents the czar."

Everybody leaned forward to try and figure out what the young man with the small spectacles and curly hair would do next.

"The ring round him are his ministers, and the ring around them are the priests and capitalists. All round the outside are the workers and peasants."

The audience nodded to one another. They smiled. It was so clear, so easy. And it was true. But was it revolutionary? This was something new? This was something they didn't already know?

Lazar felt an uneasiness in the pit of his stomach. It was not that simple, it couldn't be. It was not all that it appeared to be. While the other listeners clucked and wagged their heads in agreement, Lazar kept still. He watched Trotsky's face. He was playing with the crowd. He was giving them a few moments of glory, and then he would pull the plug. He would unmask their naiveté, their lack of intelligence. He would show them why he was a leader, or should be.

Trotsky looked up from the table. His face still had the same stoic expression that Lazar remembered from the first time he had seen him. The eyes offered no clue as to what he was thinking.

Both hands quickly descended to the table.

"Now I jumble them all up."

His hands flew all over the table, moving beans every which way until they were in complete disorder, beans filling the table everywhere, no longer a center, no longer the rings, just one huge mess of beans.

Trotsky didn't bother looking up again. He kept his eyes on the table. His voice dropped in tone and in volume.

"Tell me," he asked quizzically. "Tell me, which one is the czar?"

He turned abruptly and walked away. The audience didn't move. There was silence.

It didn't take Lazar long to realize what he had to do. The answer, at least to him, was now crystal clear. He had to get off center. He had to make a decision on one movement. He had to align himself with one direction. He would join the party of Trotsky, whichever one it was.

By the end of that year, 1911, new problems had been presented. The family had met and decided on its direction. America was the only answer to what troubled them. They could not embrace what they saw as the inevitable. Trotsky and Lenin and Martov and all the others represented a threat unlike the czar and his Cossacks, and they knew these men would never help them.

Word was filtering down that if Lenin ever came to power, repression would be tenfold what was seen under the czar. There were rumors that Trotsky himself had said he would raise the Cossacks to the first rank of Russia's troops, granting them more privileges than they now enjoyed.

"Don't you see?" Morris said. "The czar is at least a known quantity. We know what to expect. But Lenin and his people? No. Better to deal with the known than the unknown. At least under the czar we can own something. Under the Bolsheviks we would own nothing."

They understood, as did everyone in Kabany, that the czar's days were being ticked off. Time was not on his side.

Uncle Levick and his family, including Morris, would be heading to the country far to the west. His mother and father and sister would remain. Lazar would have preferred it the other way around, but he kept those feelings to himself. He had already learned from attending the political meetings that sentimentality had no place in revolutionary work. If that was their decision, then they would have to live with it. He had made his own, and, as he was told, he had to put the "blinders" on.

The day that Uncle Levick and Morris would leave, Lazar decided to take himself as far away from Kabany as he could. He could not risk the surfacing of emotions that attached themselves to good-byes. He couldn't afford a display of such feelings. They would be reserved for the birth of a new Russia. He would pour his energies in that direction, not waste them on family matters that would not be productive. He held strictly to what Trotsky had preached: "No diversions, no unproductive work."

He decided to leave for Vil'ca in the early morning hours on the day Uncle Levick and his family were scheduled to depart Kabany. There was a meeting of the Bolshevik party, and although it wasn't until the evening, Lazar knew he had to be away from his own village on what would be an extraordinarily emotional day.

Just as the sun rose, he headed out the door of the house. Morris was waiting. He had a smile on his face, and his tousled brown hair showed that he had been there for quite some time. He knew what Lazar would do, but he was a step ahead of him. He would have some final words with him, no matter what they were. After all these years together, there were still some questions that had to be asked.

"You waited for me?" Lazar said as soon as he saw him.

"You knew I would."

Lazar nodded, and the two walked across the road to the edge of the woods and sat under one of the oak trees. If they were going to talk, Lazar knew it had to be away from the prying ears of the others. Public speeches were one thing; personal talks were meant to be simply that.

"It is foolish to ask whether you would come, isn't it?" said Morris, a smirk breaking over his face.

Lazar sniffed at the cool morning air. Dew was everywhere. He reached down in the wet grass and picked up a stone with a sharp edge.

"Will you stay in Kabany much longer?" Morris asked.

"No."

"I shouldn't bother asking about Rosa or your mother and father, I guess."

"You can ask," Lazar replied, not at all unkindly. He began to draw a circle on the tree. "But there is little you know that I feel. I cannot stay here and wouldn't want to. They have survived with me and without me and . . ."

"How about your own survival?" Morris was genuinely interested, not like the other members of the family, who asked questions as if they were the local matchmaker injecting herself into everyone's life, gossiping and exchanging the smallest piece of information . . . just to talk.

Lazar had etched in the eyes, the nose, the mouth. He then put the stone in Morris's hand and closed his own huge hand over it. He felt the small, thin bones of his cousin. His own hands were enormous, backed by strong arms, and his other hand easily encircled Morris's forearm with room to spare.

"*Spaseeba*—'thank you.' *Spaseeba*."

Morris put his other hand over Lazar's and squeezed. He could feel the arm pulsate, and he looked into the cold, brown eyes of his younger cousin. They offered no hint of fear, no trace of emotion. He wanted to tell him to be careful, but he couldn't. He knew then that his warning would apply to those who would deal with Lazar. They were the ones who would have to pay heed.

He removed his hand quickly. A coldness suddenly came over him. He turned and fired the stone at the tree. It missed. Lazar bent down and picked up another stone. He hurled it, and it chipped the nose he had drawn. He picked up more stones and kept throwing them one after another, each time hitting the target until the face was no longer visible.

Morris walked over and examined the tree.

"Who was this? The czar? The Cossacks? Me?"

Lazar laughed.

"Everyone. It is everyone."

Morris came toward him and placed a hand on his shoulder.

"I will hear from you, yes?"

Lazar nodded.

"You will hear about me, I am sure." He tried to smile, but nothing came out.

"Good, then I know you are safe. We leave."

He wanted to say more but didn't know what. Lazar continued to stare back at his cousin, his favorite person next to Uncle Levick. He, too, wanted to say something more, but there were no words at hand. "Yes" was all he could muster.

Morris turned and walked back across the road to his own house. People were stirring in there already. Much still had to be done.

Lazar crouched down. He wanted Morris to take a message to Uncle Levick. He wanted to tell him something, but he wasn't sure what. Perhaps it was just that he would miss him. That much he knew. He would miss him.

But by the time he had formed even those words, Morris had already entered the house. He studied the closed door for a moment and then headed up the road. He would not return until nightfall.

He joined the Bolshevik party in Mozyr. It was a simple matter. He signed a sheet of paper with lots of other names on it and was given an assignment. He was designated an organizer. He was young,

59

energetic, and a firm believer in the goals of the party. Just what they needed. He assumed the facade of Trotsky, quiet and contemplative at times, shrill and fiery at others.

Back in Kabany, members of the community were already planning to leave. There seemed to be no other choice. They could see that the clash between what they were accustomed to and what Lazar believed in was inevitable.

To Sasha and Moisev, the choice was also clear. They would stay. Perhaps because they had to in order to hold onto the remaining vestiges of their family. At least there were fewer of them to feed. Yuri and Mikhail were off on their own, working; contact was minimal. In fact, they hadn't heard from their sons in almost five months and had no idea where they were. Too many people were traveling inside the Pale to keep track even of one's own children. Nobody really cared. They had Rosa at home, the last one, and now hints were being dropped that Lazar, too, would be leaving. They could survive, just the three of them. Why leave their home, no matter how scattered the children were? No, they would all know where home was, and they could come back if need be. It would be a beacon for them, a lighthouse in the confusing fog around them. No, they would remain, eking out whatever existence they could.

To Lazar, he would be one fewer person to be responsible for, one fewer obligation. In any event, he needed to grow up faster. Unless he made the move now, he would stay mired in the mud village known as Kabany forever. He could see what was happening in the abandoned houses, in the uncultivated fields, in the closing of small stores. At least there was one good that would come of this. The Cossacks would no longer stop here. There would be nothing to stop for.

His membership in the Bolsheviks meant a lot to him. It was a group-educated party driven on the basis of a *pravdist*, or "truthful," movement. He would commit himself to struggle hard against all other groups, including Social Revolutionaries, Mensheviks, Bundists, even Zionists if necessary. That he could do, but first he had to leave Kabany.

He had to leave quickly and with little emotion, just as he had dealt with the departure of Uncle Levick and Morris. But it would have to be without any good-byes. He didn't need his mother's soulful stares and his father's disapproving comments. He also didn't need to have Rosa's sixteen-year-old superior look haunting him as if he were a common criminal. He liked his sister, especially admiring her natural beauty—the coal-black eyes and matching hair. She looked like no one else in the family. Most of them were not that pleasant looking to begin with. They were ordinary, but Rosa was different. She had a classic face, sharp nose, chiseled features, and seemed to resemble an Egyptian queen, not a Russian peasant girl.

Unlike the leaders of the Nile, however, she didn't act like a queen. She said very little and seemed introverted, concentrating on her studies. She had an idea of being a doctor. She had seen the crying need for medical attention all her life and felt the desire to help. She was the only one who did. Lazar both approved and disapproved. It was good that she felt for others, but at the same time he thought she should be more selfish. That part—what Lazar felt was a necessary quality in his world—was missing. She would have to change if she ever wanted to succeed.

He could wring out the final days with his mother, father, and sister, and all the other cousins and relatives still left in Kabany who seemed to proliferate around the small house. But then he would be subjecting himself to tears and wailings and final pats and kisses on the cheeks and advice, advice—the last thing he felt he really needed. All the advice he would ever require he would get from one source and one source only—himself.

He spent most of the time before his departure walking the fields and watching others pack and load droshkies or donkeys. Those who were leaving had exchanged sticks of furniture with those who chose to remain, obtaining a droshky, a donkey, or potatoes to carry along on their long journeys. They were scattering in many different directions, some to the south through Moldavia and eventually into Italy; others to the north through Minsk into Poland and westward. Who knew when these people would ever see one another again, or even hear from one another. It would be best not to see them. What could anyone say at this point? Who would want to say anything?

No, he had decided. His last day in Kabany would be his briefest. In the morning, he would simply pack up and leave. Taking with him whatever possessions he needed—there were few of them—in the small satchel that he had bought in Kiev, he would set out, unafraid, or at least pretending not to be. There were jobs around. There had to be. He was a Bolshevik. Wouldn't that open doors?

Before dawn, he was standing on the road outside the house. It was unnecessary to leave any notes, to exchange final *do suidaniy*. He would just go in less time than it had taken for him to come into the world. They would all understand. They would have to. And if they didn't or wouldn't, then there was nothing he would be able to do about it.

At first light, he was on the road. It seemed impossible that he would not look back, even for a moment, but he had now fixed his sight on another star, and it had to be one that was ascending.

When he came to the edge of the town, he did stop and turned around. He saw the small house where he had been raised. It was still dark except for one candle that burned in the kitchen, the Shabbat light. It would go out when the dawn rose. He paused for a while and watched as the sun came up slowly. The candle flickered for a moment, as if a gush of air had passed it, and then it was spent, trailing only a puff of black smoke.

2

He walked much of the seventy-five miles to Kiev. There was little traffic along the way. Once, a man in a droshky carrying a pen of chickens stopped and took him almost thirty miles before turning off the main road. The man had nothing to say and took two potatoes in return. Before he came to the city, Lazar stopped at a textile warehouse on the outskirts. Strong, willing, and knowledgeable workers were at a premium, so he was able to obtain his first employment on the way to another world.

Lazar was also imposing to see. He was stocky with powerful arms, shoulders, and neck. Besides, the man who hired him was also a member of the party. They took care of their own. At night, he met with other party members to discuss what was or was not happening in the country. It took only a few months for Lazar to realize that just working and meeting were not enough. He was young, energetic, and ambitious, mostly the last. Simply taking orders from those he felt were inferior was anathema to him. His father did that, the way he bent to the Cossacks. His mother did it, too, the way she bent to his father. But not him. He would bend for one reason and one reason only—to get what he needed.

He began to organize a Bolshevik union of sales employees in accordance with the directives of the party. It was illegal to do so, but much of what was going on in the country at that time was hardly in keeping with the czar's mandates. The union itself began to conduct strikes. However, Lazar had not called for any such strikes. He did not even want one. He had organized the union as he had been told to do and was waiting for the propitious moment to move forward; that had yet to be determined by those to whom he answered. But no, someone, somewhere, had decided differently. It was so unnecessary, he thought. And it was stupid. He tried to explain it to the strikers.

"You can't move without strength."

The words fell on deaf ears. The strikes rolled on until the authorities quashed them. By that time, Lazar was caught in the middle and was fired from his job. The head was always the first to go. He saw how it went. The workers were back at work, and he was back on the road. It was "his fault," no matter what.

He moved to the other side of Kiev, where he found a new job as a leather dresser in a factory. He was hired not because he was a Bolshevik but because he was better than most of the others. He knew leather. Uncle Levick had taught him well. He knew what he was doing. And, as before, young, strong people who had mastered a trade were difficult to find. This time, though, things would be different. He decided to stay away from anything to do with party organizing of the company. He would be active for what he believed in on his own. Lesson one had been learned. People were not to be trusted. If you needed something done, you had to do it yourself.

Lesson two went hand in hand: Everyone fancied himself a leader, but few were.

For the next two years, Lazar remained in this job, doing what he had been hired to do—at least on the surface—but actively working for the party outside the factory in whatever way he could, provided he kept himself insulated from the "inferior ones" around him.

With World War I now threatening, it was also important that he stay out of the limelight in order to stay out of the war. He was able to do that for two years, but by the end of 1916, he no longer could follow his own advice. As a member of the Kiev Bolshevik Committee, he actively came out in opposition to the "imperialist war."

His physical presence on the podium was imposing. He had grown a goatee in the fashion of Trotsky and taken to wearing the same sort of sloppy cap. He was unable to imitate his idol's bushy head of hair, for his was now receding rather quickly. However, unlike Lev Davidovich, Lazar was now close to two hundred pounds. His size alone commanded respect, and he used it to the full.

His voice rose immediately to a crescendo, much as Trotsky's had done many years before.

"The czar is weak. His wife is an emotional cripple. He has a son who fortunately will never see manhood and a so-called holy man, Grigori Yefimovich, who calls himself Rasputin and whose only concern is debauchery. And these are the people who we have not—not —chosen to lead us. We do not need territory. We do not need precious jewels. We do not need banquets on golden platters. We need bread. We need bread in our hands."

His first speech became his last, for the time being. He was arrested and banished from Kiev.

Once more he was on the road, this time heading eastward, away, he hoped, from the prying eyes and ears of those who sought to quiet him. As a precautionary measure, he changed his name to Stomachin (a fellow party member supplied him with the false identity papers) and set out for Yuzovka, a city 400 miles away. He figured that the farther he went, the less risk he would run of being connected with his activities in Kiev. Besides, Yuzovka was noted for being a hotbed of Bolshevik activity. It was just below Makeyevka, east of Melitopol, and not too far from the Sea of Azov. Leisure time could be pleasant with water around. In return for the new identity, he was given the task of turning all workers away from the Mensheviks and Social Revolutionaries and capturing them for the Bolsheviks.

The trip eastward took three weeks. Already the narrow roads were heavily populated. The war had seen to that, as more and more of the population retreated toward the country's interior to escape the raging battles on its western border. While World War I blazed away, the revolutionary forces could be heard all over Russia.

With the entry of Turkey and Italy into the war, the Germans, no longer able to forge ahead in Europe, turned their attention to the east. That sent Russia into a panic. The Russian front was enormous, and the czar decided to take the reins as the supreme commander, a job for which he was ill-equipped. It was obvious to anyone of any intelligence that the czar had too much to contend with. Putting out small brush fires, which was what the war now demanded, was not his style.

He liked to sweep through an area en masse. It would be his problem and eventually his downfall.

Lazar didn't have the czar's problems. He had simply to wend his way from one end of the country to another. Hitchhiking was a common form of travel, and as long as you had a few rubles in your pocket or items, like food, that could be bartered, it was relatively easy to get from one place to another. Even if you had to walk, there was so much movement on the roads that you could find a traveling companion to walk with so as to make the time go faster.

Lazar stopped at Yekaterinoslav, below Kharkov on the Dnieper River some 300 miles from Kabany. Here he worked as a shoemaker in a factory. And here he was involved in setting up an illegal shoemaker's union, rising through the ranks of unknowns to become the leader of the group. Together with other leaders of Yekaterinoslav's Bolsheviks, he actively worked and agitated against the "imperialist war." Within months, he became a member of the Borough Committee of the party and also a member of the City Committee.

He organized and led a strike at the shoe factory. He was quickly fired from his job, but he only smiled. This had been his strike, one that he had controlled and of which he knew the outcome. The workers of the factory, in a strike that lasted six weeks, demanded that Lazar be rehired in exchange for stopping their walkout. They were unified, as Lazar had ordered, and the owner of the factory capitulated. The workers' demands were satisfied, and Lazar was hired back.

It should have been enough, but this time somebody thought that the factory owner had to be "taught a lesson." He was beaten to a pulp, and once more the police looked to the leader. Lazar was arrested and physically taken to the city's limits.

He moved on to Melitopol, just below Yekaterinoslav, a few miles from the Sea of Azov and now 400 miles from Kabany.

Again, he changed his name—this time to Goldenberg—and secured work once more as a shoemaker. With his experience broadening, he became chairman of the underground shoemakers' union and an organizer of illegal Bolshevik groups in the area.

Once the organization was established, he headed to Yuzovka. He was employed in the shoe factory of nearby Novorossiysk, becoming a leader of the Bolshevik party there. The shoemakers' professional union organized by Lazar undertook strikes, all successful. The strike movement was reaching a peak at which 50,000 workers struck in the area, demanding a 50 percent wage increase.

There was no question that the two giant unions—the shoemakers in the east and the leather dressers in the west—were now controlled by the Bolsheviks and were already playing a large revolutionary role. And Lazar was in the thick of it all. Party officials considered him intelligent and tough, a fighter who had already known what it was like to be arrested, and a persuasive speaker. Uncle Levick would have been proud, he thought. "I can stir a crowd much like Trotsky did back in Kiev."

In addition to organizing workers, Lazar was given the job of recruitment. He was to look for new people to join the party. He found not only a future member of the Bolsheviks but someone on whom he could rely, who could watch his flanks and carry out what he needed. He first met the man called Nikita Sergeyevich at a meeting of leather tanners. The man had never worked in leather goods before. He was principally a coal miner and was only one year younger than Lazar.

Nikita Sergeyevich Khrushchev had come from the small village of Kalinovka, southwest of Kiev. His father, Sergei, was a poor peasant who worked as a coal miner. The son had begun working in mines when he was nine years old. By the time he was fifteen, he was repairing equipment and machinery. At the age of seventeen, he was already married. Now at twenty-one, his question seemed proper and relevant.

"And you?" he asked Lazar. "Where is yours?"

Lazar looked over at the short man with the thinning blonde hair. He watched the pudgy fingers deftly cut an apple in two, although unevenly. Khrushchev gave the smaller half to the thin girl with the bulging eyes sitting beside him. She looked emaciated. Lazar assumed it was his wife, but his dinner partner had said nothing about her all evening, not even introducing her.

Lazar's eyes surveyed the man's boyish round face and wide grin over which a bulbous nose with a large wart looked back at him. Wide spaces separated large front teeth, and Lazar could see that a number of the back teeth were missing. The man was indeed ugly. He resembled a pig, and the way he ate his portion of the apple gave all the more credence to Lazar's analysis. He crammed the entire fruit into his mouth, core and all, chomping down until pieces could be seen at the corners of his mouth. Lazar waited until he had finished the noisy chewing. Any questions beforehand might be met with an open-mouthed response, something he didn't wish to see.

"You think I should be married? Well, I am not married and have

67

no intention at this time,'' Lazar replied. He looked at the thin girl again. It was interesting how little he had even thought about women. They were not important to him. In fact, they seemed to be unimportant to his fellow Bolsheviks as well, or at least to those with whom he had contact. Some had wives, some even girl friends, depending on which city they were in, but most of the concern, the conversation, the interest, was centered around the country and its future: What was it doing, what was the czar doing, what was Lenin doing, what would they do next? Women were in the background. Oh, not that he had no interest in them, but it was minimized, kept at a distance.

Every now and then, he would find himself in the company of a woman, which usually meant at the neighborhood social hall where the party members and workers would congregate to drink and exchange gossip. Here it was not unusual to have a single woman who worked in the factory sit at a table next to his, drink whatever was being served that night—from cheap vodka to cheap cognac—smoke cigarette after cigarette, and listen to the conversations of the men.

By evening's end, with too much to drink and too little to eat, she would entertain Lazar in some strange bed that, when sober, she recognized as her own.

There was little style or substance to any of these relationships. To Lazar, it was over before he knew it, which was just as well, for his attention span was minimal. It was simply relief and nothing more. It couldn't be anything more.

He would look down at the woman and see almost a mirror image of himself: stocky, hairy and especially unattractive. Russia did not pride itself on good-looking women. As workers, they were second to none. As interesting and seductive lovers, they left much to be desired. Revolutionary work was serious business, and there was no time, or little of it, for relationships that didn't advance the political cause.

But men were different, and among them were even greater differences. Lazar saw in the person before him an accomplice, an associate who would do what he was told and would work tirelessly. Khrushchev was uneducated—he had little schooling—but he was a hard and steady worker. That was what was needed. Lazar would let him in on certain of his activities, but he would keep a watch on him, a close watch, until he was sure that he was totally trustworthy.

"*Puskat' kozla v ogorod*—'to let the goat into the kitchen garden,' '' was the expression he had heard often in Kabany. Khrushchev would be his goat, and he would see how well he tread. One thing about his garden Lazar saw immediately. Both he and Khrushchev had considered it a "tool," a means of raising the political activity of the masses. The line of reasoning was one of innumerable examples of how leaders could, under the right circumstances, trample upon logic, facts, and intelligence.

They listened intently as a man known only as V. V. Grishkin, a factory worker who had no papers to his person and who talked little, related a meeting he had seen in Zimmerwald, a village in Switzerland. Apparently, a conference of European socialists had taken place with thirty-eight delegates from eleven countries. Most, he said, were pacifists. Only a few, led by Lenin, wanted to "turn the imperialist war into a civil war," a policy known as "revolutionary defeatism." The man's head bobbed.

"You see, to Lenin it is a simple concept. He feels that they must use the disarray of international capitalism to open up a second front at home. Our enemy is at home, he claims. But Lenin also knows that German revolutionaries have been imprisoned for expressing similar views."

"What about Trotsky?" Lazar asked. "Does he back Lenin?"

Grishkin shook his head.

"Trotsky disagreed with Lenin's call for a civil war back here. He was even asked to draw up a manifesto denouncing war."

Lazar knew that it was no secret the war had succeeded in driving many Russian intellectuals toward Bolshevism. Even Trotsky, as self-confident as he was, had to understand his own talents and his own limitations. Even he had to admit that things were moving Lenin's way in Russia. Strikes, mutiny, defeatism were all apparent at the front. Everyone spoke of it. Food shortages and peasant unrest were easily seen at all times around Russia. But maybe there was a difference in how the people now perceived things.

The one thing that separated Lazar from people like Lenin and Trotsky was that he never had to leave the country. Most of the revolutionaries had been hounded out of a number of countries, in addition to Russia, because of their opposition to the war. Many, like Lenin, utilized Swiss neutrality and took refuge in Zurich. Trotsky was expelled from France as a "suspect alien" and eventually went west, to the United States, although for only ten weeks. Perhaps he was not recognized as being important enough to deport.

Lazar kept changing his name and changing towns at a rapid clip.

Up to now the pattern had been simple. He would reach a town under an assumed name, get a job, organize workers, set up a strike, get arrested, be shipped back to the previous town, change his name, and begin the procedure all over again in a different direction. He was not the only one, either. Hundreds and hundreds, thousands and thousands of men experienced this new gypsy way of living. It became almost a ritual, a ritual based on obsession.

This he did not find acceptable. He wished to be treated differently from all the others. There had to be another procedure between the treatment afforded to Lenin and that meted out to those beneath. There was, and his wishes were answered, but not in the manner he wanted.

He had just finished instructing six new workers, explaining the best way to remove the hair of the animal skin and then going over the process known as tanning, which involves the use of tannins, organic compounds obtained chiefly from the galls of oak-tree leaves. The tannins were used to tan animal hides which contain gelatin that combines with the tannins, converting the hides to leather. He had also given them a good sprinkling of his own propaganda: He had warned the five men and one woman (who he had bedded just the day before) that they should answer only to him, and no one else. In return, they could expect preferential treatment—less demanding work and a better position in the party.

They had left his station when he was approached by four members of the czar's army. They looked rather harried. They all needed shaves, and their long gray coats were frayed at the bottoms, cuffs were torn, and buttons were missing. The leader of the group, a man of at least sixty, with a full white beard, seemed indifferent to what he had to do, but he, like the others, had few alternative choices. The czar was still the czar.

"We have a new way of dealing with illegal organizers and dissidents like you," he announced to Lazar.

"Better you should concentrate on the war. How many more can you lose?" he said.

The bearded man looked back into Lazar's eyes. He didn't bother to respond. Thirty years before, when he was younger, he would have raised a riding crop and slashed the impertinent upstart across the forehead. Now, he was simply too tired from the long, unrewarding hours to do anything more than advise Lazar of the throne's disposition.

"You are under arrest," he said. "You will be stripped of your livelihood, your money, your very means of existence. And you will be sent back to the very people who need you least. Your own.''

Lazar's ears perked up. His eyes widened. He knew what this meant. The townspeople would not want him around. Who needed extra grief? There was enough without having troublemakers returned to stir up more problems, to bring the czar's Cossacks back down on them. Oh, no, the people themselves would take care of such as he. They would make sure that he didn't bring any more grief to the town.

Maybe he should not have wanted so much. Now he was not returned to the last town. Now he was returned to the first one.

He was taken back to Kabany, to Kabany no less, a fate worse than death—or was it death itself?

Most of his papers, except for a few he was able to hide in the seam of his belt, were lifted from him, and he was physically escorted by train westbound, along with a number of other prominent revolutionaries. *Prominent*, he thought. That part he liked. Soon he found himself standing on the outskirts of the village, and what was once a dead feeling was now replaced by depression. His stomach soured, and his face twisted itself into hatred. He walked toward the small house at the bottom of the hill. This time it was devoid of any flickering candle.

"Where your mother gave birth to you, the ground is dear." Those were the last words he heard from the laughing troops who had deposited him at this godforsaken place. "Fuck you" was his response.

He had returned against his will to see what remained of the village that had given him birth. From a distance his house still looked the same. As he got closer he began to see the differences between then and now. The small vegetable plot encircling the house was all dirt. Not even a weed had grown. The chicken pen was empty. The front door no longer had the mezuzah attached to its frame, and paint was peeling off in large portions. One window had been replaced by a slab of wood, while the others were encrusted with mud. No light could sneak its way in even if it wanted to. He dreaded seeing what the inside looked like.

A knock was answered by a huge man in dark clothes and an even larger woman in a black dress. They said little. They didn't know what had happened to the prior inhabitants. In fact, they had never seen the people. They had arrived in Kabany from Lvov on the Polish-Russian border far to the west. Like many others, they were fleeing from the ravages of war. There was no place to go but deeper into Russia. From the look in their eyes, Lazar saw this was not deep enough.

The man explained that the people next door had said the house was for sale, and for two chickens, a bushel of potatoes, and three loaves of stale black bread, the small dwelling was theirs.

"The people next door?"

Perhaps Uncle Levick had returned. Even Morris or cousin Herman. No, Herman was dead. He remembered that. Maybe they were all . . . After all, who would have been able to sell the house? He rushed next door. But a knock on the door met him the same way. Another man dressed in black and another woman in the same color greeted him. A young boy hid behind her skirt, his bones pushing at his skin. The hunger in his eyes told him what had happened. They, too, had fled from the west. The war was benefitting no one and nothing except the egos of its leaders. He could offer these people nothing more than his understanding; he had little else to give them. And without food in their bellies, they were not interested in speeches about any revolution. They didn't care who ruled them. Only a potato would be their god.

He roamed around the village, or what there was of it. The changes were dramatic. Many of the buildings were gone: the school, the bakery, the stalls where chickens and books were sold. Most of the trees in the woods were now stumps, having been felled to provide heat during the long winters. Vegetation was nonexistent. Kabany now looked more than ever like a mudstop on the way to nowhere.

There wasn't a face he recognized except for the peasant who was sitting along the edge of the town, just between the beginning of the woods and the militia house. He looked vaguely familiar, a thin, tall man with a gray cap that he kept pulled down over his eyes.

Lazar remembered him from the years past. He didn't know his name, but he did know that he assisted the constable at the militia house and also worked around the village, doing odd jobs ranging from collecting manure to be sold as fertilizer to cleaning out chimneys as a sweep.

The man watched Lazar carefully before he would venture anything. One had to be cautious these days. There were too many undesirables going through the countryside, preying on people. Not the Germans. They were too busy fighting a war to worry about the ragged peasant. But the czar's troops, the Cossacks, and the revolutionaries—those were the ones you had to keep your eyes open for. In other words, your own.

When he felt that he was on safe ground, he spoke in measured words, as if he were trying to say them for the first time.

"They all left." He stared intently at Lazar. "They all left, I said."

His gaze moved off into the woods, and his head nodded as if it were confirming the accuracy of his words.

"Where did they go?" Lazar asked, repeating the same slow cadence.

The man turned his body slightly, and his bottom lip curled up. His eyes moved from side to side, and his head dropped again, deep in thought.

"Out there," he pointed, his finger indicating beyond the woods. "They all go out there."

Lazar stood and followed the direction of the finger. *Out there*, he thought. *Somewhere out there*. "And they will never return again?" he asked.

"Never," the man answered.

He was now confined, or so it was said, to this town, where the old inhabitants were no longer around and the newer ones looked as though they were simply using the place as a way station en route to another village for a similar purpose, or as the last station. He had no choices. He would have to leave. Again, it seemed as though this was not only the starting point but the ending point and the restarting place. It would be a continuous springboard until either it no longer existed or he himself no longer existed.

He started to ask the man why he hadn't gone with them, but he knew the question would serve no purpose. He wasn't interested in any answer the man could offer, even if he had one. Peasants were to be disregarded, so why even waste time with them? He had other, more important things to consider.

There was now one major difference from before. He was alone, truly alone. There was no support line. He had few acquaintances and fewer friends, just those necessary to advance his own cause. He held allegiance to no one and nothing except what would bring him success.

He had reached twenty-three years of age. He last remembered being only seventeen and setting out to work. Six years seemed to have gone by in a blur. During that time, he had thought little of anyone except himself.

He walked around the village again and nodded in agreement with his thoughts. They had confirmed what he felt. It would have been

73

unproductive to think of anyone else. The proof was before him. The people he once knew were no longer here. And he must go, too.

He discovered to his delight that there were no guards at the village limits, so people could come and go as they pleased. It all seemed silly. They escort you back to your prison and then leave you. Stupidity. If you're going to imprison someone, then do it right; lock them up and throw the key in the deepest river.

The country was revolving on a wheel of nonsense. If he ever had the opportunity, he would change it. No one would have this kind of freedom.

Money was no problem. He had saved enough rubles from his prior jobs, and he had sewn them into the seam of his wide belt. He was able to keep most of the wages because as a party leader he took food from the shops of party members whenever he wanted, all without paying. It was one of the advantages of leading rather than following.

Travel would prove no problem, either. When asked at checkpoints to show identity papers, he would have to show the small yellow card that he was required to carry. Everyone carried more than one card. He would shave his beard and change his name. However, instead of heading east, as in the past, he would go north to Gomel, where he knew the party had a strong union with the local bootmakers and leather tanners.

Once more he set out from Kabany, but this time he got no farther than the edge of the village. A large, green truck stopped his progress.

A bearded Cossack stepped down from the cab.

"Thinking of leaving, Lazar Moiseyevich?" he bellowed. The beard opened to reveal a mouth of broken and yellowed teeth. "The czar has found a better place for you."

He was shoved into the back of the truck. It was filled with boys, some as young as eleven years of age. He realized instantly what had happened. He was now in the military. He was a member of the Russian army.

The truck rumbled along the country roads for at least two hours. At one point, it stopped to watch Cossacks train. They were training to meet the Germans in their own inimitable way. A number of young boys in torn brown uniforms took the role of the Germans. As these "Germans" attacked, the Cossacks swung themselves beneath their horses' girths in their favorite style, pretending they had been killed. The trick would be used to deceive the Germans, who would mount to ride after what they supposed to be riderless horses. Thereupon, the Cossacks would suddenly reappear in the saddle and cut them to pieces.

Lazar watched as the long, curved swords sliced at the young boys. The bearded Cossack roared with laughter. He emptied half the truck of boys "for replacements." He looked at Lazar. "You are too old for this. We need you for more than just training."

An hour later he found himself on a cattle train heading for the Forty-second Infantry Regiment in Saratov, on the Volga River across from the town of Engels. Lazar would now be 700 miles from Kabany and even farther from his original destination of Gomel.

He was assigned to a unit with no orders as yet for any combat action at the front. Thus, he found himself with enough free time to become active in the Saratov Party Committee. With his years of experience, he quickly became a member of the Executive Committee of the Soviet Workers' and Soldiers' Deputies. Most of the other members were considerably younger and less experienced. He was popular among his constituents because of his background and knowledge of Russian and even went so far as representing them at a conference of Bolshevik army organizations.

He knew the Bolsheviks must organize for the end of the war. The conflict could not last forever, and it was important that they be prepared for the fight that still lay ahead. The czar's troops kept trying to convince the Bolsheviks that they were working together for one cause, for one country. It was a noble effort, Lazar thought. Noble and stupid.

To the outside world he smiled. Of course, he would cooperate. That's what everyone should do. But inside he had drawn his own way of dealing with those around him: He would trust no one. He would use people, as he was used.

He was rising quickly in this small area of Russia. He was elected a member of the All-Russian Bureau of Military Party Organizations of the Central Commitee of the Russian Social Democratic Working Party of Bolsheviks. But perhaps he was rising too quickly. The long title was not without recognition. For his propagandist activities in Saratov, the word had been passed that he was to be arrested again. He changed his name—this time to Zhirovich—and ran from the city.

He had no choice but to flee to the other side of Russia, to where he knew the party was looking for added strength, to Gomel, just below Mogilev, with a railway junction that served the heart of Byelorussia. It was an area known to him from his many trips with Uncle Levick. He was well remembered and well liked and soon became a member of the local bootmakers and tanners union as well as the provincial Polissky Party Committee. It was 1917, and all hell was breaking loose. He saw it on every building:

POLICE PROCLAMATION

During the last days disorders have taken place in Petrograd, followed by force and assaults on the lives of soldiers and members of the police. I forbid every kind of assembly in the streets. I warn the population of Petrograd that commands have been issued and repeated to the troops to use their arms and not to stop short of anything in order to assure tranquility in the capital. Khabalov, Lieutenant-General Commanding the Forces in the Petrograd Military Area, February 25, 1917.

Its effect was quickly seen. Within hours, three hundred people were killed across from Nicholas Station. And it would not end. By the beginning of March, a bread riot followed by more killings took place in the city, and on March 13, there was heavy fighting in the streets of the capital. On March 15, the czar was gone. He and his family had been put on a train to some destination in Russia. In those early days following the overthrow of the czar, it was not easy to get information. There was little in the way of newspapers or magazines, and being far from the seat of power, much of what came down throughout the country was secondhand. When newspapers did arrive, they were either weeks or months late or were new ones that had to be viewed with suspicion because of their obvious biases.

What one did learn came through the *samizdat* or "underground," or through the officially sanctioned publications, whenever they appeared. Other information came through word of mouth, but one couldn't be sure of its accuracy, from one town to another, from one dialect to another, from one viewpoint to another. Of certain facts, however, Lazar could be sure, and he was able to piece together what was happening in the country.

On April 16, Lenin, dressed in his traveling cap and knickers and sporting a short-clipped beard, arrived at the Finland Station in Petrograd. (When Russia went to war against Germany in 1914, St. Petersburg's name was changed to the Russian Petrograd, which means "Peter's City." It was done to get rid of the German ending *burg*.)

His speech astounded the audience. He called for the direct seizure of power by the working class. It shocked the Bolsheviks for it seemed that he had now abandoned the orthodox dogma and wanted to bring the Bolsheviks into line with his new position, one that was virtually identical to Trotsky's idea of "permanent revolution." "You must struggle for the socialist revolution," he shouted from the train platform. "You must struggle to the end, till the complete victory of the proletariat. Long live the socialist revolution!"

But the Soviet leadership—Mensheviks, Social Revolutionaries, and others, including some recalcitrant Bolsheviks—always believed that it was a "law of Marxism" for power to be transferred to the liberal bourgeoisie. I.G. Tsereteli, a Menshevik leader in the Soviet, had already written about the necessity of compromise with the bourgeoisie: "It's true that we have all the power, and the government would go if we lifted a finger, but that would mean disaster for the revolution."

As a result of this dogma, a number of Soviet leaders actually looked to the liberals of the provisional government—a government in name only—to take power. Lazar had heard all this, not quite fathoming what was being done. It seemed that there were too many factions, too many parties, too many politics. It was chaos. Apparently, Trotsky's predictions had come true. Here was the absurd contradiction of victorious workers handing over power to a "weak, vacillating bourgeoisie."

He knew that he would have to watch carefully how things developed. Perhaps he would have to join in the flow of information, in the stream of politics, as strange and awkward as it seemed right now. Maybe it was time to put aside the speeches, the organizing of illegal unions, the calling of strikes. He was able to connive, as it were, on his own. That had never been a problem. But what he was now facing was an interaction with the political structure of the country, dealing with others of equal or better intellect, and trying to persuade these same people to his way of thinking. Up to now, he had done quite well in the small towns and villages, but he also realized the mentality of those with whom he was dealing. They were ready to be pushed around, to be led. They were able to be dealt with in the simplest, perhaps most childlike ways.

However, the people in Petrograd and Moscow were quite different. They were thinkers. They were not peasants who could be manipulated at will. This would take a different approach. Lazar knew he would have to get on their side first in order to be able to reduce them to the one-to-one relationship he so favored. In early May, Trotsky arrived in Petrograd. He went straight to the Tauride Palace, where the Soviet was then in session. His speech was quick and to the point. He summed up his position before anyone had a chance to respond or, worse yet, to boo him off the podium.

"Remember three commands: Distrust the bourgeoisie; control your own leaders; and rely on your revolutionary strength!"

Mensheviks and other socialist leaders of the Soviet dissociated themselves from Trotsky. They would support only a bourgeoisie coalition government. The door was open. Within a few weeks, Trotsky and his group aligned solidly with the Bolsheviks.

The words of Trotsky cascaded from Petrograd throughout Russia. Now he had joined with the Bolsheviks against all others. To Lazar, it meant crossing the point of no return. Trotsky's words on that day in May became a beacon for Lazar. They became his symbol, a calling to a stance. They became his own three commandments, like signposts indicating the path of his future: "Distrust the bourgeoisie; control your own leaders; rely on your revolutionary strength."

He also knew that within the next year, he would have to make a move to the north. No longer could he afford to cross and crisscross the width and breadth of Russia. He had to get caught up in the flow of events before they passed him by. The time was drawing near for him, and, he thought, for Russia.

From May to October, an intense struggle went on inside the Soviet between moderate socialists and Bolsheviks. Lenin called for an end to the war waged by capitalists for purely capitalist interests. In July, a mass uprising in Petrograd brought everything into sharp focus. The insurrection was defeated. The Socialist Executive of the Soviet disarmed the workers with the help of the dreaded Cossacks. Bolsheviks were under heavy attack. Trotsky was arrested, and Lenin was accused of being a German spy. He went into hiding in Finland.

Bolsheviks all around Russia were now on the defensive. Everyone knew that Kerensky, the socialist prime minister of the provisional government, had conspired with his commander in chief, General Kornilov, to overthrow the Soviets. But at the last minute, Kerensky backed down. Kornilov did not.

"I, General Kornilov, son of a Cossack peasant, cannot betray Russia into the hands of the ancestral enemy, the German. It's time to hang German supporters and spies with Lenin at their head, and to disperse the Soviet of Workers' and Soldiers' Deputies so that it shall never reassemble. I am shifting the cavalry corps so as to bring it up to Petrograd.''

Sailors from the Kronstadt Soviet, though, got orders from Trotsky: Defeat Kornilov first and then we will settle with Kerensky.

Kerensky quickly rearmed the Red Guards and begged the Bolsheviks to get Kornilov's soldiers to mutiny. He figured that Bolshevik propaganda would defeat Kornilov, who would find himself a general without an army. The tactic was successful. The soldiers deserted Kornilov without a shot being fired. Another roadblock was removed.

By October, the Bolsheviks had obtained a majority of votes in the Petrograd Soviet. Trotsky was elected president. In Moscow and elsewhere throughout Russia Bolsheviks gained majorities in the soviets. The green light had now been given for a workers' revolution.

"Land, bread, and peace" became the slogan of Bolshevik agitation. Long lines of people waiting for food snaked around the streets. Thefts were commonplace. The daily ration of bread dropped to the point where it was almost nonexistent. It was obvious what was happening. Basic human needs were in jeopardy. Conditions were becoming catastrophic. From the tiny roads of Kabany to the major thoroughfares of Moscow, the situation was the same. Peasants, workers, students were restless and they were angry. And, they had united.

In the meantime, Lenin returned from Finland to Petrograd in disguise and appeared before a secret session of the Bolshevik Central Committee. The decision was made for an immediate revolutionary seizure of power. To Lenin, it was crystal clear: "Much time has been lost. The question is very urgent, and the decisive moment is near. The majority is now with us. The situation has become entirely ripe for the transfer of power . . . insurrection. We cannot wait any longer.''

On October 25, the Military Revolution Committee of the Petrograd Soviet launched a successful insurrection. Lenin's influence was decisive, although the organizer was actually Trotsky. Lazar read every piece of paper floating down from the capital, including one by a man named Joseph Vissarionovich Dzhugashvili:

"The entire labor of practical organization of the insurrection was placed under the immediate direction of the president of the Petrograd Soviet, Comrade Trotsky. It can be stated with certainty, that the party owes the rapid coming over of the garrison into the camp of the Soviets and the skillful work of the Military Revolution Committee above all and essentially to Comrade Trotsky."

Lazar read and reread the statement. It was important because of the fact that it did not, like other statements from leaders at the time, extoll only the virtues of Lenin. Here was a man who was recognizing another, the one who Lazar saw as the true leader of the revolution. Such a man showed courage and perception, and such a man, he thought, must be caught and cultivated.

The seizure of power by the Bolsheviks in Petrograd had been characterized by many as a mere "stroke" on the part of the Bolshevik leadership, not a true revolution. Lazar had heard that the takeover of the machinery of government was bloodless and that there was an absence of mobs in the streets. The speed in which it progressed then was irrelevant. He knew that the revolution had been going on for what seemed like eons now so that the ultimate seizure of power became only a minor part of the surgery. The very fact that there were no crowds in the streets, no barricades or military army regiments, showed what extraordinary power stood behind the scenes. And to some extent Lazar felt a part of this. He had organized the Gomel Bolsheviks so well that the passing of power was also without bloodshed. No doubt the people in Petrograd would see what he had accomplished.

People all over Russia now saw a chance to escape from domination. Separate governments began to form around the country. Decrees and laws now flowed out of Petrograd in a torrent. Nothing like it had ever been seen before, not even under the czars. Every day brought something new. One day the stock market was abolished, another the right of inheritance was struck down. Banks were nationalized, other industrial enterprises were nationalized. Even the fishing fleet was nationalized. Private ownership of land was abolished. A law was passed that suppressed the conservative newspapers "temporarily." Gold was declared null and void, the old courts were replaced by new revolutionary tribunals in which any citizen could act as judge or lawyer. In fact, the old, strict marriage and divorce laws were revamped by new, extraordinarily lenient codes of procedure. The ancient Russian calendar was discarded in favor of the Western calendar, and the Russian alphabet was modernized. Titles of aristocracy were swept aside, replaced by "citizen" or, more commonly, "comrade."

The edicts extended to religion as well. Although the Church was left intact, its lands were seized. Even prior religious teaching was forbidden in the schools. Of course, word came down that it was the

Jews who did this. After all, wasn't the revolution prepared and fashioned by Jews? Both of Karl Marx's grandfathers were rabbis, and Lenin's grandfather was also Jewish. And wasn't Yakov Sverdlov, the first chief of state, a Jew, as was Trotsky himself? But most people believed the Jews could be dealt with, as they always had been dealt with before.

That Trotsky, unquestionably the most outstanding man among the Bolsheviks, was a Jew did not seem an insuperable obstacle in a party in which the percentage of Jews, 52 percent, was rather high compared to the percentage of Jews (1.8 percent) in the total population.

Lazar would have to keep a close eye on this. Would the people accept the revolution orchestrated by the Jews, or would they accept only one aspect and discard the other? Deep down, he already knew the answer; he had only to decide what he would do about it. For the time being he would ride along with the tide of change, trying desperately to stay on the crest.

Elections during the new All-Russian Congress of Soviets showed a clear Bolshevik majority: fourteen Bolsheviks, seven Social Revolutionaries, and three Mensheviks came onto the Presidium of the Soviets. Lazar, too, became an elected official. He was named a member of the Constituent Assembly and by the end of the year was named a chairman of the Third Soviet Congress of Mogilev province. Mogilev was just above Gomel where Lazar had formed a Bolshevik party. Mensheviks were driven from the organization, and a "pure" Bolshevik group was established.

One key to the success of the party was the "agitation showcases" that appeared in all the large cities. These showcases consisted of trucks, trains, or other methods of transportation that traveled around a city. They usually contained photographs of one particular subject, a party official, with short propaganda slogans. In Moscow alone, it was not unusual for as many as sixty showcases to be displayed simultaneously. In Petrograd, there were around twenty. Throughout the country, there were "agitation trains" on the railway lines and "agitation steamers" on the rivers. In fact, these new methods of propaganda raised agitation to what critics said was "a level of art." The press actually became more and more outspoken. Even *Pravda* (Lenin's paper, the name of which means "truth") reported, with its own biases:

"They [the people] wanted us to take the power alone, so that we alone should have to contend with the terrible difficulties confronting the country. So be it! We take the power alone, relying upon the voice of the country. But having taken the power, we will deal with the enemies of the revolution and its saboteurs with an iron hand. They dreamed of a dictatorship of Kornilov. We will give them the dictatorship of the Proletariat.''

So much was going on within the country that determining where to watch next was difficult. Kiev became the focal point for a show of strength. Lazar could see the strength of the spirit of the revolution in the bullet-riddled walls of the Arsenal factory, whose workers rose up to defend Soviet power. A separate armistice agreement was signed with the anti-Bolshevik Ukrainian government, which had initially seized control. The Social Revolutionaries wanted land to be owned by the people, while the Bolsheviks wanted the land nationalized. Lazar already had a hand in the agreement itself. He began a movement throughout the Ukraine to bolster the Bolshevik cause and anything else that would give him visibility.

He knew that the agreement was simply a temporary measure. Lenin would never accept the sharing of power. One way or another, the armistice would be only as valuable as the paper on which it was written. It was all a matter of time, like anything else.

Finally, he thought, the great mass of people were in motion. After centuries of oppression, after being treated like cattle for a thousand years, there was movement. Czars and generals, noblemen and priests were now being challenged. Against them was hatred for their position backed by a flood of ideas, ideas that would change those of the past. The world as Lazar once knew it was being destroyed, and a new world had still to be erected. He would become part of the foundation.

For now, Lazar was succeeding in making his mark. He had been elected a deputy to the Constituent Assembly on the Bolshevik list. More importantly, he was appointed a delegate to the third All-Russian Congress of Soviets in Petrograd. It meant he would now see firsthand what he had been only reading and hearing.

In December 1917, he set out for the capital far to the north. This time he didn't have to hitchhike, and this time he didn't have to worry about false identity papers. He was once more Lazar Moiseyevich Kaganovich. He was even provided transportation by the new government, a train ticket that would take him through Mogilev, Orsa, Vitebsk in Byelorussia, and northward to Dno and Bateckij. At each station along the way, he saw platforms jammed with people. It was as if the entire Russian populace was on the move.

The train was crammed with delegates from all over the western part of Russia. Talk was plentiful and food even better than he expected. Huge mounds of *salat stolichny* were heaped on metal plates and passed around. It was a dish that Lazar could not get enough of. It consisted of diced potatoes, cucumbers, carrots, onions, peas, and a hard-boiled egg all folded into a thick dressing. Sometimes there would even be pieces of ham or chicken. Lazar heard it was the main staple of Petrograd, thus the name "capital city salad."

Although most of his traveling companions were inside their bottles of vodka within two hours, Lazar stayed with sipping tea and lemon. He was still not much of a drinker. For a while when he was in the east he had tried to compete with the others as they literally inhaled drink after drink, but he found he could not. He would simply get sick to his stomach. Perhaps it was conditioning. He had seen very little of drinking or drunkards when he was growing up. Most of the people in Kabany would have a glass of wine once a week on Shabbat, and the men might even have a small thimble of schnapps every now and then, but there was none of the heavy drinking that was so much a part of the average Russian's life. Thus, drinking was unimportant to Lazar. He considered himself a social drinker, and his intake was moderate.

But the conversation and camaraderie were good, and the trip went faster than he expected, notwithstanding the crowded conditions. Most of his fellow travelers—practically all men—had never been to Petrograd before. It was new to them, an adventure that they eagerly awaited.

The countryside passing by was barren. War and revolution had indeed taken their toll. Village after village along the way was either empty, burned down, or consisted of too few people occupying too many ramshackle dwellings.

At times, he would tune out the cacophony surrounding him and simply stare out the window, trying to catch the eyes of the people who stood at the edge of their towns watching the train with the bright red flag chug by. He was looking for recognizable faces, people that he had traveled with, worked with, and, yes, those he had lived with. For the first time in years he thought for more than a moment about his own family, long since scattered. He had heard relatively little

83

about what had happened to them. His mother, father, and Rosa were somewhere other than Kabany. He felt they were still in Russia, but he was unsure where.

Someone way back had told him about a large engagement party that had been held in Mozyr for the son of a well-to-do leatherworker. The family name was Kaganovich. From the description given, it sounded much like Uncle Levick and Morris, but this had been many years ago, and his own visit to Mozyr within the past year had revealed a community of poverty-stricken people who knew nothing about lavish engagement parties.

The only one he knew something about was Mikhail. He had become chairman of the Military Revolution Committee in Arzamas in central Russia. And, Lazar reasoned, wherever Mikhail was, Yuri had to be close by.

By sunrise of the third morning, Lazar saw his first sight of Petrograd. He reviewed the history of the city in his mind. Stories had it that in 1703, Peter the Great knelt on a bank of the River Neva, thrust his bayonet into the marshy earth and proclaimed, "Here shall be a town."

Needless to say, the czar's command was obeyed. Twenty-three thousand workmen began the project, and when they were finished in 1712 (with 40,000 more men recruited), Peter had himself the capital of Russia. It had been called St. Petersburg—Lazar remembered that name from when he was a boy—now, it was known as Petrograd. Lazar chuckled at this. Had the czar thought that a change in name alone would, or could, defeat the Germans?

As the train pulled into the station, Lazar could immediately see what gave the city its widespread reputation. Except for Kiev, he had seen only villages or small towns that looked to be nothing more than train stops between major cities, towns that were ugly with factories lining the streets, towns devoid of any beauty or charm whatsoever. Now he saw hundreds of bridges, both simple and decorative, linking the various islands and islets of the city. He saw palaces of immense proportions, impressive plazas, church spires, domes, cupolas, and parks filled with classical statues, all under a layer of sparkling white snow. It was a veritable feast for the eyes. Even now, with a wind whipping outside and a gray sky, the city was appealing. Lazar surmised that it must be spectacular in spring when, it is said, the "sky turns to an azure blue with streaks of green punctuated by a golden sun."

84

The delegates were being housed at various places around the city, most of them, though, at the Smolny Institute, a grand, white-columned building that was originally designed as a boarding school for daughters of the eighteenth-century Russian nobility. The War Committee under Trotsky, which ran the Bolshevik revolution, actually plotted the take-over from its headquarters inside the institute.

Cots were everywhere, and Lazar made himself a makeshift bed-room along the side of a hallway. At least he had a window just above his head and could see the Smolny Cathedral next door. It was an impressive piece of work. Built by the prolific Rastrelli in the mid-eighteenth century, the church was considered a glorious example of onion-dome architecture, with its exquisite symmetry and light-blue color.

He decided to take in as much of this city as he could, although his days would be filled with meetings and his nights with endless talk about the direction Russia would now take. And then there were people to see and people to talk to and listen to, faces to connect with names and reputations.

The first day he toured the Nevsky Prospekt, which had been the main thoroughfare of the city from when it was first laid out. The long boulevard ran three miles, ending at the Nevsky monastery. Lazar had heard talk of changing the name to October Prospekt in honor of the revolution, but he also heard that no matter what the decree might say, everybody would ignore such a change. The Nevsky, after all, belonged to the city and the people, and it wouldn't be likely that such an important—the most important—part could be altered so quickly, not even by the government.

Lazar passed the cathedral of the Virgin of Kazan, so reminiscent of St. Peter's in Rome. He had never been outside Russia, but he could imagine the similarity. The church had a semicircular colonnade of 136 Corinthian columns. More intriguing was the fact that it was the spot where Alexander II had been slain.

He saw more churches as he walked, plus monuments, bridges, and shops. The Nevsky Prospekt was indeed the main artery of the city. It was Lazar's first experience in such a large city, except for Kiev, and it was made even more dramatic by the fact that this city was now the center of his world. He thought he saw Trotsky at one point and even Lenin, although on closer scrutiny he found it was not them. A lot of people seemed to look alike.

He roamed up one street, then down another, across one bridge, and onto another. Petrograd was a maze of hundreds of bridges, some simple, some ornate, which linked the islands that made up the city. It was the most beautiful city he had ever seen. Some said it was called the Venice of the North, and he could see himself living here without any trouble; of course, he could get away from his bedroom in the hallway.

He returned to his "room" well after dark. He knew he might have missed some meetings that day, but for the first time he didn't care. Whatever it was could wait for another day. He had to know where he was. He had to know what was around him before he could concentrate on the inside.

When he returned to the institute, he found someone sitting on his cot writing a letter. Lazar's eyes immediately shifted to the paper, and he could see the words "My beloved Catherine." The man writing was at least fifteen years older than Lazar, and he introduced himself as Kliment Yefremovich Voroshilov from the industrial town of Lugansk.

He said that during the February Revolution he had been in this city representing the Izmailovsky Regiment but was later sent back to Lugansk to organize the Bolshevik party there. He had become chairman of the party in that area and was elected to be a member of the All-Russian Central Executive Committee. He was now back in Petrograd as a deputy to the Constituent Assembly.

Lazar found him a rather pleasant-looking man with wavy but thinning hair and a pencil-thin mustache sitting under a rather large nose. His physical makeup was also on the slender side. Obviously, he had kept himself in good physical condition, unlike Lazar, whose weight bobbed all over the place. He didn't seem to be terribly intelligent, but he had an infectious smile. He was instantly likable.

Lazar reached back in his mind to see whether it would come up with anything on the man. He thought that someone, somewhere had said his record in fighting for the Bolsheviks was a good one, that he had extraordinary courage, with little fear of anyone or anything.

Standing behind was a short man with rich, black hair and an equally black mustache that curved onto his cheeks. He introduced himself as Ordzhonikidze, and he also seemed to have a pleasing personality. He obviously loved to tell jokes, for he was keeping a group of other men in hearty laughter, regaling them with one story after another. He didn't seem to stop, and only after a little while did Lazar realize why. He was hard of hearing and continued telling stories as long as there "appeared" to be laughter.

"Lazar Moiseyevich?" asked Voroshilov.

Lazar nodded.

"I bring you greetings from your brothers in Arzamas. I was passing through there on my way here. In fact, Mikhail was even supposed to be here, but he took ill."

Lazar frowned.

"Oh, nothing serious. Just a cold. The usual Russian winters, eh? *Delat' pogodu*—'If only we could make the weather,' eh?"

He smiled. "I was just writing to my wife, and since my friend there is too busy occupying my bed with his jokes, I hope you don't mind my using yours."

He referred to Ordzhonikidze, who had launched into another tale, although his audience was constantly diminishing.

"You're new at this, eh? So I guess you have some questions, eh?" Voroshilov said.

Lazar relaxed. He sat down beside him.

"Actually, I'm not sure who is who. I keep hearing names like Rosenfeld and Trotsky's brother-in-law. Do I understand there is much nepotism here or . . ." He looked around but lowered his voice. "A lot of Jews?"

Voroshilov let out a chuckle. "No, no. Let me explain, eh? First, there is Lev Borisovich Kamenev. His family name is Rosenfeld. He's Jewish. He's also Lenin's literary executor and editor of his papers. Some say if Lenin ever puts his work together, Kamenev would be the head man. Now, he's Trotsky's brother-in-law. The second is Grigori Yevseyevich Zinoviev. That's Lenin's closest assistant and co-editor of all his publications. You see the difference, eh? One does his personal papers and one does his personal papers."

Voroshilov looked around. It was the end of the day, and the corridors were beginning to fill with delegates returning from various meetings.

"And they are both Jewish, right?" said Lazar.

Voroshilov nodded. "But there are also two who are not. You may come across a man, Nikolai Aleksandrovich Bulganin. He's another favorite, having spent a lot of time in Japan. I don't know what that has to do with it, but Lenin considers him one of the Bolshevik's leading theorists."

He paused.

"And then there is Koba."

His voice lifted a bit, and Lazar noticed that those within earshot immediately fell silent. Even Ordzhonikidze stopped with his jokes.

"Rumor has it that he wields much influence with Lenin. I don't know about this. Supposedly, he was a member of the secret police and knows what everyone is doing and where. Rumor also has it that he had been in the czar's secret police force as well."

Lazar looked around. There was quiet in the hallways as Voroshilov spoke. Some men shook their heads as if to question what was being said, as if to say "Keep still. These are not matters for publication."

"What does he look like?" Lazar asked.

This time Ordzhonikidze spoke up.

"Joseph Vissarionovich is unlike any other man you will see. He is from Georgia, which to some may be bad enough. He is stocky. He has a sallow complexion. He has yellowish eyes." Ordzhonikidze chuckled to himself. "He has a bushy mustache and . . ."

He leaned forward and in almost a conspiratorial tone whispered, "And dirty fingernails." And then he threw back his head and laughed. And all around him followed suit.

At the Congress of Soviets that opened the following day, Lazar was appointed to the All-Russian Executive Committee of the Russian Soviet Federation. He wasn't sure how this came about, but when he looked around the room after the confirmation, which seemed to be a fait accompli, he saw one face staring back at him, the face of the one who was known as Koba. He acknowledged the stare with a nod. The man with the sickly complexion didn't respond, but Lazar could detect the start of a smirk behind the black mustache. He thought of asking Voroshilov, who was standing next to him, whether his appointment was indeed a result of Koba's influence, but then he changed his mind. If this was his benefactor, then he would let him do what he wanted to. He wasn't in a position to challenge it. He would simply enjoy his new position, whatever it was, and his new city.

The enjoyment, though, was short-lived.

During the afternoon of March 11, 1918, the Bolsheviks dissolved the only democratically elected constituent assembly at the Tauride Palace. By nightfall, the new Soviet government was moving from Petrograd to the giant city 400 miles south—to the Kremlin in Moscow. Once more Lazar found himself on a train, but this time going south.

The Kremlin. The fortress. Lazar stood on the top of a hill that overlooked the Moscow River, supposedly where Russia began. Originally, there were buildings of wood under Ivan the Terrible, with white stone walls encircling them for defense. In fact, starting with the fourteenth century, the city was referred to as Holy Mother Moscow with the White Walls.

It was said that all of the city was really inside those walls. This is the ideal capital, thought Lazar, even better than Petrograd, for here was a true fortress against any evil.

Lazar walked around the area known as Cathedral Square, which is really the heart of the Kremlin. He saw the massive Cathedral of the Twelve Apostles with the bell tower of Ivan the Great, which was built in 1600, and the Cathedral of the Archangel, with its forty-six tombs of the czars of Russia. Then there was the Cathedral of the Annunciation, where princes and czars were wed. The oldest public building in Moscow, the Granovitaya Palace, then met his view. It went back to 1490, and it was here that Ivan the Terrible celebrated his victory over the Tatars at Kazan.

He touched the old Czar Cannon, which was cast in 1586 for Czar Feodor I, the feebleminded son of Ivan the Terrible. But he knew that no one ever fired the gun for fear it would blow up.

Just before him he saw the triangular-shaped yellow building that had once been the meeting place of the czar's Imperial Senate. Now it was to be the meeting place of the new Soviet government.

There were more buildings surrounding him, but Lazar had already seen enough. The Kremlin was immense. He had never before seen so many buildings clustered together, each grander than the next, all with precious works, from icons to frescoes to gold domes.

But only a few people knew and could enjoy these things. Only a precious few. And then he understood what the Cossacks had meant, for this was where his father's bread had gone; made up in all the wealth and beauty of the buildings was the sweat and agony of those who lived in Kabany and other villages throughout Russia.

"We had all toiled for the jewelry and icons and frescoes that were behind these doors and only enjoyed by the very few who locked themselves in."

He was whispering to himself, but he felt the whisperings getting louder and louder. "Towns were raped, children killed, so that these few could have more, more than they even knew what to do with, more than they could even appreciate."

He stood before the Grand Cathedral of the Assumption, where coronations had been held. It was trimmed in bronze and silver, with its doors plated by black-lacquered copper and embroidered in gold. Inside was the carved throne of Ivan, and a vermilion-colored gallery of icons encrusted with precious stones. A forty-six-branched silver chandelier weighing 880 pounds hung from one of its five golden domes.

Lazar walked around the cobblestoned streets of the Kremlin.

"This is the reason we never had enough to eat," he said to no one in particular. "This is what my cousin died for. This is why my mother had to be in dung-filled holes. This is where our lives have come."

Tears began forming in his eyes. He could not believe this could be happening. He never cried. He never showed emotion. But this had a greater effect on him than he realized. He could not quite nail down why. Was it resentment? Was it envy? Was it sorrow? Was it a touch of all three?

He found a small room on the top floor of a building on an unnamed alleyway just off Razin Street. The local people termed it Rybny Pereulok, or "Fish Lane." Here the Muscovites bought their sturgeon, carp, and caviar. During the winter months, the fish would be piled like a wall, their insides filled with snow to keep them fresh. Lazar didn't particularly like where he was. The constant smell of fish was nauseating; besides, two streets away was the Zaryadye, a slum area known for abject poverty and crime.

But where he lived and what he saw was quickly pushed to the back of his mind by the events that he was constantly exposed to at the Organization of the Workers' and Peasants' Red Army.

The infant Soviet Republic was still threatened by German armies in the Ukraine. Peace negotiations with the Germans had broken down again. The Germans had demanded independence for Poland, the Baltic states, Finland, and the Ukraine. Trotsky was horrified. He refused to sign any such treaty. Lenin, on the other hand, felt that there was no choice. He urged the signing. Much to Lazar's chagrin, the Ukraine decided in favor of the German proposal. Others screamed for independence as well, and a White army, opposed to the philosophies and direction of the new Soviet government and its Red Army, emerged. Anyone with any sense knew there was little time to play games. Lenin insisted, and the treaty with Germany was signed.

But now the new government faced another problem: civil war.

The czarist White generals were preparing for a counterrevolution. The Allied powers, annoyed by the peace negotiations, were ready to support the Whites. This war would see the Bolsheviks fighting against not only forces led by White generals such as Denikin, Vrangel, Yudenich, and Kolchak but also 50,000 British, American, Italian, Serbian, French, Czech, Polish, and Japanese troops. They had all joined in what was considered a holy crusade against the Red Republic. Their aim was simple: to crush the world's first workers' state.

Already the czar and his family had been taken into custody and shipped to the remote city of Yekaterinburg. On July 16, they were executed. The Romanov dynasty was formally ended. The era of the czars was over.

But the civil war had now swung into high gear. Trotsky had the responsibility of organizing the Red Army because of his already proven military success during the October uprising. Lazar was assigned as organizer of the first Red Army detachments. The task was to mold the army into a fighting force without equal. Even some former czarist officers would be used; the army urgently needed experienced military men.

All the while, Moscow was in an uproar. Factions rose and split. The new government, already in chaos, seemed about to be toppled at any moment. On August 30, an attempt was made on Lenin's life. It did not succeed. The following day, an attempt was made on the life of Uritsky, the chief of the secret police. It did succeed.

Lenin moved quickly. The word came down. Over a thousand people were arrested in Moscow and Petrograd, accused of taking part in the assassinations. They were all executed. Lazar could see what was happening. Lenin the God, Lenin the Hero, Lenin the Savior, had ordered the executions. It was crystal clear to all within the Kremlin. The founder of the Soviet State had no intention of letting his years of revolutionary activity and dreams wash away in a sea of his own blood. No, others would pay for his dream, and they would pay with their own blood.

At the end of 1918, Lazar was sent to Nizhni-Novgorod, a city 275 miles east of Moscow and not too far from Arzamas, where Mikhail and Yuri worked. Lazar had been thinking about his two older brothers for the past year, ever since leaving Kabany. Perhaps it was because he saw others with their families around them, like the father and his three sons with whom he remembered sharing some bread on the train to Petrograd or the cousins (there were five of them) he worked alongside at the military organization in Moscow.

His job in Nizhni-Novgorod was as an agitator for the Province

Committee. It would be a good place for him. Many Bolsheviks were flooding into the city, and it was fast becoming a Bolshevik stronghold as well as a base for Red Army detachments. Besides, his new assignment brought him back in contact with Nikita Sergeyevich Khrushchev, who Lazar had not seen in many years. Khrushchev had not changed much in the intervening period.

He still wanted food, not talk. From the moment he and Lazar had hooked up again to work with the Red Army, Lazar began to understand what fueled his friend. Once he ate, he would be able to relax and tell his jokes or make caustic remarks about the restaurant, the service, and even the food, which he devoured in what seemed like milliseconds. The young girl who Lazar had last seen with him and who someone had said was his wife was now nowhere to be seen. Questions about her whereabouts were met with a vacant stare.

Most of Lazar's fellow workers wanted little to do with the balding, rotund man. They found him crude and boorish. Lazar found him possessing all of those things, but he knew of his hardworking abilities, and he knew he could be counted on. Time after time, that had been proven. Nikita Sergeyevich was always there when Lazar needed him. He did what he was told and never tried to share or steal the limelight. No, people like this were rare among the Bolsheviks. Too many talked but never worked. Too many sought the laurels but didn't know why. Too many were devious (like those he saw in Moscow) but didn't have the gray matter to make their deviousness work for them.

There was at least one who wasn't in that category, and Lazar hoped to see him that night at the local eating place, the National. It seemed that every city had a restaurant called the National.

He saw him sitting off to the side, a smallish man with a thin mustache. He was slight of build, and his eyes seemed to dart about nervously. He was sitting with another man who was some six to seven years younger but who already had flecks of gray running through his small goatee.

"There," Lazar said to Nikita, pointing a finger in the direction of the table. "There. I told you."

Lazar walked directly to the table. He gripped the back of the small man's chair and whipped it around. The man started to rise but Lazar's strong hand pushed him hard in the chest. Then their eyes met.

"You!" the man cried out. "You!"

His outburst was answered with a laugh.

"Mikhail, you *pizdasos*—'bastard.' You recognize me?"

The two brothers hugged each other. It was easier for Mikhail to do. He had always been more demonstrative than Lazar. Perhaps too much so. Lazar had the more difficult time. He rarely showed emotion, and the closest he came to any sort of openness was when he saw the beauty of the countryside on the train trip from Moscow. That touched him.

Most of the time he felt anger, a deep, seething anger that had still to escape in any definitive way. He was able to succeed, he knew, because he could control his emotions while those around him, like Mikhail, went from one extreme to another. He also noticed that those at the top seemed to relish their own sense of power and command. They gave orders as if they were born to do so, and this was coupled with supreme arrogance, an arrogance born of a confidence that only they knew the difference between what was right and what wasn't, that only they could criticize with any degree of accuracy, that only they understood the problems of their own people and what was necessary to alleviate those problems. It was all too familiar, too close a pattern to what Russians had been used to all their lives. However, none of these qualities could be attributed to his older brother.

Mikhail introduced the man he was sitting with, a fellow of twenty-three years of age named Nikolai Aleksandrovich Bulganin. He said he was from this city, and Lazar instantly liked him. He was not only pleasant looking with a round face, puffy cheeks, and twinkling blue eyes, but he appeared to be totally calm. Nothing seemed to ruffle him. He had a short goatee, a high pompadour, and wore an army uniform that was a little too big for him.

He smiled half the time and wanted to the other half. Mikhail said that he was with the secret police and had only become a Bolshevik in the past year. Lazar thought it odd that so new a recruit would be pressed into the secret police. After all, how could he be trusted with so short a track record?

Lazar glanced at Khrushchev and gave a slight nod. Immediately, his friend began a conversation with Bulganin, while Lazar turned his attention to his brother. Nikita would find the answers. He always did.

"You look well," he said to Mikhail, first getting the pleasantries out of the way.

"You, too. I heard about your work in Moscow, and before."

"I wasn't there that long to make such waves."

"Nikolai knows of you. He works for Joseph Vissarionovich."

Lazar's eyes widened. The name again.

"The man called Koba?" he asked.

Mikhail chuckled. "Only to his friends."

Lazar looked at Nikita. He was deep in conversation with Bulganin. He could now afford to shift topics. There would be no need for the four of them to dwell on one man.

"And what do you hear of anyone?" Lazar said.

Mikhail chuckled again. It was as if he were getting a charge out of knowing something his younger brother didn't.

"I was waiting to hear something from you that was not all business. I don't suppose you're married, right?"

Now it was Lazar's turn to laugh.

"I wouldn't know what it would mean, anyway."

"I am," Mikhail answered. "So is Yuri. He lives in Arzamas, not too far from here. We both met our wives there. And we both actively work for the party, although I would say that my position is much more important. I am chairman of the Military Revolution Committee."

His chest puffed out.

"In fact, you could say that I was responsible for getting Nikolai here into the party, and you can see where he is going."

Lazar grinned. He would let Mikhail play the part of the older brother. It obviously made him feel good to do so, but he knew that the answer to any advancement would not lie in a local member of the secret police. No, the answer could be found only in Moscow, in the person who made the appointments. To Lazar, the party members were all the same, all stuffed with their own self-importance as if they would now replace the czar. The irony of it all.

"And Rosa?" he asked. "Where is our sister?"

Mikhail practically stood in his chair. A big smile crossed his face.

"With me, of course," he exclaimed proudly. "With me, of course."

"Of course," Lazar mumbled. Where else would she be?

"And" he started to ask, but stopped when he saw Mikhail's eyes drop.

"Rosa will tell you. Uncle Levick is in America. Morris, too, and his wife. You may remember her. Hannah Gutman from Kishinev. They met in Mozyr and were married. They, too, are in America. Doing well, I understand. Something to do with the dress business. Who knows? They're probably all capitalists now. You know Uncle

Levick. I think they live in the city of New York, although somebody told me they moved to a city named Philadelphia. I don't know about children.''

He was going to continue in that vein, but the look on the face of his younger brother suggested that he stop.

Mikhail sighed and stared into Lazar's eyes.

"I don't know much more. Rosa I found working in a hospital in Suradj. She said very little then. Even less now. All I could get from her was the fact that she wanted to be a doctor. I mean, of all things. She's only twenty-three, and she wants to be a doctor. Better she should get married and raise children. Those the country needs. Good children for the party. In the middle of a revolution, in the middle of a civil war, she wants something unattainable. I don't know anymore.''

Lazar nodded. He turned to Nikita. Both he and Bulganin were still arguing over where the country was going. They were in a war, Nikita was stressing, and economic emergency measures had to be imposed. He was pushing for tighter state controls, more expropriations, and confiscation of grain from the hard-pressed peasantry.

"War Communism" was Bulganin's response. "That is what you are advocating, and this would mean a virtual militarization of the Soviet Republic, with the Bolshevik party as the general staff.''

Lazar already knew what this would mean. He had heard enough of it in Moscow. What would be considered now as a temporary measure would later become a permanent one. It would never change.

Rosa didn't change much either. He saw that as soon as he entered Mikhail's small apartment. She was already there, setting the table for coffee. Nadezhda Bulganin, Nikolai's wife, was also there. She had just finished putting Kaddish lights on the sidebar that occupied a corner of the kitchen. He realized that she was Jewish and wondered what effect it would have on her husband's career.

Rosa still had the same pitch-black hair and eyes the color of coal. She was even more beautiful than Lazar remembered from her childhood. She wasn't too tall, but she seemed to exude strength, not only physically—he could see strong legs—but an inner strength that obviously would make her resilient to the trials of the world around her.

She was quiet for most of the evening, and although she appeared happy to see Lazar, it was a restrained happiness. He sensed that she was not quite sure of where she was going. She needed help. Yet, she

95

was making sure that all defenses were up, that she was in complete control of the situation. Lazar admired that. It reminded him so much of himself.

The others were different. Mikhail and his wife ran a gamut of emotions, from an outburst over the deceitfulness of the armies of the world that had invaded *Rodina*—Mother Russia—and how they must be "crushed" to the sad, quiet reflection of what has happened to the family.

"They are gone forever."

Yuri was the same way, although he echoed most of what Mikhail said. Lazar would not have even noticed him if it weren't for his cigar, which he kept lighting and relighting, striving for attention. But Rosa was unlike them. She said little, but whatever she did say was calculated, every word measured for its import and effect.

It wasn't until the Bulganins had gone home and his two brothers had retired to bed that Lazar and his sister had some time to themselves, to sit around the kitchen table and talk. What she had to say came out in almost a rhythmic way, a pattern, as if it had been rehearsed and rehearsed, waiting for a performance—like this one.

"We were forced out of Kabany. They just came and told us we have to leave. Just like that. Someone said that the Germans were advancing and we had to burn our houses. We couldn't leave anything for them. Others said we were being sent to a settlement farther to the east where we would be given new homes and new plots to farm. Some said it was by order of the czar; some said it was by order of a new revolutionary government. We didn't know. There was so little information. All we did know is we had very little left to eat and even less to barter. Papa's eyes were nearly gone. He had trouble even distinguishing me from Mama. He wouldn't admit it, though. He went around the house bumping into furniture, into doorways, and said nothing. Then he simply memorized each stick of furniture, each route around the house. We made sure, Mama and I, that nothing was moved, that Papa's sight was left intact. We two looked the other way, like it didn't exist."

Rosa glanced at the Kaddish candles flickering in the corner. Lazar followed her look but said nothing. He would wait, and she eventually would tell him.

"Things got worse. There were so few of us left in Kabany. It seemed that more and more would have to leave each day, but nobody seemed to know where. People would simply make up routes as to where they would go, some to the north, some to the south. They reminded me so much of Papa, groping around. I could almost see them following the bends in the countryside much like Papa touching his way from one room to another.''

She closed her eyes and put her head back against the chair. She was thinking now of every detail, and Lazar could see her wince at those she didn't wish to share with him. There were just so many to remember but even fewer to relate.

"We left. We sold what we couldn't carry and left. A blind man, an aging and broken woman, and me, their daughter. We went out to find a home, even a place to live, along with thousands of others. We were all searching for the same thing, but I'm not sure what. Our home then was what we carried. Mama would not leave her pots, or even one dish. We had a donkey that she was able to buy from the rabbi's son and a small cart that Uncle Levick had given her—you remember, the one he took with him on his trips.''

Lazar remembered it quite well. He used to sleep in it on the way back from those trips, on top of the hard, leather lasts. Sometimes he would use the soft animal hides as a blanket, especially on chilly nights.

He looked up at Rosa. She had stopped talking to give him time to reminisce. He nodded to her in appreciation, and she began again.

"Strange how things happen. We didn't get too far. We buried Mama in a field by the side of a road. I'm not sure where. It was her heart. She was talking one morning, sleeping that afternoon, and in the ground that evening. We had no sign, no warning, not even a good-bye. Papa said nothing. Some people helped us and that was all.''

A smile flashed across her face. She had obviously thought of something both amusing and painful.

"You know, I even left one of her dishes with her. I put it in her hands. It seemed only right, don't you agree?''

She fixed her eyes on Lazar.

"Papa and I continued. The trip became heavier to bear. There was one fewer of us, and yet it was more difficult now. Papa still said nothing. I don't think he ever said more than two words at a time to me after that. He just kept looking off into the countryside, his eyes closed half the time and opened the other half. It was all the same. He saw what he wanted to see.

97

"I think he left a part of himself—perhaps all of him—in that hole by the side of the road." She paused.

"I knew Mikhail was in Arzamas—we had been told that—and Papa insisted we get to his oldest, or, as he would say, 'the next in line.' I found Mikhail here. That was not too difficult. He is doing well, you know."

She surveyed the small apartment. Lazar followed her gaze, and his eyes picked up certain dishes that looked familiar and a large pot on the sidebar that reminded him of his past. The Kaddish lights were beginning to die now, and his mind shot back to the morning he left Kabany, the first time, when a Shabbat candle had glowed in the kitchen in the early sunrise. Now they were lights for a different purpose, but they still seemed to glow in much the same way.

Rosa watched her brother, and when their eyes met he could see moisture had formed in the corners of hers. The control was leaving her. She welcomed its departure.

"We can see Papa tomorrow if you want," she said. "We can find some flowers to put where he sleeps."

She cupped her face in her hands. Her shoulders began to heave.

Lazar studied the Kaddish candles. They had only a few seconds more of life.

3

The civil war proved costly, very costly. It killed off a generation of the most politically conscious workers, and it ruined Russia's economy. Apart from the war deaths, some 9 million people perished in just two years, from 1919 to 1920, of cold, famine, and disease.

In 1919, Lazar was sent south to Voronezh, where, with a group of other workers, he personally participated in fights against General Denikin's mounted army, which was coordinated by the White Guard cavalry of General K. K. Mamontov.

It was here that he learned the tactics of war, which included how to shoot a gun and how to kill with it. He remembered the first time. He had simply fired the small pistol into a crowd. Somebody clutched his throat and fell forward. It was a direct result of what he had done. It seemed so easy an act and yet so final.

After the Red Army captured the town of Voronezh, Lazar was assigned there as the chairman of the Province Revolutionary Committee. It was Bulganin himself who sent word back to Moscow about Lazar's effectiveness. Whoever was then making the decisions in the capital was basing them on firsthand, eyewitness information.

From this position, Lazar was able to erect a solid party structure in the region. He coordinated the rehabilitation of both agriculture and industry, which had been destroyed by the White Army.

"Let those," he stated, "wreak havoc on the people's minds. I will concentrate instead on first filling their bellies."

He set about feeding the stomachs of the area. Then he turned to the people's minds.

He was an "agitator" in the purest sense. He traveled the province on an "agit" train (a political indoctrination train filled with agitators and indoctrinators), "educating" the peasants about the revolution. The train would stop at various villages, and Lazar would cart out a Victrola with a huge shell speaker. He would play martial music first followed by speeches of well-known members of the government, with Lenin as the grand finale. People would come from every nook and cranny in the area just to hear some music—a form of entertainment and diversion that had been absent for much too long—and some words that were not the highly cultivated tones of a czar.

By 1920, Lazar's work had so impressed the Central Committee of the party that he was sent to Central Asia to become a member of the Turkestan Commission of the All-Russian Central Executive Committee and the Council of the People's Commissars. At the same time he was appointed a member of the Turkestan Bureau of Central Committee of the All-Russian Communist Party of Bolsheviks. If that were not enough, he also worked as the people's commissar of workers and peasants inspection of the Turkestan Republic, not to mention being one of the leaders of its Revolutionary and Military Council.

He collected titles and positions quickly, as was the vogue then. He was one of a select few who knew how to organize and weren't afraid of hard work. He even took on the chairmanship of the Tashkent city council in his spare time. There was little opposition. Those around him were less organized and infinitely lazier.

He was already receiving the support of Moscow, and that was plenty to carry him forward against any recalcitrant members of the former city council.

The only other person who seemed to work with the same speed, although not with the same intensity, was a fat, round-faced man whose fingers looked like sausages. He was a professional *apparatchik*, this Georgi Maksimilianovich Malenkov, but he had a card-file mind that was incapable of forgetting anything. He had been in the personnel department for the Central Committee and was able to help promote people from the ranks. He was then working on the Turkestan front in what was called the Political Administration.

Lazar found Malenkov a good conversationalist. He was able to dissect rather quickly, and with accuracy, what was happening in the country. He could split the hairs as well as anyone.

"You know, Lazar Moiseyevich, there is a difference between what we have heard before, from Marx, and what we hear now from Lenin. It may be heretical to say, but the distinction is quite apparent."

There was a singsong quality to his voice. It was rather high in pitch, and that, coupled with the round body, made Lazar begin to entertain doubts as to what was beneath the man's surface. But what mattered more was what he had to say.

"Let me draw the new parallel lines for you. According to Marx, the dictum is 'From each according to his abilities, to each according to his work.' That's the true socialist philosophy. But Lenin's principle, as I have heard it, is 'From each according to his abilities, to each according to his needs.' "

Lazar remained silent. He listened carefully, but he could not make up his mind which he preferred. His head grappled with "work" and "needs." Couldn't they be combined? Was it only one or the other? He could not quite decide which one he believed in, or was it neither? He realized that he had not really given any thought to an overall philosophy—to coping with a specific problem or taking a direction, yes, but as to a basic concept, no. There was a flaw in his character, in his thinking process. That much he recognized, but he didn't know what to do about it. It would require more study. For now, he must continue to work and work hard.

He struggled tirelessly to consolidate the young Turkestan Soviet Republic. Moscow would take even greater notice of him, he was sure. But Moscow's attention was turned elsewhere. The Kronstadt uprising captured the spotlight.

The Kronstadt soviet was a strong naval fortress on an island off Petrograd. Its sailors were famous as the vanguard of the revolution and as loyal Bolshevik supporters. Many of the sailors, as "sons of peasants," wanted an end to the grain confiscations. They demanded a free market place, which the emergency laws of war Communism had abolished.

But Trotsky, Lenin, and the Bolshevik Central Committee weren't listening. Before the winter's ice could melt, they sent the Red Army, commanded by the famous Tukhachevsky, to crush the sailors' mutiny. Many Communists, like the influential writer Victor Serge, were sympathetic to the Kronstadt demands. In the long run, however, the party was supported against the sailors.

Lazar heard what was happening and felt the same way. If the party fell, there would be chaos, and what would evolve out of the debris would be another dictatorship, perhaps even the return of a czar. They would be back to where they had started.

While Kronstadt saw fighting, the Tenth Party Congress opened in Moscow. A new fight emerged.

Lenin told the congress, "The poverty of the working class was never so vast and so acute as in the period of its dictatorship. The enfeeblement of the workers and peasants is close to the point of complete incapacitation for work." In order to save the revolution, Lenin ordered a compromise, a word that became anathema to Lazar. Lenin decided to give the peasants full freedom to cultivate their land and market the fruits of their labors.

The peasant was now being encouraged to produce more so that his share of the surplus would be more. This was known as the New Economic Policy (NEP); while the state controlled industry, foreign trade, banking, and transportation, agricultural production was to be controlled by the peasants themselves.

Lazar heard all of this and wondered, as he sat along the banks of the Chirchik River in Tashkent, between the Caspian Sea and the Tien Shan Mountains, what effect this would actually have on the people. He looked around him. The surrounding land was flat and sandy to the north, rising to form mountains in the southeast. Rivers from those mountains flowed inward, disappearing in the desert sands.

The known history of the area began at the time of Christ, when much of it belonged to the Chinese Empire. Tibet, China, and Turkey have all contributed to the vast region. Now it was Russia's turn to follow Marco Polo's famed Golden Road, which went through the heart of the territory.

Some of the people made their living here by farming or raising cattle. Private entrepreneurs (nepmen) made profits in the towns while in the rural areas, rich peasants (kulaks) prospered. They were in the minority although they controlled much of the industry. How would they benefit from this new mixed economy, which Lenin dubbed "state capitalism?" Would it change anything, or create new problems? And on the workers and poor peasants, how tough would this NEP be?

NEP was opposed inside the Bolshevik party by the newly formed Workers Opposition. This faction, led by the commissar of labor, Alexander Shlyapnikov, demanded the management of production by the unions. "There must be control."

The demand, for the most part, fell on deaf ears. "Let trade unions have the right to strike," responded Lenin. "But they must remain subordinate to the party."

With Trotsky claiming that trade unions must be "fused with the state," oppositionists within the Bolshevik party didn't have a chance. The leadership voted to prohibit the formation of groups within the party, to limit criticism, and to carry out a purge which, by the beginning of 1922, would result in the expulsion of more than one fifth of the membership.

Lenin had now successfully banned all opposition parties. The main forces against him had either collaborated with the Whites or threatened to do so. Not taking any further chances, the Tenth Congress went a step beyond and banned even factions. "If you ban other parties, it seems inevitable to curtail dissent in your own," said Lenin. He insisted, however, that the measure was only temporary, but when Malenkov told him of the remark, Lazar could only smile. He knew that the civil war had been just about won. There was no real threat to the Soviet State. Why ban factions? It was obvious that to Lenin and to Trotsky the "liberal" measures of the NEP must be imposed even at the cost of silencing dissent within the Bolshevik ranks.

Lazar kept his opinions to himself. He had already seen the expulsion of too many of his associates. He would not jeopardize his own position.

Lenin knew what he was after. In reality, the emergency measures of war Communism, combined with the NEP, had actually strengthened the apparatus of the state and the party at the "temporary" cost of democracy. It had to be invoked, for if this apparatus fell into the wrong hands, the government would be in grave danger.

Lazar remembered what he had been told many, many years ago on that first droshky ride back from Kiev.

"Whatever is good for the Jews," Uncle Levick had said to him. "Follow only that line of reasoning."

Lazar had heard all he wanted to. The decision to ban any dissent and to eliminate all opposition seemed more important to him than an economic idea such as NEP. He would be less concerned about where the economy was going and more concerned with the inherent right to change or alter direction. This now marked the beginning of a philosophy for him, one that became another signpost, one that said the party was to be considered invincible.

"The party can never be wrong," Lenin had believed, "and can, therefore, never admit to being wrong. It is indeed the party of the working people, and their party cannot be wrong, by definition."

His allegiance to Moscow was quite clear. Any negative or rebellious thoughts would be squelched first within himself. He would also not let anything surface on its own. He would hear what the rulers had decreed, and then he would gleefully join in, but only after he was sure the opposition had been disposed of completely. He would make Moscow notice him. That he was sure of.

Lazar saw a different city when he returned to Moscow in 1921. Its population was now 2.5 million, a dramatic increase. People were flooding into the capital, and it had become the commercial center of eastern Europe. There were trolley cars with cables, horse-drawn carriages, bonfires in the streets, and red banners with white lettering: BROTHERHOOD AND FREEDOM.

Lazar took a small flat atop a bookstore on Gorkovo Street just across from number 14, where Yeliseyevsky's Food Store held forth, the best in all Moscow. His new assignment was as an instructor of the All-Union Central Soviet of Professional Unions. He wasn't sure how he had got this post, who was responsible for it, other than Bulganin's remark to him when he was going through Nizhni-Novgorod that "You'll understand what is happening in time." Lazar always disliked cryptic remarks, and as fond as he was of Nikolai, it was just as easy to fire back, *"Idi slonu yaitsa kachat' "*—'Go swing on an elephant's balls.' " Sometimes, Bulganin could be a little old lady. He dreaded seeing what Bulganin would be like when he aged.

Lazar studied his own years. He looked in the mirror and was surprised at what he saw. The years in Turkestan had served him well. He had slimmed down a lot. The weight loss even gave him a taller appearance. His face had a narrow look, from the high forehead sloping down to the goatee that some said reminded them of Lenin's. He didn't know whether he would accept that as a compliment. Those who worked in the government were not all that trusting of Lenin. Those closest to the seat of power had privately compared him to the czar. It was more of the same. Only the faces and names had been changed.

Lazar adopted new facades. He spent moments each day in front

104

of the mirror, much as he had in his youth, perfecting a smile to be used with superiors and a frown for those beneath him. He would exhibit faces of indifference, faces of deep thought, and faces of arrogance. They would all be used.

Soon he would be thirty. He remembered what the old man who owned the bookstore downstairs had said to him as he headed for work just this morning.

"You should know where you are at thirty. You should be on the track. But most of you have no idea what I am saying."

Lazar knew very well. He felt like he wanted to tell the old codger that his words were not wasted, that he, probably more than any of the others, would be on the right track when the right time came.

He headed toward Red Square, where he was scheduled to meet with the members of a new Italian Communist party group who were engaged in agitator work similar to what he had been doing. The streets bustled with people who seemed to have a purpose in where they were going. Red Square was really a rectangle. It got its name in the seventeenth century from the Russian word *krasnaya*, which means both "red" and "beautiful." To Lazar, it was one of the most imposing sights he had ever seen, even more breathtaking than his first trip to Moscow a few years earlier.

A giant red flag now fluttered over the Kremlin above the cupola of the building where the new Council of Ministers held meetings. To his left stood the immense GUM, the State Universal Store that was quickly becoming Mecca to shoppers from all over Russia.

In front of him was St. Basil's Cathedral with its nine onion domes, each different in color and design. In back of him was the three-story Nikolskaya Tower. The Bolsheviks in their long, gray coats had poured through the gates of this tower four years earlier to overpower the White Guards. Today, the guards manning the main Kremlin Tower —the Spasskaya—were dressed in brown uniforms with flat caps emblazoned with a red star. Their pants legs were tucked into boots that came up to their knees; long carbines were strapped over their left shoulders.

Prior to the revolution, a picture of the Savior had hung over the entrance, and anyone passing through the gate had had to uncover his head in respect. The picture was no longer there. There was now a new savior on the premises.

Perhaps someday Lazar would meet him, even catch a glimpse of him flitting around the hallways. Lenin, though, never flitted. He never

105

roamed. He was noted for moving directly, swiftly, and decisively from one place to the next, from one meeting to another, from one problem to a solution.

He gave his name to the one guard who carried no rifle. Those in charge had pistols, not rifles. He then lined up with a group of other men, eight of them. In a few minutes a small man dressed in a black jacket, open-necked shirt, gray pants, and a small gray cap that was two sizes too small came out of the entranceway. He read names from a small card he fished out of one pocket. Lazar heard his name and stepped forward, as did the other eight when they heard theirs. They followed the man back through the entranceway. No one removed his cap.

The group walked silently up a set of steps, through a large wooden door, up another flight, and across a small, dimly lit hallway. Lazar wasn't sure where he was. He could only guess he was in the senate building but heard nothing in the way of activity. It was quiet, as though the building were totally abandoned.

After walking up another flight of steps, he began to hear voices. The group was heading toward a lighted doorway. He could see a number of people chatting, all in a language foreign to him. Someone in his group whispered, "Italians, waiting to see Lenin."

Lenin? His heart began to beat faster. Was it possible he would see this man for the first time? He had heard his voice on the Victrola that he played from the agit train, and he had seen pictures of the leader, but he had yet to see him in the flesh.

The men stopped before the doorway. Four others stood there talking in Italian with a small, dark-haired woman whose soft but forceful voice could be heard above anyone else's. The same person in the group whispered again. "Nadezhda Krupskaya—Lenin's wife."

Lazar immediately sized up the group. Four Italians and eight Russians. It was common practice to have more people, double if possible, than your guests. It was a form of one-upmanship as well as protection.

When they approached the Italians, their escort gave the card to Nadezhda. She glanced at it quickly and, with a facility that comes from years of teaching children in schools, began to tell the guests who these eight men were. She mentioned no names but simply told them what they did for the new Soviet government. When she had finished, she asked both groups to follow her and went into the lighted room.

This was Lenin's bedroom, Nadezhda explained. It was a small

106

room, perhaps only forty-two square feet. By the window was a desk covered with a blue broadcloth, a wooden armchair in front of it. A few books sat on the desk. To the right was an iron bed, a simple plaid blanket was folded on top. Nadezhda said that Lenin's mother had given the blanket to her son the last time they were together, in 1910, in Sweden. A photograph of Lenin and Nadezhda hung over the bed. To the left stood a bookcase with a small sofa in front of it.

The next was the dining room, a smaller area of perhaps only twenty-four square feet. There was an oak table in the center with a white tablecloth. Chairs with wicker seats circled the table. A large clock on one wall and some pots of flowers in the corner completed the room.

In answer to a question, Nadezhda said that the family (consisting of Lenin, his younger sister, Maria Ulyanova, and herself) ate the simplest of foods. For example, lunch would be a bowl of soup, some black bread, cheese, and tea.

From there they went into the living room, which was more dimly lit than the other two rooms. There were two sofas, one facing the other, a few tables, and some lamps. They all surrounded a large Oriental rug that captured everyone's attention. The colors of blue, green, orange, red, and yellow shot out at them. Along one wall was a spinet made of dark wood.

Most of the group focused on the rug—it was so riveting—until they detected something, or someone, in the far corner. At first, Lazar saw two green eyes staring back at him. Then he realized that they were the eyes of a cat. He studied where the cat was sitting. He shifted his gaze upward, into the face of a man who had thin lips, high cheekbones, arched eyebrows, and a smooth-skinned forehead that ran clear to the back of his head.

Dark eyes studied the group in front of him. There was no question as to the identity of the man in the rocker. It was Lenin himself.

One Italian stepped forward and bent down to kiss Lenin on each cheek. This was Bordiga, the head of the delegation. He started to make a speech on the future of Soviet-Italian affairs, but Lenin quickly put a hand out and gripped the man's sleeve.

"No, no. We have already listened to so many speeches at the congress. Let's just have a casual, friendly talk." He smiled. The voice was soft. The words came out slow, in almost a cadence. Lenin appeared to be in a talkative, friendly mood. He switched to Italian.

He was known to be fluent in German, English, and French. He could also read and translate in Polish and Italian, and he understood Swedish and Czech, not to mention the Latin and Greek he took in school.

He explained to the group, in both Italian and Russian, that he was always busy with state and party affairs and had little time to relax. He told how his favorite forms of relaxation were hunting and occasional outings in the country. He said he also liked to take walks in the woods and could ski, skate, swim, and bicycle. The delegates looked at one another as if to ask why they were being told all this. It was obvious that Lenin was not going to discuss party business during this "audience." It was simply to be social, and nothing more.

He related his interest in theater, but with the press of government, he wasn't always able to attend performances of even the Bolshoi. Now he would just stay in his living room, rock in his chair, stroke his cat, and listen to his sister, Maria Ulyanova, play Beethoven's sonatas, or perhaps Mendelssohn, Grieg, piano notes of Wagner's "Tannenhausen", and Tchaikovsky. He especially liked Beethoven's "Appassionata."

"I know nothing better than the 'Appassionata.' I could listen to it every day. It is hard to believe that such fascinating music was written by a human being. I always think with pride, somewhat naively, what wonders men can do." He began to wander.

The Russians shuffled their feet. The Italians grinned outwardly, but Lazar knew that there was confusion behind the smiles. It was all show, and it would not last very long. After another minute had elapsed, the small man in the gray cap returned, and the group was ushered out into the hallway. Nadezhda had disappeared, and the members of the group turned to one another, wondering what more would happen. The Italians pretended that they were pleased with what had taken place. Lazar felt differently. He had hoped there would be more to the visit than this. The one revealing aspect was that Lenin looked small, thin, frail, and his speech seemed to be slurred. This was not the Lenin he had imagined. No matter. At least he had seen the "Great One," as some had termed him, and he had listened to his voice, even though it was primarily in a foreign tongue. Yet, he could still say he had met Lenin, was even in his bedroom, and he could describe it if pressed. Information like this was always useful. After all, he was fast approaching thirty, and he intended to be on the right track no matter what.

The right track headed south. As 1921 turned into 1922, Lazar found himself on a train bound again for Turkestan. He was being sent as a representative of the Turkestan Bureau of the Central Committee of the Communist Party of Bolsheviks, a title that was more important, it seemed, than the job behind it. He was to quell a separatist movement that had started, but what he didn't realize then was that the success or failure of his actions would determine his fate for some time to come.

Lazar didn't remain in Tashkent long. He was able to crush dissident movements that wanted to draw away from Moscow rather easily. Red Army detachments were at Lazar's disposal as well as a tight organization he had helped to create. Within three months a messenger came with orders recalling him to the capital. He could not have been happier. Although he was somewhat autonomous in this region of the country, with little competition from other members of the local committee, except for Malenkov, he knew that he was still out of the center arena where the giant searchlights of attention held forth. He had made his mark here. That was good. He had found a useful springboard, not so much in the people, over whom he had ruled, but rather in the results he had obtained. Clearly, as far as Lazar was concerned, the end had justified the means.

He discarded fellow committee members with no remorse. He would just refuse to recognize their existence. If he felt they could not serve his purposes, then he would simply toss them aside. He would bother only with those he felt would be important now or could be important in the future.

But now the word had come down. His success, a relatively effortless one, at least to him, had been noticed, and once more he packed the few belongings he had, all fitting into three canvas bags, and boarded the train to the north. He would make his customary stop along the way.

Nizhni Novgorod was only 265 miles east of Moscow, and Lazar couldn't understand why his brothers weren't elevated instead of him. Mikhail was not only closer to Moscow but was older than Lazar and had already risen to a post as member of the presidium of the province's Executive Committee.

Also, unlike Tashkent, Nizhni Novgorod was fast becoming an industrial center in Russia. Located at the fork of the Volga and Oka rivers, it was one of the oldest cities in the country, known as the

109

Cradle of the Russian Empire. Back in the Middle Ages, the city was an important commercial center when west-east travel along the Oka River through a low pass in the Ural Mountains met north-south travel on the Volga River.

The upper part of the city contained a fortress and a host of historic cathedrals, while the lower part held all the manufacturing factories. Already armaments were in production there.

No, Lazar thought, this was a far better place to be if one wanted to move up the ladder. Mikhail and Yuri were both here plus Nikita and Nikolai, two new people he would soon meet, and, of course, Rosa.

One primary reason Lazar stopped at Nizhni Novgorod was to see Rosa. He had taken a deep interest in her well-being. When they were children back in Kabany, he couldn't give her the time of day. Actually, he didn't really like her. She was cold and aloof, ignoring him and having time only for their mother. Sasha seemed to be the center of her world and, to a lesser extent, Moisev.

But things were different now. For some unexplained reason, she had warmed to Lazar. Perhaps, it was because he had succeeded to the position once occupied by her parents. That was a possibility. Yet, it could not be only that, for both Mikhail and Yuri were older than he. No, it had to be something else, but what he did not know. What he did know was that she liked to talk with him especially about where the country was going and its relationship with the rest of the world. She once met a woman from Canada and was told that there was great beauty, great wealth, and great opportunity in the Western Hemisphere. She tried to find out everything she could about Canada.

The only other person she spoke with at any length was Nadezhda Bulganin. She, too, had lost her parents at an early age, and in Nadezhda, Rosa found some solace.

To Lazar it seemed that she simply needed a boost in her confidence. If she could only come out of her shell and let herself see and taste and experience life about her. But he knew he could not force the issue. She had to do it herself; she had to want to do it.

It was a good time to visit his brothers for a number of reasons. Yuri's new son was the first to be named after Moisev, and although Lazar found the name Misha Moiseyevich rather amusing, he still engaged in balancing the one-year-old on his knee. He hadn't thought he was capable of sharing this much affection. He really hadn't thought of children or marriage or family, other than scattered flashbacks to his childhood.

But perhaps this small show of interest was what propelled the shy, tall girl to him. It wasn't that she was so tall. Actually, she was Lazar's height, but compared to the others in the room she was a giant. Mikhail, Yuri, and both of their wives were short. So were Bulganin and Nadezhda, as was Nikita, who now had an ample but rather pleasing woman in his company.

This new woman was the kind of person to whom Lazar immediately felt attracted. He wanted to make sure it would be good for him politically. If all the important people in the party were married, then his course was clear. It would be just another obstacle to hurdle.

Her name was Maria, and she worked in a textile factory. She had long, brown hair that was bunched in a knot on the back of her head. Her eyes were hazel, which Lazar thought blended perfectly with the beige and green dress she wore. You couldn't say she was beautiful, but she was certainly pleasant looking, and her voice was soft, somewhat like Rosa's.

She worked with Nadezhda at the factory, and it was Nadezhda who had invited her to meet Lazar. The Bulganins were like that. No one, in their mind, should be without a companion. First, it would be Lazar, and then, when the time was right, they would turn to Rosa.

Maria talked a little about her background. She said she was from the area and that her mother and father had originally supported the czar. They had once been merchants. Now they were simply laborers. Lazar could sense a hint of resentment in her voice. But there was a difference. Unlike his own family, Maria's had not had to endure the pogroms and the Cossacks and the anti-Semitism that had been so much a part of his life. She didn't have to. She was Russian, not Jewish.

One person at the party, who was neither Russian nor Jewish, stood out. He was introduced as Anastas Ivanovich Mikoyan. He had been sent by Moscow with a mandate to work in the Provincial Party Committee of Nizhni Novgorod. He was to be the party secretary. Immediately, he had met with some distrust by the local leadership. Lazar could have told him this. Most people sent directly by Moscow had faced the same circumstances. He certainly had in Tashkent, so he could empathize somewhat.

Lazar liked Mikoyan instantly. He was a small man, perhaps only

111

five feet three inches, with olive-colored skin, black wavy hair, and a small, pencil-thin mustache that Lazar felt would be better if thicker. The sharp nose reminded him of a chicken hawk, and the upturned lips gave him a sour expression. Only when he looked into the large, brown eyes did he see a combination of softness and intelligence.

It was obvious that he kept himself in good physical condition, unlike Nikita and Nikolai, who already sported large bellies. His wife, Ashken, stood by his side. She, too, was small and quiet.

Mikoyan came from the Armenian village of Semain but had been educated in Tbilisi at the famed Nerseyan Seminary. Immediately, this told Lazar he was a man to be reckoned with.

Lazar's feelings about people in general were divided into four groups. There were those, like Nikita, who he could control; people who, although beneath him in importance, would still be of some benefit. There were those—the majority—who were nothing more than a step above a peasant; these people Lazar simply dismissed as not being worthy of much attention. At the other end of the spectrum were those who were either on an equal footing with him or were above him but whom he didn't like or trust. Basically, he still trusted no one, although he could certainly share likes, dislikes, and views about where the country was heading and who could lead it. More often than not, these were only exercises in gossip, exchanging tidbits of information —the juicier, the more secretive, the better.

But then there were those who were on an equal footing with him, although not in the same sphere of interest, and whom he genuinely liked. Nikolai and Anastas were two in that category. Both were highly intelligent, educated (something he knew he wasn't), and had a firm grasp on what was really happening in Russia. They also seemed somewhat honorable, which was good for him as he was somewhat dishonorable. What he needed was information, a good pipeline that would help prepare him for the events still to come in Moscow. These two were the perfect sources.

Bulganin was especially useful when he drank, something neither Lazar nor Anastas did to any extent. They both nursed their drinks as long as possible, watching as their friend Nikolai's nose (which was prominent enough) reddened and seemed to grow larger with each glassful of cognac. He was one of the few Russians who did not like vodka all that much. Most Russians preferred vodka over any other drink but in its absence would gladly down practically everything else, including straight rubbing alcohol. Bulganin did have class. That was for sure.

"The word is already out. Lenin has had a stroke," he said, staring pensively into his half-filled glass.

"What kind?" asked Lazar.

"What kind?" Bulganin mimicked. "How many kinds are there? Ask Rosa. She wants to be a doctor. It's a stroke. It means he's not going to be able to move around so much. Parts of him are paralyzed, I hear. I don't know how much it has affected his mind."

"I know," said Lazar. "When I saw him it looked like he had already had a stroke. This can't be the first."

Mikoyan, as usual, simply listened. Invariably, he had little to say. He was a superb listener, and Lazar envied that attribute. He himself was a poor one. He wanted to talk too much, to take over the conversation, to have someone else on the receiving end of his voice.

This time, though, he decided to follow Anastas's lead. He remained quiet. Bulganin was drinking good now and talking even better. Let him continue.

"You know, that reminds me. You could do something with Rosa. Why should she remain in this ugly place? Get her to the university in Moscow. She would make a fine doctor. You just tell Stalin what you want to do. With Lenin out of the picture, he'd be the one to see."

Lazar's ears pricked up. Stalin. He had heard the name Joseph Vissarionovich before and even the family name Dzhugashvili at times and then the nickname, Koba, that only his closest comrades could use. Now he had heard the latest. Joseph Vissarionovich Dzhugashvili, alias Koba, had taken the name Stalin.

"Means 'man of steel,'" said Bulganin, head still buried in his glass. "But to me he's still a pocked-faced, little twerp."

He looked up at Lazar and Mikoyan.

"*Gavno*—'shit'—I shouldn't have said that. He's my boss, you know, and who knows if I can trust you two."

He smiled, reached for the bottle of cognac, and turned it upside down over his glass. Nothing came out.

"*Gavno*—'shit'—again," he murmured and got up to get another bottle from the cupboard.

Lazar watched him carefully. He didn't have to say more. He had already given him the clue, the tip he wanted. Lenin was slowly dying, if he was not dead now, and Trotsky seemingly had no power. Who else was there? Being stuck in the middle of Central Asia, he had lost track of the power brokers in the party. Names floated in and out, like Kamenev and Bukharin and Malenkov. But they didn't seem to matter. In effect, Nikolai had told him who was responsible for his return to Moscow. And that was the one he had to cultivate.

The Eleventh Party Congress in March 1922 was the last one Lenin attended. Following this, the Central Committee elected Stalin as general secretary of the Communist party. Word had floated around that this was done over Lenin's objections, and, in fact, Lenin was supposed to have said, "This cook will cook only peppery dishes," one of his few attempts at wit.

During Lenin's illness it was obvious that the party leadership was being passed to a triumvirate: Zinoviev, Kamenev, and Stalin. The fact that Kamenev was married to Trotsky's sister didn't prevent him from siding with Zinoviev and Stalin against his own brother-in-law. In fact, Trotsky's own position as chairman of the Military Revolutionary Committee was now deemed an honorary one, and everybody knew that his abilities were not being sufficiently used. In effect, he was being sidetracked and not given any key work in the party apparatus.

The bitter struggle for eventual succession had begun. Lazar had been recalled by Stalin himself; yet he had not seen his new boss after two months back in Moscow. He was given an apartment on the top floor of a building at Sobachaya Ploshchadka, which meant "Dog Square," so named because the kennels of the czar's estate had been located at this site in the seventeenth century. The square was formed by the streets Maly ("small") Nikolopeskovsky and Bolshoi ("great") Nikolopeskovsky.

Each morning he reported to building on Gogol Boulevard that housed the Ministry of Defense, where he was given lists of names to review. He had to determine those who were members of the party, which ones he knew personally, and what he thought of them. He was not sure what this all meant, but he would look at names from the width and breadth of Russia. There were literally hundreds of thousands of names. It was as though the government were now trying to compile a master list of every single person in the country.

He understood that what he was seeing, in its infancy and at its very base, was the accumulation of power by Stalin. Lenin's stroke had obviously forced him to relinquish a lot of the active leadership of the party, and Stalin's new position as general secretary was becoming increasingly important. But Lazar had still not even met him. It was as though he existed in name only, like those on the lists. He knew Stalin was working from inside the Kremlin, but he had not passed through the Spassky Gate since seeing Lenin there a year ago.

By June, he had been given the task of not simply checking names but actually organizing a list of instructors for the party. From that he graduated to the responsibility of posting the instructors, disseminating names throughout Russia.

Lazar realized that his importance to Stalin would be measured by the people he posted. By carefully analyzing the names, he made sure that only those favorable to Stalin would be given the plum jobs. He had now taken sides. In effect, he had declared his allegiance to one man; he hoped that such devotion would be felt by the man in the Kremlin.

Orders flooded in from Stalin "suggesting" one person over another, "asking" whether certain people could be assigned to specific posts, "questioning" a particular individual. In each instance, Lazar made sure that his loyalty would be unchallenged. He understood the orders for what they were and carried them out swiftly and accurately.

If there was to be any kind of "shadow cabinet"—waiting in the wings for Lenin's death—he would make sure he was a member of it.

It was obvious that Stalin was creating his own power structure notwithstanding the fact that Lenin was still alive. It was also obvious that Trotsky still had considerable influence while a few others, like Kamenev and Zinoviev, had their fingers in the pie. It didn't matter. Stalin had moved Lazar around at will, bringing him up through the ranks, slowly but surely. He would do nothing to change that direction.

For the next two months, he worked eighteen-hour days—every day—to give his leader what he wanted. He had no social life. He never went to restaurants anymore, taking his meals either in his room or at his desk. He even ceased writing Maria.

Now he would rise at five each morning, be at his desk well before the regulars arrived, and stay rooted there until eleven at night when he would go home to sleep. Five hours later, he was at his post again. If he faced an especially knotty problem, he would sleep in the office just to save the walking time between his flat and the ministry.

Within two months, his loyalty was rewarded. He was named chief of the Organizational-Distributing Department of the Central Committee of the All-Union Communist Party of Bolsheviks. He was now the head of the Personnel Department of Russia, one of the more important and pivotal spots in the new government. Now, surely, he would meet the man who was responsible for all this.

He did, but it was not for another two months, and then it was only with a group of other people. The road was still slow and painful.

The second time he passed through the Spassky Gate it was different. Activity was everywhere. Now there were people rushing from one end to the another, going in and out of buildings, carrying papers, talking constantly. In a short period of time following the centralization of power by the Bolsheviks in Moscow, one could see clearly that this was indeed the main seat, the focal point, the center of the entire country.

But it was no longer an armed camp. Although soldiers of the Red Army could still be seen, they were not in such numbers as before. They were less conspicuous than during the early days after the revolution and certainly nowhere near the number during the war with the Whites. There seemed to be less fear of another uprising. The Bolsheviks were ensconced in the Kremlin. That was for sure. World War I had ended, the Whites had been defeated, and opposition parties had been outlawed.

The rest of the world was feeling the euphoria that came with the end of the war, and business was booming in the West. The twenties were beginning to roar. Who wanted to worry about what was going on in the massive country to the east? A Communist government was now in power? So what? "They won't last long," said the capitalists. "And if there is money to be made, we'll sell to them." Who cares who buys—the Communists or the czar? Who cares?

Ten of them showed up at the Spassky Gate that morning: nine men and one woman. Most of the names meant little to Lazar except for their backgrounds, which he had read in their records. But certain ones he seemed to recall from his days in Petrograd: Kirov, Ordzhonikidze, Kuybyshev. The group seemed relatively cheerful. They laughed among themselves, even going so far as teasing the one woman among them who worked in the agricultural division. The men compared the increase in production of watermelons with her breasts, which were of enormous proportions.

Whatever euphoria they were feeling quickly left when they entered the small office of the man they had come to see. Malenkov, newly appointed as secretary to the general secretary, ushered them in.

Stalin was standing behind an enormous desk. A line drawing of Karl Marx hung from the wall. There were no other pictures; in particular, there was no photograph of Lenin.

The only other items in the room were a wooden chair in front of the desk and a small table in a corner. To say that the room was Spartan would be an understatement.

Stalin looked different from close range. His face was indeed pock-marked, the result of a childhood disease, and his eyes were yellowish. He was short, shorter than Lazar had realized, and if it weren't for the bushy hair and equally bushy mustache, Lazar thought, he wouldn't look too imposing. In fact, he seemed rather frail. He was also not a typical Georgian, for they are noted for their outgoing manner and outpouring of emotions. Instead, he was cold and unemotional on the surface. It was clear from his demeanor that he liked to have others do his dirty work.

He wore a brown, long-sleeve shirt that was buttoned at the collar. It seemed too hot in July for such clothes and, to make matters worse, the one window in the room was closed. Stalin was also holding the bowl of a lit pipe, cupping it in his hands. It was clear to Lazar that the man suffered circulatory problems and was unable to feel the warmth of a Moscow summer.

A sort of Cheshire-cat grin leaped across his face. Lazar couldn't remember what he said. He seemed to be mumbling some sort of welcome. It looked as though he were solely interested in matching faces to names and positions and perhaps letting his subordinates know who he was and that, despite his appearance, he was the one to be reckoned with. Whatever it was, it worked, for Lazar could feel the power exuding from this man. He knew that this was not someone to be trifled with, that this was a person who had and wanted control.

The entire audience lasted fewer than ten minutes, and all Lazar could recall were the final words. "I will see you all again. I hope I will." He let out another Cheshire grin, and the group departed.

He did not see Stalin again until the end of December, when he attended the Bolshoi Theater, but not to see a ballet. The First Congress of Soviets of the USSR was scheduled to convene at noon on that day.

Originally, the Soviet republics consisted of the Russian Federation, which included the peoples of the Volga and the Northern Caucasus areas and Turkestan; the Ukrainian Republic; the Byelorussia Republic; and the republics of Transcaucasia. But now the government wanted to conclude an agreement on the formation of the USSR itself. The attempt would be to establish a multinational state that would, it was hoped, endure for centuries to come.

Lazar was invited to attend the congress meeting on the next-to-last-day of the year. By then, a document issued on December 14 was making the rounds of the inner party members. In his position, Lazar had been one of the first to see it. It was a sheaf of papers that Lenin had written, a testament that critically assessed all potential candidates to succeed him, stating that none alone was capable of replacing him. Lenin wrote that Trotsky had "exceptional abilities but that his too far-reaching self-confidence and a disposition too much attracted by the purely administrative side of affairs" made him unqualified to be the successor.

He dismissed Zinoviev and Kamenev as "unreliable," bypassed Piatakov because of his "inability to grasp political problems," and removed Bukharin as a possibility because of his alleged "failure to comprehend Marxist dialectics. The favorite of the party; but also a soft wax on which any demagogue can inscribe whatever he likes."

That brought him to Stalin. And, "Joseph Vissarionovich does not know how to use power with sufficient caution. I can only suggest that our party members remove him from his position, and quickly."

Lazar could only weigh the words and determine for himself who he would support and in what direction he would move. He could not stay stagnant, not now. He would keep his eyes and ears open and make his decision at the best possible moment. He would know more at the congress.

It was held at the Bolshoi Theater starting at noon on December 30. Lazar had constantly seen the outside of the building with its great portico because it was within eyesight of where he worked. Tall stuccoed columns were surmounted by four rearing horses harnessed to the Chariot of Apollo, clearly a monument to the imperial age. But he had never been inside the gray building.

The interior of the Bolshoi was all red plush. Founded in 1776, the Bolshoi, which means "great" or "big," had five tiers of red and gold, a massive crystal chandelier, and a stage as large as the auditorium itself. Even at the third tier to the side and to the rear, where Lazar sat, the acoustics were magnificent.

It was said that in the 1850s Richard Wagner conducted here and amazed the audience by not facing them (as was the custom in Russia) and facing the orchestra instead. That was only one of many stories. Today would be another.

The congress was opened by Lenin's close associate Pyotr Smidovich. His speech was clear and to the point. He said that the unification of the Soviet republics was a "wonderful source of tremendous new forces of resistance and construction . . . attracting workers of all nations."

Lazar looked around at the audience. Many were in their early twenties, and they listened to the speech of the veteran delegate with bated breath. Lazar realized he was only a few years older, but his experience had already aged him considerably, and his present job gave him a perspective that the majority of those here could not equal.

Mikhail Frunze was given the floor. The working people of the Ukraine had elected him a delegate to the congress. He stated that the conference of the delegations of the four unifying republics instructed him to put on the agenda a "declaration on the formation of the Union of Soviet Socialist Republics and a treaty on the formation of the USSR."

He read the declaration:

"Since the formation of the Soviet republics, the nations of the world have been divided into camps: the camp of capitalism and the camp of socialism. Reigning supreme in the camp of socialism are mutual trust and peace, national freedom and equality, peaceful coexistence, and fraternal cooperation of nations.

"It was only in the camp of the Soviets, only in the conditions of the dictatorship of the proletariat, which rallied the bulk of the population around itself, that it became possible to uproot the national oppression, create an atmosphere of mutual trust, and lay the foundation of fraternal cooperation of nations.

"The years of war have left their traces. Devastated fields, plants standing idle, destroyed productive forces are making it impossible for individual nations to cope with economic development single-handed. Economic rehabilitation is unfeasible without the unification of the republics.

"Moreover, the unstable world situation and the danger of new attacks necessitate the establishment of a united front of Soviet republics that would replace all capitalist governments.

"Finally, the very essence of Soviet power, which is international by its class character, is prompting the working masses of all Soviet republics to form a single family.''

He paused, looked at the ceiling, and thrust his right fist into the air.

''Declaring this before the whole world, we delegates . . . decree the signing of a treaty on the formation of the 'Union of Soviet Socialist Republics.' ''

The historical moment had arrived. The audience rose to its feet and cheered. By voice vote, the delegates unanimously approved the declaration and the treaty on the official formation of the USSR. Within minutes, the heads of the delegations, from all the republics, were walking to a table covered with red velvet; they would sign the appropriate documents. It was a solemn procession. Each signature evoked loud applause.

Lazar looked around. People sat on the edges of their seats, their faces anticipating the final signature. He searched for familiar faces, but there were few. He didn't see Stalin, but he did see Voroshilov standing to the side of the stage. He didn't see Trotsky or even Lenin, but he did see Ordzhonikidze sitting in the front row next to Bukharin.

And then, when the last delegate had departed the stage, Mikhail Kalinin, the tall, stately president of the Central Executive Committee of the USSR, rose to give the closing remarks.

''For millennia the best minds of mankind have been trying hard to evolve structures which would enable nations to live without strife, to live like friends and brothers. The first stone on this road is being practically laid only now, at the present day.''

The audience again erupted into spontaneous applause. And then it truly began. The strains of the ''Internationale'' could be heard from Victrolas on both sides of the auditorium below, rising like a wave and engulfing tier after tier. Men began weeping openly. Others were cheering. Many were singing, many embracing one another. Some, though, a few, remained silent, as if trying to analyze, to understand exactly what was taking place. Others were contemplative, some serious.

Lazar's eyes swept the exquisite auditorium. It was an amalgam of people, a mélange of voices and faces. He looked at the magnificent crystal chandelier. It was swaying almost in time to the music. He quietly studied what was going on around him. No longer was he the innocent, naive youth, listening to fiery speeches in Kiev. He was well past that. He would be thirty next year. He thought of Uncle Levick and of Morris and even of his mother and father and Rosa and his brothers and all the others from Kabany, and he realized that none of them knew what was really happening in the country of their birth. He, though, was a part of history. They would all read about what was going on here, but he was present—on hand—an eyewitness to the event that would have a lasting effect on his world, his life, and perhaps worlds and lifetimes of others in the future.

He was no longer a youth. It was time to assume the mantle of adulthood completely. He thought of Maria and decided he would marry her and bring her to Moscow. It seemed the thing to do.

His eyes scanned the crowd once more. They were searching, seeking out the short, stocky figure in a corner of the stage, out of sight from most of the delegates. He stood there with his arms clasped behind his back, the ever-present pipe hanging from the side of his mouth. Lazar could see the yellowish eyes even from this distance. They seemed to glow. He was waiting, biding his time, waiting for the propitious moment.

Lazar remembered Lenin's testament again. It had made one additional, important demand: that Stalin should be removed as general secretary. But nothing had happened. The Politburo had not even mentioned the testament. There had been no reference to it at this congress whatsoever. Why? Why?

Lazar zeroed in on the eyes until he caught them staring back at him. They pierced his. No acknowledgment. Just a watch. A purposeful watch.

Five days later, in a postscript to his testament, Lenin described Stalin as "rude and capricious." From Lazar's vantage point, it was an understatement, for Stalin had set a course of planting his own men throughout the party structure. He was determined to change the governmental operation to his liking, no matter what the means.

During his illness, Lenin had time to think about what was happening around him, and his thoughts were being disseminated immediately. "Our workers' state is deformed." "The weight of bureaucracy is too great." "The division between Trotsky and Stalin spells disaster." There was a steady stream of such statements flowing from the small room in the Kremlin.

Lenin saw that Stalin was creating this enormous bureaucracy for his own advantage. He tried to stop it. While the party planned for its March congress (the twelfth), Lenin attempted to censure Stalin for ordering a Red Army invasion of Georgia over the previous decision of the Politburo. Lenin felt that any attempt to crush the Georgian dissidents would be best accomplished through political means, not by military force. Stalin thought differently. Accordingly, Lenin sought to have Stalin removed as general secretary.

It went nowhere. Stalin was too firmly entrenched. He had support in almost every branch of the government. The only question remaining to be answered was how far he could go.

Two groups of pretenders to Lenin's throne had surfaced. The first was headed by Trotsky, a member of the Politburo, and chief of the Red Army, who was considered a man of great learning, a gifted writer, and a capable organizer. At the forefront of the other group, known as the *troika*, or "triumvirate," were Zinoviev, Kamenev, and Stalin. All three were also Politburo members.

Zinoviev was a well-known, long-time associate of Lenin, leader of the party's powerful Petrograd organization and the head of the Comintern. Kamenev, too, was an old-time associate of Lenin and head of the influential Moscow party organization. In actuality, Stalin was really the least known, but as the party's general secretary, he was in a position to control its administrative apparatus and thereby to pack both party and government organs with his own people. This he was doing.

By October 1923, Trotsky had assailed Stalin's manipulation of party membership. He labeled it "the dictatorship of the Secretariat." He even brought this criticism, endorsed by forty-six high-ranking party members, before the Central Committee. Stalin, whose men formed a majority in the Central Committee, branded Trotsky's critique not only as a "grave political mistake," but "an anti-Leninist factional move that threatened the party's unity." In fact, at a party conference he condemned Trotsky's views as "petty bourgeoisie deviations from Leninism." He warned him that such behavior "was not compatible with party membership."

It was apparent that Stalin would give no quarter to anyone. He would take on the great name of Trotsky if necessary. No one was sacred.

The attacks on Trotsky took their toll. By the beginning of the following year, he left for a rest in the Caucasus. Lenin's illness worsened, but Trotsky did not know this. Stalin took no chances. He sent Trotsky a telegram: TROTSKY. GEORGIAN LINE. POLITBURO THINKS BECAUSE STATE OF HEALTH YOU MUST PROCEED TO SUKHUM. REPEAT. PROCEED TO SUKHUM. STALIN.

Stalin knew that Lenin's days were coming to an end, and he would make every attempt to see that Trotsky would be unable to attend the funeral.

During the past year, while Stalin was waiting for Lenin to die, Lazar was moving ahead with his new life. Maria had become pregnant almost immediately after the small wedding that only his brothers, sister, and the Bulganins attended in Nizhni Novgorod. She had given birth to a girl who they named Maya, after Moisev. Lazar didn't know what possessed him to follow the Jewish tradition of naming a newborn after a recently deceased member of the family. He had always ignored his heritage. Of course, it was Maria who had been desperately trying to instill some sort of commitment in her husband other than what he felt toward the government. She hoped that perhaps he would become "Someone with more passion for what really counts—people." Whatever it was, Maria was at least successful when it came to their daughter.

However, she began to wonder whether she had won only the proverbial battle and not the war, for Lazar spent even less time at home, occupying himself with what was happening at the Kremlin. It was hard not to.

As 1923 turned into 1924, rumors flew thick and fast among those in the government about Lenin's condition. Apparently, it had worsened drastically. Those he saw around him in the ministry building were now making wagers, for bottles of vodka, or bushels of tomatoes, or cartons of French-made cigarettes, on the precise day, hour, even the minute, that Lenin would finally die.

It was a perverse delight that seemed to seep into every corner of the bureaucracy. Every *apparatchik* was responding in some way to what was happening. It began to resemble an enormous lottery. However, it never went beyond the walls of the government buildings. The general populace, for the most part, thought Lenin had a firm hand on the wheel. It was typical of the enormous success of the system that the average Russian was kept totally in the dark about what was really taking place in his own country.

Lazar was changing Maya (one of the few times he did) when news of Lenin's death, at age fifty-three, arrived, on January 21, 1924. Despite his position in the government, he learned of Lenin's dealth by the commotion in the street below. Rumors had always traveled quickly, especially bad ones, and he hurried to the ministry building, where he was greeted by silence. It seemed strange that those he worked with were going about their business matter-of-factly, talking in hushed tones about the possible successor, while the average citizen in the street was racing from one group to another to exchange tidbits of information.

To the Muscovite, there was great excitement. The founder of the Soviet state had died. A father had been pulled away from them. Men, women, and children wept openly, an outpouring of emotion. Their grief was genuine. But to many working within the government's walls, within the Kremlin itself, there was less agony over what had passed than over what would happen next. Sorrow was replaced by fear. Most knew how ill Lenin had been for the past year, growing progessively worse each day, and most knew of the inner-party struggles that were taking place. Lenin's death did not seem half as important as what would follow.

Much of what Lenin had said over the last years of his life was already being disregarded. It seemed as though he had served his purpose and now would be relegated to the pages of a history book.

But there was so much that wouldn't be there, too. Bulganin knew that Lenin was looked upon as a god, the messiah who saved the country from the terrible czar, but as he told Lazar at dinner that night in the privacy of his dining room, "How many knew the ruthlessness of the man? Did they know how he increased the activity of the Chekists, the secret police, who now have access to practically everything and everyone in the country? Did they know about the mass execution orders that Lenin signed? Did they know about the martial law that he imposed on many villages? Mikhail used to tell me how questionable party members in Vyksa would not only be stripped of their jobs but in many instances actually executed because they simply wouldn't conform to party requirements. They were considered traitors to the new Soviet state and as such they were deprived of their lives.

"Did people understand that Lenin, our great benefactor, had given the orders for the closing of many churches? Did they know how many religions were outlawed, how many people with religious beliefs who were no longer working or even alive?"

Nikolai did not have to tell Lazar all this. Violence and ruthlessness had always marked Lenin's reign. He had been there on the inside, and he knew that the "Great One" was primarily responsible for the policy of terror, of arrests and executions that had actually set the stage for the mass purges and murders that would mark Stalin's days. To him, Lenin was simply an opportunist with a holier-than-thou attitude and self-righteous words. He heard Bulganin's speech, and he wondered whether he was not also hearing a description of himself.

But Lenin was gone, and his lieutenants from the top to the bottom expressed to the public profound sadness. Lazar was unsure where Lenin had actually died. Everybody seemed to have different opinions, ranging from a seaside resort on the Black Sea to a dacha just outside of Moscow to the Winter Palace in Petrograd. Some said he was in Finland at the time.

All he knew was that on January 23, a funeral train (Engine 4-127) had come into Moscow bearing the coffin of Lenin.

It was carried with great ceremony to a mausoleum in Red Square, where his embalmed body was placed on permanent display.

The funeral was an emotional one—at least on the surface; Lazar could sense that beneath the surface most of the emotion was not real. He himself felt little. He knew too much of what had been going on, and as he stood among the crowd in Red Square on that January day, a sharp wind blowing, he was overwhelmed more with the planned "show" that was being paraded before him than with any true feelings. Lenin and "Leninism" were being elevated to a quasi-religious status. Lazar had heard that Lenin's birthplace of Simbirsk on the Volga was being renamed to Ulyanovsk, and that Petrograd would become Leningrad.

The public outpouring was nothing short of splendid. Red banners floated everywhere. Even Stalin's eulogy was a masterpiece of what Lazar termed "emotional propaganda." It ended, "We shall guard and strengthen the purity of party membership, of party unity, the dictatorship of the proletariat, and the worker-peasant alliance."

The cheers were deafening. Stalin, without Trotsky's presence, had publicly presented himself as Lenin's rightful successor. Privately, he would maneuver ruthlessly to make sure it was so.

The funeral was quickly forgotten in the events that followed. Almost immediately, Lazar was caught in the machinery of the government's inner workings and what was indeed a race by many people

125

toward the chair left vacant by Lenin's departure. Events were happening fast. The party's name was officially changed from Bolshevik to Communist, new positions were formed both inside and outside the Kremlin with astounding speed, and Lazar even found himself named as a candidate-member for the Central Committee of the All-Union Communist party. Other names and positions surfaced as well. Mikhail had become a deputy of the people's commissar of heavy industry, Yuri was a secretary of the Nizhni Novgorod city committee, Rosa had received her entrance to the medical facility in Moscow, and Mikoyan, Bulganin, and Voroshilov were all in Moscow, too. Even Khrushchev had been recalled and was assigned as a deputy to Lazar. He also began to see a new name coming into view: V. M. Skrybin, better known as Molotov ("the hammer"), a name he had assumed when evading the imperial police. He was now heading the Central Commission and was Lazar's immediate superior.

Molotov was a short, frail-looking man with cream-colored skin, an extraordinarily thin neck, a jaundiced complexion, round rimless glasses, and a high-pitched squeaky voice. He was just the opposite of some of the strong and forceful men who were near the pinnacle of power. Yet, unlike these pretenders to the throne, who took themselves too seriously, he had a rather pleasant smile, whenever he did smile. Lazar liked him because he posed no threat to his own advancement.

While Lazar had raced past his thirtieth birthday, Stalin was closing in on his fiftieth. Lazar's own busy schedule had afforded him little opportunity to dwell on age coupled with the goals in front of him. Oh, occasionally he even flirted with the daydream of he and Stalin exchanging positions. *Flirt* was the only possible word. It was not a reality until he was called to Stalin's office for his first private meeting with him.

He appeared at the Spassky Gate a little before ten that December morning. Much had happened during the year following Lenin's death. Lazar had been given the task of compiling major, and confidential, lists of who was sympathetic to whom, names he painstakingly scrutinized before he posted them in their new positions. The job had come from Stalin himself, and even if he was unsure as to whether he wanted to align with that man or not, he recognized that there were few options open to him. He had seen firsthand what was happening.

Stalin, through his careful organization and manipulation of party members, had successfully forced Trotsky to approve him publicly

126

and to criticize the doctrinal "mistakes" of Zinoviev and Kamenev. To strengthen his hand more, Stalin had persuaded Britain, France, and Italy to recognize the Soviet government.

But now Trotsky tried to counter Stalin's activities. He published a volume of essays, *Lessons of October*, that was critical of the NEP and of the behavior of Zinoviev and Kamenev in 1917. The attack backfired. It drove them right into Stalin's arms, not as equals, but rather as subordinates. As a result, Stalin could cleverly use them to help mobilize the party's propaganda machinery against Trotsky. They did. They exposed Trotsky's disagreements with Lenin, questioning even his contribution to the Bolshevik victory. Stalin's plan was to identify Trotskyism as "distrust in the leaders of Bolshevism" and, therefore, a heresy. The starting point would be to have him abdicate even his nominal leadership of the Red Army.

Lazar was ushered into the same room where he had first met Stalin. The Soviet leader was already there, reading papers on his enormous desk. He did not sit but stood behind it in order to make sure he could see everything that was spread before him. Lazar measured Stalin's height with his eyes. He calculated him at five feet five inches— considerably shorter than his own five feet seven inches, and also much lighter. Lazar was topping the scales at 185 pounds and he reasoned Stalin was at least twenty to thirty pounds lighter. He thought he remembered him as being much heavier. However, the pockmarked face was still there as well as the yellowish eyes and a facial expression that did not reveal feelings.

"Feelings are womens' concerns," Stalin was quoted as once saying. Very rarely, in fact, were any women around him. He seemed to enjoy the company exclusively of men.

Lazar knew that Stalin had been born and raised in Tbilisi, the capital of Soviet Georgia. He had been there once on a trip from Tashkent, and he recalled that the city was built along the lines of an amphitheater, lying in a bowl of some 1,500 feet above sea level and surrounded by mountains. The city was fifteen centuries old, and it looked it. Streets were narrow and steep, houses had carved wooden balconies and little courtyards, and churches were all cone-shaped, the most famous being Mtatsminda ("Holy Mountain"), a twelfth-century church with a graveyard located on a slope overlooking the city, which was home to a pantheon of Georgian poets, actors, and educators. Black cypresses surrounded the gravestones as did gladiolus and tangerine trees.

The turbulent Kura River ran through the center of Tbilisi, and the headlong rush of its waters was said to have inspired many poets. Lazar wondered whether it had also inspired in Stalin his forceful way of doing things.

He also knew that the Georgians had been conquered successively by the Romans, the Persians, the Arabs, the Turks, the Mongols, the Tatars, and the Iranians. Finally, they sought the protection of Orthodox Christian Russia, and the area was annexed by Czar Paul in 1801.

The man standing in front of him, Joseph Vissarionovich Dzhugashvili, who had taken the name Stalin, meaning "man of steel," would never take off his armor. He would always be on the alert, always ready. He was one Georgian who was determined not to be conquered.

Lazar had studied Stalin considerably. He tried to find out all he could about him. He discovered that except for his taste in good food, he was a man of Spartan, rather uncouth habits, with his only luxury being power. In fact, so basic was this man that he often went to sleep fully dressed under a blanket, removing only his boots. He was a man who had little tolerance for pretensions, yet his ego was often said to be the size of Russia itself.

Stalin motioned to the one chair in the room other than his. He said nothing, not even a greeting. After Lazar had sat down, Stalin settled in his own chair. He picked out a cigarette from a small wooden box and then, as an afterthought, offered one to Lazar.

"No, thank you. I don't smoke."

"Good."

Stalin lit the cigarette and gazed at the ceiling. Lazar watched the smoke curl upward just below the bushy beard of Karl Marx. When Stalin spoke next, it was with rapidity and in a low voice.

"Mikhail, he is now chairman of the Nizhni Novgorod Council of the National Economy. I think this is also good in addition to his post as the people's deputy commissar of heavy industry. You agree? And Yuri is a member of the council, too. Good, no? Rosa? Yes, she will go to medical school and she will succeed. We need good doctors now. It is a plus."

He paused and looked at Lazar. The bushy mustache could not hide the smile.

"And you, Lazar Moiseyevich? What about you? Shouldn't you, too, have something good happen to you?"

Lazar smiled back. His was a nervous one. He hadn't realized until then how much power this man had already accumulated, and how it could be used.

"Yes, Comrade Stalin, it would be nice."

"I think we should drink to that, eh?"

He pulled a full bottle of French cognac from the side of the desk and uncorked it. He squinted at Lazar.

"You thought vodka perhaps? Eech! That's a peasant's drink. Besides, I know that Lazar Moiseyevich does not drink vodka. In fact, Lazar Moiseyevich does not drink anything. But I am sure Comrade Lazar will not want me to drink good French cognac alone. True?"

He plunked two small glasses on top of the sheath of papers on the desk. He poured a little of the liquid into each glass, carefully recorked the bottle, and held one glass in the palms of his hands, feeling its warmth. Lazar remembered that the man always seemed to be cold.

"*Vashe zdarovye*"—'To your health!' "

When they had finished drinking, Stalin opened the top drawer of the desk and lifted out a small stack of papers. He turned them over to Lazar.

"I am sure you have seen these."

It was Trotsky's volume of essays.

"You know what is happening, I am sure."

Lazar nodded.

"Good," said Stalin. "You know that until this year, all Bolsheviks, including Lenin, maintained that the success of the revolution and of socialism was dependent on assistance from a victorious proletariat in the industrially advanced countries of western Europe, and they believed that by using our resources, they had an obligation to help bring about such a revolution."

He paused to catch his breath, and then continued.

"Trotsky has become the most vocal advocate of this course of action and the greatest critic of my handling of the Comintern-sponsored insurrections in Germany, Bulgaria, and China."

He paused again and looked at Lazar.

"You may speak if you wish."

Lazar did wish.

"But you, Comrade Stalin, agreed with Trotsky that the revolution was not an end in itself but a stage in the world struggle against capitalism."

129

"That was then," Stalin sniffed. "I need to do more. Your suggestion, Lazar Moiseyevich?"

Lazar's eyes widened. It had come so fast. Now he was being tested, and he didn't know if he was prepared. He said the first thing that came into his mind. It was dangerous, he realized, but he had no choice.

"You must reverse yourself, Comrade Stalin." He stared intently into the man's dark brown eyes.

"You must brand Trotsky's permanent revolution as a variety of Menshevism and as a lack of faith in the strength and capabilities of the Russian Revolution."

"You are suggesting that I negate and repudiate Lenin's own theory of proletarian revolution?"

Lazar nodded again. Stalin looked up at the ceiling. He thought for awhile.

"It will, therefore, be my theory and mine alone. This Bolshevik regime can maintain itself without any aid. We possess all the necessary tools to establish a powerful socialist base by our own efforts, and once that base is established, then we can assist the workers of other lands in their revolutionary struggle. Hah!"

He slammed his hand on the desk and then leaned back in his chair.

"I have thought of this often. This is not the first time for me. It is socialism in one country. You realize that, don't you?"

Lazar, too, slouched in his chair, the hard wooden back rubbing into his neck.

"The difference between your position and Trotsky's is not in the objective—the final worldwide victory of socialism. Rather, it is in the timing: you are calling for the establishment of socialism in Soviet Russia first. Trotsky's concept has the order reversed. But, Comrade Stalin, you control the party organization. Your view should prevail."

The word *control* caught Stalin's ear. He sat upright in his chair. Lazar quickly did the same.

He studied Lazar, eyeing him suspiciously. Then he leaned back in his chair again and fingered the butt of his cigarette.

"You understand what you are saying, Lazar Moiseyevich?"

He understood precisely what he was saying.

"And you understand the consequences, Lazar Moiseyevich?"

He knew exactly what would happen. He had decided to cast the die again. There were not too many options open to him at his age and position. The decision had to be made. He could only hope it was the right one.

Stalin waited a moment. Then a smile crossed his lips, and he reached for the phone. One hand cupped the mouthpiece. Lazar could not hear what he was saying. The receiver was returned to the cradle and Stalin moved forward in his chair. The door opened and Molotov walked in. He was carrying a sheaf of papers. Stalin rose from his desk and took the papers.

"Comrade Molotov, Comrade Kaganovich."

Lazar stood and shook the small man's hand. There was practically no feeling in the clasp. He had delicate, soft hands, like a woman's. Lazar could see that behind the stoic facade were twinkling blue eyes.

Lazar's mind played back what he remembered from the files:

"Molotov. Began career at Nizhni Novgorod in 1918 as party secretary. President of the Regional Soviet. Jewish wife named Paulina. Considered taciturn and tough. He and Stalin play a good guy-bad guy game; he plays the latter. Has ability to generalize about what is happening based on scant indications. Has great perception."

Stalin thrust the papers into Lazar's arms.

"Comrade Molotov, here is our new chief of Central Personnel and Assignments." Lazar could feel his jaw dropping.

"Now, Lazar Moiseyevich, let us discuss what you do with these."

The next two hours were a lesson in patience. Stalin went on and on about the revolution, the people responsible for it, his part in it, even his role in the czar's secret police force. Lazar listened intently, but he also began to formulate in his own mind the chances of Stalin's success. The man in front of him with the sallow complexion would be formidable. It was true that Trotsky was the most intelligent, but as had been proven time and time again, the gifted intellectuals did not always rise to the very top, and Trotsky was simply too smart for his own good. The others, Lazar sensed, were by and large dolts whom he felt Stalin could brush aside if he had help. Lazar despised intellectuals because of his own lack of education. He knew that Stalin's chief enemies after Lenin's death were intellectuals. He would get rid of those people.

Lazar wanted to be a part of this. He would help, no matter what. He had seen what had happened in his first thirty years, and he knew that if he wanted to live another thirty years but in a better style, he would have to align himself properly with the right people. It was

131

nothing new or even onerous. Everyone did it. Everyone. Except that he would do it better.

Stalin's modus operandi was simple. He would purge his opponents from the party and admit thousands of new members to strengthen his position against the "old guard." On Stalin's instructions, Lazar was to evolve a pattern of direction and control of all party and governmental activities in the country, the intention being to afford Stalin the means to make or break anyone in the Soviet state. After all, the Personnel Department could transfer or depose an individual from one minute to the next, often as a prelude to arrest by the OGPU (secret police), with which the department had close ties.

Lazar realized that even a long record of successful work combined with exceptional talent, expert knowledge, and loyalty did not automatically insure any post. He would have to do more. What he did not know then but would find out was how he could insulate himself as best as possible. One way was to stay close to Stalin, and the opportunity to do that had been presented. He had to seize it.

Stalin would bring in new people, and the head of Central Personnel—the primary source of information—was to be right beside him, filtering the names.

For the next six months, Lazar saw Stalin frequently. Occasionally, they were alone as they reviewed lists upon lists. More often, he was in the presence of other men like Voroshilov and Ordzhonikidze, who had been members of the Military and Revolution Council and were now members of the Presidium. Voroshilov was extremely noticeable around the Kremlin because he had become commander of the Moscow military district, replacing Trotsky's friend Muralov.

Mikoyan was also on hand as more and more responsible duties were being entrusted to the man from Armenia.

Closest to Lazar and Maria at that time were Molotov and his wife, Paulina Zhumchuzkina. Not coincidentally, their daughter was named Svetlana, the same name given to the daughter of Stalin and his wife, Nadezhda Alliluyeva.

But although the wives would socialize and even the children, because of the restricted schools they attended, were together frequently, the men did little socializing outside the Kremlin. Suspicious eyes and ears were everywhere. You had no assurance that the job you were doing today would not be filled tomorrow by the man standing over in a corner watching you work.

To Lazar, this meant one thing and one thing only. He had to do exactly what Stalin wanted and he had to do it letter perfect. If there was any other person who had the same attitude and gifts of work, it was Molotov. Both men worked long hours. Their loyalty would be unquestioned, and their hard work would be rewarded. They knew this had to be, and it was.

In March 1925, Stalin called Lazar to his office, but not to review more names and positions. Instead, he handed him a communiqué from Kiev. The Ukrainization process was not working, and party officials were asking for help, a solution to the problem.

Just two years before, a campaign had been inaugurated by government decree. In effect, it elevated the Ukrainian language to equality with the Russian, making it compulsory for all party and government officials in the Ukraine to learn the language in one or two years. But now the process was stalled, and Moscow's aid was being sought.

The policy was originally intended to advance Ukrainians in the governmental apparatus and to foster the language in all areas of life, particularly the schools. At the same time, it tried to keep the reins on runaway nationalism. The objective was to meld the Ukrainian into the Russian. After all, you couldn't have too strong a Ukrainian party working at odds with Moscow. First you win them over, then you take them over.

Stalin's orders to Lazar were direct, leaving no room for compromise.

"You are to organize the Ukrainian party, to purge it, and the governmental administration of everyone whose loyalty is not absolutely sure. And you are to rid it of inefficient officials."

Stalin had selected Lazar for a variety of reasons. One, Lazar knew the language. Two, he knew how to get things done. Three, his forte was not necessarily his efficiency, but rather his philosophy that the end result totally justified the method used.

Again, he was being uprooted to another area. It seemed as though he was constantly on the go, never able to settle in one place for longer than two years. He felt like a gypsy, but with less freedom. At least a gypsy had a choice of where to live.

He took Maria and Maya with him. They gave up their apartment in Moscow, which they were outgrowing, and set up residence in a larger apartment at 17 Levamovski Street in the most fashionable section of Kiev. Once more, he had returned to the heart of his birth-place, the Ukraine.

The only other person he took with him was Khrushchev to handle most of the petty chores, like visiting the smaller villages—in partic-ular, Kabany. Lazar had no desire to see that mud stop. It would serve only as a reminder of the past, one that he would just as soon forget. If there were anything to be done there, then Nikita would take care of it. After all, he, too, spoke the language, although not perfectly, and he would do what was necessary as his surrogate. Other than Khrushchev, he kept no one else close to him.

His intention was to work solely by himself, keeping a single, open line between Moscow and Kiev. If Stalin needed anything, he would call only Lazar. Intermediaries were not needed, or wanted. He would function within the framework of keeping one mentor (Stalin) in front of him and a protégé (Khrushchev) behind. Naturally, he would keep an eye trained on each.

Lazar was appointed secretary general of the Ukrainian Communist party with specific instructions to remold the party according to Stalin's wishes. The return to the Ukraine involved mixed emotions for Lazar. The last time he had been sent here it had been against his will, as an outcast, a rebel, a prisoner serving a term of punishment. Now, it was different. He would arrive clutching a piece of paper in his hand that said he was the authority, he was the one all had to listen to. Everyone would have to grovel at his feet. It reminded him of the Cossacks storming into Kabany with the leader waving a yellowed decree and demanding whatever he wanted "in the name of the czar." Now it was his turn to wave the paper. Now it was his turn to demand. And he would do just that.

Lazar had learned what was involved in exercising the rights of his position by watching Stalin. He understood that on rising up the ladder, once you stepped onto even the lowest rung, it would be exceedingly dangerous to stop. As in the feudal hierarchy, your fate was closely linked to your immediate superior, who in turn was dependent upon his immediate superior, and so on up the ladder to the summit.

Here in the Ukraine Lazar was the immediate superior. He had returned as the supreme boss.

The politics of the new Soviet government at the time were extraor-dinarily complicated. Each of the areas comprising the new republic was made up of hard-core nationalities, and no one wanted to give up any independence. Lazar thought that perhaps he could cultivate the Jews. They generally rallied behind the Bolsheviks. They had seen enough of the pogroms that had invaded their households under the czar, and anything seemed better. Moreover, in the Ukraine, Jewish youth represented more than half of the students then attending universities.

But as Lazar consolidated his position, he found that the Jewish revolutionaries, to whom Lenin owed so much, had to be beaten down. There was no choice. They would not yield to the party line. They were too intent with keeping their own identity.

"Goddamn them," he screamed at Khrushchev, his huge fist slamming against the door. "What do they think I will do? Bend over backward and kiss their ass? They won't learn Ukrainian, they won't use it, they insist on staying apart from what we are doing. They speak only Yiddish. They resist. Those *pizdasosy*—'bastards'—resist. We try to do something better for them and they want the czar back. They fight us. What do they want, anyway, their own country? I wish there were such a place. I would send them there—all of them. *Pizdasosy!*"

Lazar now saw the road dividing before him: Stalin went one way, and the people among whom he was raised and, yes, of whom he was a part by blood went another.

Caution was not a hallmark of Lazar's work pattern. He moved quickly and efficiently in doing what he had to. He prepared the agenda of all meetings and formulated the matters for discussions. He even directed the discussions in such a way that all the committees at the meetings would unanimously vote on what had already been recommended up front.

The first order of business was to rid the local party apparatus of all those Lazar thought "undesirable." He already had a good breakdown of who came under this label by virtue of the lists prepared back in Moscow. His tenure as personnel head had given him an advantage second to none. He moved people in and out of jobs seemingly at will. Those who he knew would adhere to the party line would find themselves with positions; those who still had too strong a nationalistic feeling would find themselves demoted to a lesser level if Lazar felt there was still a chance for them to be won over, and those who Lazar felt had no future would simply be out of a job. The modus operandi was to elevate those sympathetic to the cause and remove any dissidents.

He would force his views on anyone. V. Chubar, the chairman of the Ukraine Economic Council, and A. Shumsky, a member of the Ukraine Party Central Committee, were two of many who opposed him. They would take the arguments as far as they could. Then they would contact Moscow. Shumsky even demanded that Stalin recall Lazar, but he found no support. Lazar's argument was too politically strong.

"Comrade Stalin, I am dealing with a prejudice. You can see it all over. I am being criticized because of my name. I am doing what Comrade Stalin has directed, and they find fault only because of what I was."

Lazar knew exactly what button to press. Whenever opposition became too vocal, Lazar simply yelled, "Anti-Semitism." Stalin, who was already trying to walk a fine line with the Jews, was not too eager to rock that boat, at least not yet. He stood behind his secretary general of the Ukraine.

In less than a year, Lazar had trained the party's secretaries in the Ukraine in the Stalinist method of party work, which meant that a secretary must first learn to work with his committee to decide all matters collectively. It was to be the same with municipal and factory committees whether on party or on governmental levels.

With Khrushchev at his side, Lazar completely overhauled the entire Ukrainian operation.

One thing he needed to do was to keep the economy strong in that area and to build up the inflow of money. He industrialized the region as best he could: He had a hydroelectrical power plant constructed on the Dnieper and brought heavy equipment in to develop the sagging agriculture. He also filled managerial slots with those Bolsheviks who supported him, and thus created a solid working force. His goal was to unite the Ukraine into one "indivisible fighting collective devoted to further the cause of Lenin." Actually, he meant the eventual cause of Stalin.

Back in Moscow, Stalin was having his own not too dissimilar problems. The struggle for party control had begun years before, in October 1923, when the "Letter of the Forty-Six" was issued. This was a statement signed by forty-six prominent Bolsheviks against the party leadership, meaning his own. The letter demanded an emergency party conference to review the matters of economic planning and an open debate on freedom of criticism. It went nowhere. The letter was suppressed by the Central Committee, Trotsky was censured, and the forty-six were warned that they were breaching the 1921 ban on factions.

Trotsky knew that his fight had to be a combination of the legal and the political. Yet, he could bring himself to use only one weapon: the time-honored socialist method of appealing to the workers.

For eighteen months following July 1926, Trotsky struggled against Stalinism. He was leading a new United Left Opposition, which had a membership of 8,000 Bolsheviks inside the party. It was no secret that on the outcome of this fight could rest the fate of the entire revolution. But unlike the revolution it was a struggle in which the general populace was not directly involved. Clandestine meetings of the Left Opposition were held in workers' homes outside Moscow, almost like old times; almost, but not quite. The leaders of the Left Opposition were pitting their policies against the strong party apparatus, and they were doing so without any organizational trump cards to play. Stalin had already labeled them a "Social Democratic Deviation." Who would take them seriously?

During that time, at the First All-Ukrainian Party Conference in Kharkov, Lazar was heaping ridicule and scorn on all those who claimed that democracy within the party had been wiped out. He knew that the party hierarchy was manipulating language to support their own ambitions, yet he toed the line handed down: "Intra-party democracy does not mean that everyone has the right to question the decisions of the majority. It simply means drawing the masses into the political activity under the party's wing."

But the new front, led by Trotsky, Kamenev, and Zinoviev, was determined not to attack the principle of party unity but rather the party bureaucracy, which they blamed for many defects such as for the lag in industrial development, and for the deplorable conditions of factory workers.

At the Fourteenth Party Congress in 1926, everything surfaced for all to see. Although Trotsky remained silent, even aloof, Zinoviev and Kamenev split openly with Stalin, who had already formed a new coalition with Bukharin. The struggle for control was locked into the future of the Soviet State. Stalin proclaimed his theory of "socialism in one country"—putting the safety of the Soviet Union's own economic development first, above any international policy of revolution. Bukharin supported this vociferously. He kept telling the wealthier

137

peasants, the kulaks, "Enrich yourselves!" They were intent on letting Zinoviev and Kamenev take the blame for all of Russia's internal and foreign failures.

Trotsky, however, was in an enviable position. He was being courted by all sides, but he did nothing about it. Instead, his actions only helped to seal the fate of those opposing Stalin. During the Central Committee and Politburo meetings, he sat back and read French novels. He refused to become part of any discussion. It was his way of showing that he was thoroughly disgusted with what they were doing.

Stalin responded to this inactive challenge by dismissing a large number of opposition members from party and governmental positions. The opposition leaders now had no choice. They issued a declaration in which they actually admitted to violating party discipline and promised to discontinue their factional activity. They even repudiated many of their left-wing followers. It was clear to see that the power struggle was coming to an end.

Though these opposition leaders capitulated, Stalin never returned them to their former posts. On the contrary, in August 1927, he expelled Trotsky and Zinoviev from the Central Committee, and when in October Trotsky publicly revealed the existence of Lenin's testament, with its criticism of Stalin, both he and Zinoviev were expelled from the party along with some seventy-five of their constituents. (Both Kamenev and Zinoviev were executed in 1936, and Bukharin and Rykov in 1938.)

Of course, it was not without a final gasp.

Adolph Abramovich Joffe, a revolutionary emissary to China, and Trotsky's friend, committed suicide in 1927. He had become depressed by what was going on around him. A letter he sent to Trotsky said, in part:

> *I have always believed that you lacked Lenin's unbending will, his unwillingness to yield, his readiness even to remain alone on the path that he thought right. Politically, you were always right, beginning with 1905, and I told you repeatedly that, with my own ears, I heard Lenin admit even in 1905, you, and not he, were right. One does not lie before his death and now I repeat this to you. . . . But you have often abandoned your rightness for the sake of an overvalued agreement, or compromise. This is a mis-*

*take. I repeat, politically you have always been right and now
more right than ever.*

    *Some day the party will realize it, and history will not fail to
accord recognition. You are right, but the guarantee of the victory
of your rightness lies in nothing but the extreme unwillingness
to yield, the strictest straightforwardness, the absolute rejection
of all compromise: In this lay the very secret of Lenin's victories.*

The letter, which might have affected the opposition groups against
Stalin, never saw the light of day until well after Trotsky had delivered
his last speech before the Central Committee in January 1928. Lazar
had seen to that, for the remaining personal effects of Joffe had come
to him through his own "contacts" in Kiev—the people who had
manifested absolute allegiance to him—and the only person who was
told the contents of the letter was Stalin.

    Thus, the attempt to paint Stalin as the "gravedigger of the revo-
lution," according to Trotsky, fell on deaf ears. It was almost over.
Even his opponents now realized they were witnessing the fall of a
titan. In fact, he was totally ignored. He was abused, heckled, and
insulted.

    The leaders of the Left Opposition were all expelled from the Central
Committee and even from the Communist party. Many were arrested.
Stalin had issued the edict: "It is no accident that the opposition is
led by Jews. This is a struggle between Russian socialism and aliens."

    Lazar's ears perked up. He knew that Stalin had no love for the
Jews, but that was in private. Now it had been made public. He watched
quietly as the decimation of the opposition reached completion. Trotsky
and his family were to be exiled to Alma Ata in Central Asia. Later,
they would be deported from the country, inaugurating a journey that
was to end with his murder in Mexico City in 1940.

    Lazar realized that he would have to do something dramatic in order
to survive. As a Jew in Russia, he was already in a precarious position,
and as a Jew in the hierarchy of the party, his position was even more
tenuous. With Trotsky gone, Lazar had emerged as the most important
Jew in the government. It was not a position to be envied.

    In 1928, he returned to Moscow at Stalin's call. During the Eighth
Professional Unions Congress that year, Lazar was elected a member
of the Presidium of the All-Union Central Soviet of Professional Unions.
What secured such an election was the way he dealt with what was

ultimately the last of Stalin's opposition—Lenin, himself, in the figure
of his widow, Nadezhda Konstantinovna Krupskaya.

A lot had happened during Lazar's absence from Moscow. Stalin
had emasculated Trotsky, dropped Zinoviev and Kamenev, and associated himself with Bukharin and the staunch "rightest" backers of
the NEP. With that support, he embarked on a policy of easing peasant
tax burdens, and at the same time he isolated his political adversaries.
Stalin had already determined the membership of future congresses.
He now was triumphant, to the delight of his own hand-picked supporters, who insulted all anti-Stalinists, including even Lenin's wife.

Lazar garnered two more titles: secretary general of the Central
Committee of the All-Union Communist Party of Bolsheviks and secretary general of the Central Committee of the Ukrainian Communist
Party of Bolsheviks. As such, he was now permitted to attend the
meetings of the Central Committee.

He was surprised at the location of these meetings. He had always
been under the impression that the committee met just a few doors
down the hall from Stalin's office in the Kremlin. It seemed logical.
After all, it was what the average citizen thought as well. But now he
found that the committee met at 4 Staraya Ploshchad', not behind the
Kremlin walls. In fact, very few people knew that the country was
being run from a small room on one floor of a rather nondescript
building a good three blocks from Red Square.

The people were stupid, he thought. They would congregate in the
square, on their way to GUM, the main department store, or they
would visit St. Basil's Cathedral, the building of the nine multicolored
onion domes, and they would think they were in the center of everything. He chuckled at the thought. "The imbeciles stand in the middle
of this huge cobblestoned area that they call a square but which is
really a rectangle and watch what little traffic moves in and out of the
main tower, the Spassky Gate, and they believe, actually believe, that
the government is run from within those walls. Good. Who needs them
to know that it is run from a shabby building with only a number on
the door. As long as nobody knows where you are, you are safe."

That day a meeting had been convened to discuss the possible
industrialization of the country. It was a topic that had come up a
number of times before. The Soviet Union, with the largest area of
any country on the face of the earth, had yet to enter the Industrial
Revolution. It seemed incredible, but survival had taken precedent.

Now, however, plans were being made to make the leap, but Lazar knew that based on what he had seen at other meetings, there was still one open matter to be resolved.

He always arrived early in order to get a chair with a full view of Stalin, and with Stalin having a full view of him. The room was small, just big enough to hold a dozen people. It was devoid of the trappings usually associated with board or conference rooms.

True to Stalin's tastes, it was Spartan. There was one rectangular table and eight hard, wooden chairs surrounding it. The chairs were straight-backed, which encouraged people to stay awake.

Six more chairs were lined against one wall. Stalin always took two seats, one at the end of the table and another by the wall facing the door. There was only one window, and many times a drape was drawn across it. The overhead fixture gave off a solitary light, and a small sidebar in a corner had a water pitcher with metal cups. The constituency had to supply its own writing materials, and two large metal bowls served as ashtrays. Smoke quickly filled the air from Stalin's ever-present pipe and the endless number of cigarettes that the majority of the committee members lit, one after the other.

Lazar had been a chain-smoker for a brief time while he was in Central Asia. It helped to pass the time in what was a boring, stifling part of the country. The cigarettes did little to help. He found his nerves jangled, and he coughed and cleared his throat constantly. It became a source of irritation not only to himself but to those around him. Maria had let it be known that she found the cigarette smoking not only disgusting but detrimental to Maya's health. She suffered from sinus infections and allergies. All year round, she had puffy eyes and a congested nose.

Maria had literally confiscated all of Lazar's cigarettes and replaced them with a string of worry beads, which Lazar could wind and twirl around his hands and fingers. It was supposed to make him less nervous, but more often than not his temper reached such a point that he would wind the string so tight the beads would break. His hands, which were already bearlike, became more pronounced as his weight ballooned because of his not smoking. He was now tipping the scales at over two hundred pounds and no longer could wear his brown uniforms.

"You look like a whale in that suit," Maya would say, watching the brass buttons popping one by one.

He had taken to wearing the brown army uniforms that Stalin favored

141

so much. Now he would have to switch to the suits and ties that the other committee members wore. Perhaps he would have been better off taking up puffing again.

It seemed that the only other person who didn't smoke was Krupskaya. She sat upright in the straight-backed chair, her small frame dominated by black piercing eyes, commenting on practically everything that took place. Rarely did a smile cross her lips, and if it did, it was only when she said something that displeased Stalin or his supporters.

The meetings were always attended by Krupskaya, who felt she had a preeminent position because of her stature as Lenin's widow, and she constantly reminded everyone of this fact.

This day she was once more defending the economic policies of her late husband; in particular, the NEP. No matter what was said, she was ready with an answer, as if she were still in school facing a bunch of recalcitrant boys.

Lazar watched Stalin. He bristled each time Krupskaya opened her mouth, but he had to be careful as to what he could say. He could never make accusations in public about Lenin's widow. No, that would be blasphemy of the highest order. The public had still not totally accepted. Actually, it didn't know who was in charge. But inside the confines of 4 Staraya Ploshchad', Stalin was already feeding the fire.

He knew that he could not attack Lenin and certainly not openly, so soon after the founder's death. Instead, he concentrated on trying to destroy the next best person, and that was Krupskaya.

Stalin relished secrecy, and his favorite agency was the secret police. Lazar knew this, and with his own personal knowledge of who had access to what information from his years in the personnel department of the Communist party, he was able to stitch together some of the information that could be used against Krupskaya. And he would not hesitate to use it.

He began to circulate pieces of information, some fact, some conjecture. He concentrated, though, on one theory: that Krupskaya was not really Lenin's wife, but simply his mistress. Names were floated about regarding other women: Elena Stasova and R. S. Zemlyachka were two mentioned.

Lazar understood, as did Stalin, that he could not come out directly with these "suggestions." Therefore, his attack had to be well placed, and it had to be backed with a quid pro quo, something she would receive in return for something she would have to give up. Lazar emphasized the *have*. It was also important that it was he, rather than Stalin, who took the gamble. He was prepared for this. Previously, he had said little at these meetings, watching instead what was going on around him and listening carefully to what was being said.

But the opportunity had now arisen. Krupskaya was raising Lenin's testament again. The spirit of her discontent was clear. She was not happy with what had happened to Trotsky, and she insisted that the committee move to take action on the testament; in other words, they should oust Stalin.

Lazar listened intently as the rantings and ravings went on for over an hour. Some members, like Kirov and Ordzhonikidze, seemed to sympathize with what she was saying; others, like Kalinin and Yakov Rudzutah, felt the assault on Stalin was unwarranted.

Krupskaya had already heard the rumors milling about as to her true relationship with Lenin. She looked coldly at Stalin and demanded to know why he was personally directing a vendetta against her. Stalin caressed the bowl of his pipe and stared back. He did not answer.

Some committee members began to shift uneasily in their chairs, not sure of exactly the kind of support Stalin had among them. They already had seen what he could do against the likes of Trotsky, Zinoviev, Kamenev, Tomsky, and Rykov, to name a few, and no one felt ready to challenge the Georgian right now. They didn't have to, because his answer came from the other side of the room. The voice was strong, authoritative, confident.

It came from Lazar. His voice cut through the room like a buzz saw going through wood.

"Nadezhda Konstantinovna. Nadezhda Konstantinovna."

She stopped her diatribe in mid sentence. She turned to Lazar, in awe that she had been interrupted so forcefully. Silence reigned in the room. Stalin moved himself to the chair at the side of the room, as if he were disassociating himself with what was about to happen. Lazar waited until he was sure he had everyone's attention. It was not a long wait. He had already secured such attention when he spoke, but now for dramatic effect he waited just a few seconds longer. He carefully put the worry beads down on the table before him.

"Nadezhda Konstantinovna, you are not unaware, I am sure, of these whisperings about your true identity . . ."

She started to say something, but Lazar quickly held up his hand. It looked like a huge placard in the small room.

"You may, if you wish, Comrade, question the necessity of such whisperings, but that may be no end in itself. The fact is, Comrade Krupskaya, that much of what you say here is not in the best interests of our new Soviet Socialist State. I needn't tell you that those of my constituencies—and they are many—do not wish to hear further rumblings and negative attitudes about those entrusted to lead us on to greater glory, as when we began under our beloved founder.''

He paused, took a deep breath, looked down at the table, and jabbed a forefinger at the beads. His voice dropped, and what he said was barely audible.

''Therefore, Comrade Krupskaya, if you continue to be a *perdunya* [a woman who farts frequently], we will make someone else Lenin's widow.''

Lazar continued to survey his beads. No one in the room moved. After a minute, he flicked his eyes up quickly, searching out Stalin, who was looking down at his pipe. He raised his head fully to see what the other members of the committee were doing. They were watching Stalin, for some reaction, for some sign. Krupskaya had her eyes fixed on Lazar. It was in disbelief. She knew full well that Lazar had still not given his proposal.

Now she looked over to Stalin, who had raised his eyes and was staring back at Lazar. The response was evident. He, too, was ready to hear what Lazar had to offer, as if he didn't already know.

Lazar continued talking in an almost matter-of-fact way. He knew Krupskaya placed her own position, her own ego, above anything or anyone else—and that included Lenin. Therefore, his proposition was a relatively simple one. The committee would acknowledge her position as Lenin's widow. He even suggested a monument to her, to be placed in a square in Moscow, in recognition for all her services to the children of the Soviet Union as the ''leading and inspirational teacher of the land.'' In return, she was to be quiet. She would no longer be welcomed at Central Committee meetings. She would no longer give interviews. She would leave the field of politics.

''And if I choose not to accept any of these conditions,'' she said, ''or I violate them? What then?''

Lazar looked back at her coldly. He glanced at Stalin. His eyes remained riveted on him. He knew that what he had already said had met approval. He could sense it. Now would come the final nail.

''Then, Comrade Krupskaya, the only thing people will remember of you will be your statue.''

Her proposal to make the testament public was eventually defeated by the Central Committee thirty votes to ten. Lazar's foray into inner-circle politics was successful.

From that time on, Lazar became Krupskaya's shadow. He would watch her every move and report back to Stalin what she was doing and what she was saying. In effect, he became, at his own volition, Stalin's eyes and ears. He would watch not only Krupskaya, but in effect anyone else Stalin had questioned. When necessary, he would take immediate action himself, all with his leader's blessings.

With Krupskaya now being completely neutralized, Lazar turned his attention to doing what he felt he had to do and wanted to do, knowing full well that he had Stalin's support. Stalin, on the other hand, had similarly disposed of Trotsky, although in a different way, and began to formulate where he wanted to take the country. In fact, he began to adopt many of the policies of his heretical adversary, including accelerated industrialization, collectivism of agriculture, and the general abandonment of the NEP. Those who failed to approve this about-face were sent into oblivion.

Lazar did the same. In order to find scapegoats for any adverse situation in the mining industry and for the rather low living standards of miners, Lazar began to plan great show trials at which a series of bourgeois experts confessed that had they organized wrecking; in other words, they had obstructed the improvement of workers' conditions and infringed the Soviet labor protection laws. Their aim, of course, had been to disrupt the development of socialist industry.

As a result, a steady flow of victims went before the OGPU firing squads or were sent to Siberia. In fact, an underground circular in 1929 stated that on December 1, 1928, the total number of people deprived of their liberty was 113,500. However, this was separate from and did not include the number awaiting sentences as well as those who were executed. Within these figures was the disposition of Trotsky. In 1929, he was handed an order authorizing his deportation: "Under Article 58/10 of the Criminal Code, on a charge of counter-revolutionary activity. Resolved: Citizen Trotsky to be deported from the territory of the USSR."

The decision of the OGPU was handed down on January 20, 1929. He was deported to the Turkish island of Prinkipo, which had been used by the Byzantine emperors to exile their opponents. Trotsky's expulsion, Lazar understood, was not the simple outcome of a duel between his personality and Stalin's. Rather, it was a radical struggle between Trotsky's principles of permanent revolution and Stalin's bureaucratic defense of "socialism in one country."

Lazar continued making his points well known, supporting Stalin at every turn, and incurring the wrath of many party regulars.

As the decade came to an end, the emergence of two people would clearly be seen. At the age of fifty, Stalin had become the undisputed master not only of the Soviet Union but also of world Communism.

And, at the age of thirty-six, while the Western world was seeing the temporary collapse of capitalism in the crash of '29, Lazar had become the first secretary of the Moscow Party Committee and a full-fledged member of the Politburo of the All-Union Communist party.

He was now firmly entrenched in Moscow, ready to start the decade that would establish him at the top of his power. He saw clearly where he was going and what he had to do. The days of Kabany were light-years behind. He had only the stars left, and he felt close enough to reach them. After all, he was now one of them.

Sasha and Moisev Kaganovich at the turn of the century

147

Hannah Gutman and Morris Kaganovich in 1909

Hannah and Morris Kaganovich in 1911

Rosa Kaganovich in 1913

Lenin, Krupskaya and an unidentified person in 1918

Aunt Anya and Uncle Levick in the 1920s

From left: Kalinin, Kaganovich, Ordzhonikidze, Stalin in the 1920s

From left: Kaganovich, Stalin, Molotov, Shvernik, and Svetlana Stalin at the Grand Opera in Moscow in the 1930s

From left: Stalin, Molotov, Kaganovich, and Ordzhonikidze in the 1930s

Kaganovich directing construction of the Moscow subway in 1934

Commissar of Heavy Industry Lazar Kaganovich in 1938, telling a miners' conference that they must supply their country with as much coal as required

4

Although the Cheka was established as an investigative agency on December 20, 1917, it quickly transformed itself into a political police force that was committed to the extermination of all opponents to the ideological makeup of the Soviet state. In fact, statements made by its founding director, Felix Dzerzhinsky, echoed this commitment: "The Cheka is not a court. We stand for organized terror. The Cheka is obligated to defend the revolution and conquer the enemy even if its sword does by chance sometimes fall upon the heads of the innocent."

And it did, becoming the major "control" force in Russia. It was exactly what Lenin wanted. In 1922, he tried to soften its image somewhat by changing the name to the General Political Administration, the GPU, although its function remained the same. Two years later, it was renamed the OGPU so as to include the entire USSR.

In 1926, Dzerzhinsky died, and the OGPU supported Stalin. Whatever had been started with the Cheka back in 1917 was continued threefold by Stalin ten years later. Consistent with the idea that whatever serves to advance Communism was moral by definition, the OGPU murdered and kidnapped anyone they pleased, including foreigners— and even in foreign territory. In fact, in 1926, OGPU agents gunned down the Ukrainian leader Simon Petlyura in Paris, they abducted the

Estonian minister Ado Birk right in the center of Moscow, and in 1930 kidnapped the White Russian leader Alexander Kutepov in Paris.

Lazar was not blind to all this. His contact with the security agencies stemmed back to his days with personnel. It was a close contact. Copies of the lists he had prepared were sent to the head of the security agency; this was especially so after Lenin's death. It was well known that Stalin always sought to bolster his position on three primary fronts: security, military, and administrative.

But Lazar had his own interests to support. His time in the Ukraine had served him well. He had shown Stalin that he could be trusted with more than list making or outbursts against Krupskaya. Those had long been forgotten. Stalin generally looked only at yesterday, not at the days before. Lazar knew he could be depended on to get the job done no matter how, and he had proven his loyalty, his allegiance to the one person who could determine his fate.

Nevertheless, he also needed to find ways to protect himself. After all, he was still somewhat on the outside of the true inner circle. He had not even taken a pseudonym, as the others had done, and it seemed almost perverse that he remained what he always had been, Lazar Moiseyevich Kaganovich, of Jewish parentage, from the most troublesome area in the entire country. He had a lot to overcome, and it was important that he find ways to do it.

His next avenue of approach had to be a position where he could see everything happening in the regime and also one where he would be able to obtain information on a firsthand basis, preferably before anyone else. The logical progression from working in personnel was the OGPU, whose finger was on the very pulse of the nation.

He had to become an integral part of the *nomenklatura*—the people who formed the key posts in the government, the special Party bureaucratic stratum. But at the same time, he had to know who surrounded him. He remembered what Stalin told him when he returned from his successes in the Ukraine: "A hundred friends are not too many, one enemy is. To one man, two enemies together are a regiment."

Lazar convinced Stalin to let him organize an administrative group for special tasks. It was referred to as the Department of "Wet Affairs."

To those who understood, it meant a body of *mokrie dela*—"for blood."

Lazar was given an office on the fourth floor of the building at 2

Dzerzhinsky Square. This was OGPU headquarters, also known as the Center. From his window, he had a view of the square itself. This way, he could watch the comings and goings of those who went through the main entrance. The only drawback was that all the windows in the building were shielded somewhat with steel bars or heavy screens. Lazar had heard that it was Stalin who had ordered such security measures.

Many workers of the Organ for State Security arrived at the six pedestrian gates by 7:00 A.M. They arrived early just to take advantage of the cafeteria. On the eighth floor, the cafeteria offered good breakfasts of milk, eggs, bacon, and fruit, and it was all free.

The hallways of the building were painted a light green. The parquet floors were uncarpeted. Light was provided by ceiling fixtures with large, white globes.

The standard offices were spacious, but they were typically barren. They were also painted the same green color. All they contained was a wooden desk and a few straight-backed chairs. They were certainly not made for comfort. Each office had a steel safe that was sealed with wax at the end of the workday.*

The halls were patrolled by internal security troops who wore the regular beige uniforms but with bright-blue collar tabs edged with red. They were considered badges of honor, of merit, of respect, of fear.

Lazar's office was unlike most of the others. He had a massive oak desk, three wooden chairs, a separate conference, or layout, table, a portrait of Dzerzhinsky on one wall and one of Stalin on another. A number of telephones ringed his desk. Two were of prime importance: On his right, the Kremlevka line provided direct access to Stalin. On his left, the Verkhushka linked him with a special circuit reserved for Central Committee members. Behind that were other phones that connected him with principal offices throughout the Soviet Union.

One in particular was a direct line to Khrushchev, who was now in Yuzovka. Khrushchev was doing his part in making life easier for Lazar. Whenever he could find a podium, he used it to praise his mentor and especially his instructions "which we receive in our everyday work." He gilded the lily like mad.

"Lazar Moiseyevich's brilliant proposals to plow virgin land to grow wheat in Moscow province is direct guidance."

---

*A visit to these offices—now known as the KGB Center—in 1981 revealed pretty much the same color and furniture. What was conspicuously missing from the offices were portraits of Stalin and, of course, the safes. Now, all materials are fed into one main safe each night.

Lazar knew that as foolish as he looked, his protégé was no fool. He even became a "Shabbos Goy" in the Ukraine, meaning that he lit the Sabbath lights and started the stoves for the Jewish high politicos on Saturday. Nikita left no stone unturned. Lazar would now throw him a bone on which he could chew for quite some time: "Nikita Sergeyevich, I offer you the post as deputy chief of the Organizational Section of the Ukrainian Party Central Committee." He was looking to equalize the representation of workers in the party apparatus.

There was silence at the other end, a silence that surprised Lazar.

Finally, Khrushchev spoke.

"I am most grateful, Comrade Kaganovich, for the opportunity. Can you tell me where the post would be?"

"Kharkov."

More silence. Lazar realized what was happening. Kharkov was known for its ruthlessness and especially the untrustworthiness of its workers. Khrushchev knew it, too.

"Again, Comrade Kaganovich, I do thank you, and I think you're quite right to want to bring more workers into the Central Committee apparatus, but I don't want to leave Yuzovka. I'm very much at home here. I know the procedures and the personnel of the organization. Besides, I'm completely unfamiliar with the procedures in Kharkov, and I doubt if I could adapt myself to the organizational section."

Lazar listened to the short, fat peasant. He was now wheezing, as a result of saying his piece in one breath. It was the first time Lazar had heard him question an order. Nikita was learning well how to handle himself, but he hadn't learned from the masters themselves, Lenin and Stalin, and Lazar now showed how little effort there was in keeping his protégé in the subservient position.

He sighed so that Khrushchev could hear it and then spoke in hushed tones, as if he were letting the listener in on a secret.

"Well," he said. "If you put it that way, I guess the Central Committee can do without you. There's no need to transfer you from Yuzovka if you feel so strongly against it."

He paused long enough for the words to sink in. He didn't have much of a wait.

"Kharkov?"

"Kharkov."

"*Da*, Kharkov."

Lazar smiled as he put down the receiver. He had indeed learned well how to give orders, how to find the means, just like Stalin, to survive. If you were to survive, you had to have people around who could do what they were told—and understand why.

His second call of the morning was to Mikhail in Nizhni Novgorod. He was passing along the good news that Mikhail had now been elected a Presidium member. The final count was not in as yet, but it didn't matter that much. After all, it was the old axiom that whoever controlled the pen marking the ballots controlled the persons elected.

Mikhail sounded delighted, but Lazar heard an edge to the voice. Perhaps it was a tinge of resentment. Mikhail knew his younger brother had now surpassed him. He had completely underestimated what he was capable of doing. Lazar hoped that more people would do the same. Carelessness by others gave him an edge.

Yuri, too, was taken care of. He was made a first secretary in Nizhni Novgorod, but Lazar knew that was about as far as he could go. He had little ambition, little drive. He sat back, a representative of the great chunk of the party apparat, and did what he was told, offering nothing and doing no more than the minimum. Whatever energies he had seemed to be channeled to his wife and children. They represented his life, his country, his party.

Lazar's own life at home had now taken a decided turn, but in the opposite direction. Maria and Maya were inseparable, as well they might be. Lazar was never with them. He seemed to spend every moment at work. No matter where he was around Moscow, he always had a desk, a chair, and a battery of telephones at his disposal.

The third one, Rosa, had settled quietly in the city. She had become what she always wanted to be, and her days and nights were spent at 8 Kalinin Prospekt, a building erected in 1780 by Quarenzhi that had housed the Sheremetyev family. Now it was a special hospital for party functionaries.

She would have preferred doctoring the general public in one of the city clinics rather than the select few of the party in lavish surroundings. But, that would mean having to confront Lazar, who had arranged the enviable position she now held. Not a welcome task. Besides, she rarely saw her brother. Very few people did.

Lazar had little time for socializing unless he felt it would serve his purposes. He saw Bulganin frequently and Voroshilov occasionally, but the others in the hierarchy were only sporadic visitors. His principal concern was still Stalin (even more so than Maria), and he would speak with him by phone at least six times a day and see him at least twice.

To all but a few, he took on an almost imperious attitude. He offered nothing to a conversation—to a relationship—except to give orders. When asked for information by anyone other than Stalin, Lazar's answer was always the same, the one he developed at the Organ for State Security: "We receive information, we don't give it."

Moscow now was unquestionably the stronghold of Bolshevism (it had been shifted finally from Petrograd, which had been renamed Leningrad), and Lazar was one of the strongest Bolsheviks in the capital. His power was becoming so acute that if he spoke to a party member without calling him "Comrade," it might be considered as either a slip of the tongue or a sign of displeasure.

If subsequently the party member was missing from his desk for a few days without explanation, others began to realize what had probably happened. The OGPU had arrested him. One could be sure of that. Of course, there was always the possibility that the member may have been sent away on a secret mission somewhere, but no one would really believe that.

It was clear that Lazar had been given an axe to wield in Moscow. Stalin obviously liked what he saw of his services against the so-called Ukrainian nationalists and in his handling of Krupskaya and Khrushchev. But he also had to start in on the Jews. It was subliminal at first, small things, like not promoting Jews within the party. They hadn't seemed especially helpful to him in Kiev, and he knew Stalin had no great love for them. At times, he wondered why Stalin had even put up with him in light of his background, but he could not risk posing the question directly. Instead, he asked Bulganin for his thoughts, and the explanation he received seemed logical: "He needs you. Simple as that. You do what is told and obviously you do it well. As long as you don't cross him or disappoint him, you will remain fulfilling his needs. Simple, eh?"

Maria, though, took an opposite view.

"For God's sake, what are you doing?"

It was one of the few times she expressed her true feelings to him. Mostly, she kept important things to herself. Although married to him, she could not completely trust him. You could never be sure what he would do. His temper was too well known. He tried to keep it under control as best as possible, but she had seen the outbursts too often, the times when the string of beads she had given him would snap around his fist, sending beads flying in every direction. She had to replace those beads at least once a month. But when she heard that he had forced the firing of Trashunov, a respected newspaper editor in Kiev who had supported the party, simply because he was Jewish, as an example of what he was capable of doing if the people did not obey him, she could hold it in no longer. She confronted him.

"Have you no sense, no compassion, no feelings for one of your own? He is your people, not Stalin."

"I am doing what I have to do. Understand that before it is too late. My god is Stalin. Do you hear me? Hear me good!"

And again he broke another string of beads.

What choice did he have? Only Stalin had to know who was behind him. He had to satisfy Stalin and no one else. Not even himself. If only the Jews could understand that, too—if only they would stop resisting. He stared into the mirror. His face had become fuller. The mustache was now thinner and trimmer. He wore a new suit and a clean shirt. The better life was agreeing with him. Would he want to give all this up? Yet, hadn't he accused the man named Moisev, his namesake, his father, of doing just this? Wasn't he being hypocritical?

He dismissed the questions with a shake of his head. No, this is a different time, a different place, a different world. You had to be especially careful today. You had to learn the ways as they were. You had to survive. No, not survive. That was what his father had done, and barely. You had to go another step. You had to live—to live.

He looked around the room quickly to make sure his thoughts were not heard. Maria was in the kitchen. "I have to be careful," he murmured to himself. "The merest slip could be outright suicide. People live in perpetual fear of informers who listen and report what they have heard. It is ten times worse than the days of the czar. Hah, then you worried only about the Cossacks and the town constable, but now you cannot be sure of anyone. Students, the errand boys, the colleagues, wives. They will protect themselves at your expense, out of ambition, protection, or downright stupidity. He tried to lighten his mood. He chuckled at a story that best summed up the sign of the times. A Soviet citizen came home from work one day, triple-locked the door behind him, undressed completely, and surveyed his image in the mirror. His eyes narrowed, and after a few minutes he said to the reflection, as if admonishing it, "There is no doubt. One of us is certainly a provocateur."

Things were definitely changing in Moscow. He saw that humor now was finding its way into the system, even if it seemed strange.

For example, *Pravda*'s habitually austere tone had loosened. One article started with, "Through the plains of Malachite, the Khripan River unrolls its silvery ribbon. Beyond the plains, a century-old forest rises up like a bronze wall. In gaps among the pine trees, dachas appear here and there, looking like cottages in a fairy tale."

What then followed was a blistering attack on corrupt bureaucrats and lazy factory workers.

He also noticed a new effort to instill nationalistic pride in the USSR at the expense of everyone and everything else. It was almost as if a huge broom had been dropped from the skies to clean up every part of the country, to sweep away the crooks, the physically and mentally retarded, the debris of yesterday. Even the language changed.

Pharmacies now supplied "bitter salts" for constipation instead of "English salts," and bakeries now produced "city bread" rather than "French bread." Whatever was foreign was swept *za granitsei*— "beyond the frontier."

Lazar joined the parade, too, but in another way. He made sure that Stalin's name was kept in full view. Word filtered down from 2 Dzerzhinsky Square to even the schools that the young were to be taught a new concept: If there were a choice between the death of one's parents or the death of Stalin, the answer was to be the former. Maya was one of the first to learn that "Better if my parents would die because only I would suffer, not all my country."

In private, Lazar had already started to elevate Stalin past Lenin. At dinner parties, he would rise and offer a toast.

"Comrades, it is time for us to tell the people the truth. Everyone in the party keeps talking about Lenin, but we've got to to be honest with ourselves, too. Lenin is dead. The time has come to replace that slogan. Long Live Leninism? No! Long Live Stalinism!"

The rewards would now come.

By 1930 the rest of the world—especially the capitalist countries —had sunk into a depression. But the Soviet Union was already in its second year of the first Five-Year Plan, a plan that was uppermost in the government's mind. Their call was to "Fulfill and Overfulfill!" Workers were to be rewarded according to their productivity in the frantic race to set records. The intention was to triple the production of coal, iron, steel, and oil, to double the production of consumer goods, to raise the production of electricity by 600 percent, and to increase overall output in the entire economy two and one third times. Through such measures, it was believed that the workers' sense of patriotism would be tapped. It had to be, for hardly any foreign government was now prepared to provide capital, nor could they at this time.

Stalin's industrial goals were to move forward rapidly, no matter what the cost. The system Stalin saw would be based on a number of theories: that the operation of industry under Socialism would be determined by production forces, and that there would be no conflict between personal achievements and discipline. The bottom line amounted virtually to martial law under which workers were obedient—even passive—behaving simply like robots.

Along with this, Stalin now developed the collectivization program.

In order to increase agricultural exports to pay for the import of capital equipment that was needed for industrialization, Stalin reasoned that it was absolutely essential to amalgamate the 25 million peasant households in the country into larger and more economically viable arrangements. Land was then ruthlessly confiscated, and small landowners were forced into a *kolkhoz*, a collective farm. By February 1930, one half of the farms had been collectivized. Prices paid for the agricultural products of the *kolkhozy* were set by the state, which also decreed what crops were to be grown. The idea behind collectivization was to modernize agriculture, to secure a steady food supply, to get capital for industrial improvement, and to free labor for work in heavy industry.

Along with this was an edict to "smash the kulaks," those wealthier landowners who were charging excessively high prices for their surplus crops. "They must be eliminated as a class."

But the kulaks would not sit idly by and watch what they considered rightfully theirs being taken away at the whim of the government. They retaliated by killing their cattle, burning their crops, and destroying their homes; in effect, doing anything rather than allow their property to be appropriated by the state.

It was here that Lazar began to feel increasingly stronger. Stalin would send him all over the country as a troubleshooter to "iron out the difficulties," but unlike past times when he might have done more reporting and investigating than anything else, he was now invested with full power. Accordingly, he used force whenever he could, especially against the Cossacks, who were among these wealthy landowners and whom he had not forgotten from his days in Kabany. It gave him immense pleasure to have sixteen major Cossack villages removed to Siberia. If there was a revenge motive, Lazar had it.

He signed orders with reckless abandon. There was almost a perverse joy in being able to dictate to the Cossacks. He recalled too vividly what he and his family had experienced at the hands of these people. His mind flashed back to horses, boots, swords, blood, arrogance, death. Now they would all pay—men, women, children. It didn't matter who. They became one and the same. That was the key to Lazar's being. He would never forgive and he would never forget.

During this new period of reconstruction, Lazar was making an extra effort to reorganize the party ranks and "other bodies of the dictatorship of the proletariat," as he called it. He believed that the Five-Year Plan would become the key factor of Soviet life not only because it represented the entire economic program of what was then a highly centralized Socialist state—in which, according to Marxist doctrine, "economic factors dominate and determine politics"—but because the plan's basic purpose was to socialize both industry and agriculture.

Lazar reasoned that no industrial socialization would be permanent unless the peasants, who formed more than 80 percent of the population, were socialized first. He liked his role in what was happening in the country. He now saw himself being quoted more and more in *Pravda*, and then in a Polish paper and even in an article from Paris, and finally his name appeared in the prestigious *New York Times*. That unnerved him slightly, for he realized, perhaps for the first time, where his life was. It also reminded him of Uncle Levick and Morris and the rest of the people from Kabany, those he had not seen in over twenty years.

Word had already traveled back that they were living in New York. Obviously, they would see the article. Wasn't everyone there forced to read *The New York Times* like they read *Pravda* here? Weren't copies posted at almost every corner, in store windows, on sides of buildings, at offices, even in schools for the children to learn from?

He looked again at *The New York Times* of January 2, 1931, and he was pleased with what he read. He was referred to as "a new and energetic member of the Communist Party Politburo." He even found part of his speech quoted: "Already this second year of the 'Pyatiletka' (Five-Year Plan) has given us twice the total of rural socialization we planned for the fifth year of 1933."

What would Uncle Levick think of him now? What would he say?

"You have done me proud, Lazar Moiseyevich. I always knew you would bring honor to the family. I took you with me on trips when you were only ten because you were the best worker of all. I knew then you would be what you are today."

Morris, too, would feel the same way. He would be excited about his success. He wouldn't look down his nose. In fact, Lazar couldn't think of anyone from Kabany who would harbor any resentment. But then again, one person did come to mind who would—no matter, he was dead.

The following year the same *New York Times* referred to him as "one of Joseph Stalin's closest henchmen." Lazar didn't take kindly to the term *henchman* but it still meant someone to be feared. Articles continued to headline him. He loved being quoted so often and with such respect. Now he was being shown citing figures between Lenin's time and the present. He had said that when Lenin's New Economic Policy was instituted in 1921 "the total State production was 2,000,000,000 rubles annually; now it is 30,000,000,000 rubles. Then there were no collectives; today, State farms and collectives cover 80 percent of the sown area."

But behind the rhetoric, the opposite was beginning to happen. Lazar could see this as the reports flooded in from the farms. Problems were mounting. Agriculture had become disorganized. Crops had slumped to the point where Soviet citizens were now under food rationing. Herds declined even more than field crops, and within one year, the country had lost over one half of its horses and cattle, two thirds of its pigs and seven tenths of its sheep and goats. It was obvious now that collectivization could prove to be the spark for a rapid turnover in the Moscow party leadership. Lazar could only watch and wait and hope. He also had no choice but to support the government's program. An about-face now would be tantamount to an admission of error, a mistake in judgment, something unacceptable to Stalin.

No, Lazar had to take a hard-nosed, determined position to show Stalin whose side he was on and to indicate continuing confidence that the program would be effective.

Already, N. A. Uglanov, who was an opponent of collectivization, had been replaced by Bauman. Then Bauman got caught in the crackdown on excesses and was replaced by Molotov. Word began to filter back that there was more trouble on the collective farms than originally anticipated.

The Ukraine, in particular, was suffering from the worst famine in its history, a result of a combination crop failure and the collectivization program itself. In addition, high taxes had to be paid just after the harvest. More than 2 million Ukrainians died of starvation. The situation was critical, and Stalin immediately recognized the need for a stronger individual, if not in mind, at least physically. He turned to one of the strongest men in the Politburo, the one who was known for tossing caution to the wind—at least it appeared that way. He looked to his 215-pound assistant. Molotov was replaced by Lazar.

Enforcement, Stalin thought, was desperately needed, and Lazar would be the one to do it.

He was sent out under different ruses. On one such trip, he supposedly was going away on a business trip to Krasnodar, in the south. It seemed benign. He would make a stop there to check on the party membership, even have some time to sun and swim in the Sea of Azov. It would be a vacation of sorts, something that everyone agreed he needed. After all, he was known for being at his desk starting at 6:30 A.M. and could still be found there burning the proverbial midnight oil, primarily talking to Stalin, who also didn't get to bed much before 2:00 A.M.

But Lazar never made it farther south than Donetsk. Instead, he went to quash a rebellion by the Kuban Cossacks, who had gone on strike, refusing to cultivate their land and thus contributing dramatically to the famine. Lazar's answer was the same as it always was: "If they don't shape up, then whole Cossack settlements would be forcibly moved to Siberia. The rebellious ones would either do what they are told in the green valleys of the Ukraine or they would wither away and freeze their goddamn balls off."

His tactics were becoming well known. They involved a combination of expulsion and violence, and not necessarily in that order. His unique way of dealing with reluctant workers was legendary. He sat behind a desk with one pistol beside his right hand, another beside his left—and people knew he would not hesitate to use them.

This reputation for dealing successfully with factions such as the Cossacks was widespread, and Stalin had no problem in simply sending Lazar out to the countryside to put down whatever rebellions were fermenting.

Workers and peasants alike feared him. The village of Ivanovo-Voznesensk was a firsthand witness to his methodology. People there went on strike over the shortage of food. Lazar handled the situation in a ruthless yet effective manner. First, he took the party membership cards away from the province committee chairpersons with the warning that if things didn't get better within three days, such as meeting a grain procurement quota, they would be expelled from the party, relieved of their jobs, and imprisoned.

The next step would be far worse.

Lazar would make sure that the most vociferous strikers of the general public would share a cell with the ex-party member who was deemed instrumental in causing the food shortage. Lazar's face was a study in glee as he imprisoned the father of a starving child along with the person accused of causing such starvation. The punishment was self-apparent.

The more successful Lazar became, the more Stalin turned to him. After the principal grain-growing regions had been socialized with the anti-Kulak attack, the time came for the remaining vast areas of the Soviet Union, including the Moscow province. In the city itself, Lazar had mobilized 2,000 leading party workers of the Moscow party machine to organize total collectivization of that province.

But the more he did meant the more he had to do. Stalin added responsibilities one on top of another. He even gave him the task of putting his second wife, Nadezhda Alliluyeva, under strict surveillance and reporting back to him all observations about her. Rumors had been floating about for some time that she was not well and had already made attempts on her life. Lazar didn't know whether this was true or not. All he knew was that Stalin must be a difficult man to live with, and he had heard, although he had not seen, that he had even beaten her on occasion. Maria told him stories she had heard from Paulina Molotov that Stalin would lock his wife in her room for days at a time, even preventing her from seeing her own daughter.

No one seemed to have answers for such behavior. When it came to family matters, Stalin was more reserved than usual. Few people saw Nadezhda, and even fewer were able to talk with her.

In that respect, Lazar's task was easy. Nadezhda moved around very little, thus his reports to Stalin were scanty. In a way this was good because he had more than he could handle outside of Moscow. He didn't relish a job that he knew could be a no-win situation. But Nadezhda made it even simpler for him. Within a month, her next attempt on her life was successful.

He had received two messengers early one morning, ten minutes apart from each other. The first said she had shot herself; the second said she was the victim of poison.

When Lazar arrived at the Kremlin, Molotov was already there. Stalin was sitting in a wing chair in his living quarters. He was puffing absently on a cigarette and watching the smoke curl toward the ceiling. Although to an outsider he seemed to be calm, as if he were just waiting for his breakfast, Lazar and Molotov both knew there was turmoil in his head.

As soon as Voroshilov entered, Stalin began to speak. Lazar had the feeling he had said little to Vyacheslav before his arrival.

"There are rumors that she was troubled by my policies, or should I say our policies? There are rumors that she had deep political differences with what we are doing. I assume you agree. We do not pay much attention to this."

Lazar looked at Molotov and then at Voroshilov. They all knew that Nadezhda was obsessed with the supposed "viciousness" (as she called it) of what her husband and those around him were doing to the country, so much so that she had become a recluse, paying little attention to even her daughter, Svetlana, who had now turned six.

"She didn't understand, Comrade Secretary," said Molotov in the most gentle voice he could find. Lazar nodded.

"People don't always realize what is good for them," Voroshilov added.

Stalin kept his eyes on the three men. It was obvious that he didn't like what had happened, but for different reasons. It was a nuisance to him, an intrusion into his daily routine. It was unproductive.

"Funeral arrangements still have to be made," he said, lighting another cigarette with the butt of the previous.

"May I suggest," offered Molotov, in a voice that was almost a whisper, "the Novodevichiy?"

It was a good suggestion, Lazar thought. The Novodevichiy Cemetery, which means "Young Maidens," was next to one of Moscow's loveliest architectural monuments, a seventeenth-century monastery. It was the perfect setting: dignified, tasteful, nonpolitical.

"And," added Stalin, "I want this over quickly and privately."

The stories surrounding Nadezhda's death were giving Stalin great concern. Attempts were made by many in the government to substantiate a story about an unsuccessful operation. Word spread that she had peritonitis that had caused her death during an appendectomy. It went nowhere. A few believed that Stalin had actually murdered his wife. That also was without foundation. Still, the question of suicide surfaced irresistibly.

Lazar decided that he would let others think what they wanted. It would be good for his own cause. If the masses preferred to believe that Stalin had killed his wife, just as Ivan the Terrible and Peter the Great had done, so be it. On the other hand, as Lazar well knew, whether Nadezhda had held the revolver to her head or whether Stalin had helped her, there was in effect no difference. There was also no question that Stalin was the one who made living impossible for her.

Now, with Nadezhda's death, Lazar moved to isolate Stalin, to protect him at all costs, but in a way, also, to isolate himself, to protect himself. He would throw a tight security ring around him, just the tactic necessary to arouse sufficient paranoia in the man. It worked, for Stalin collapsed a week after Nadezhda's burial. The Kremlin doctors diagnosed a mild heart attack. It was mild but telling. Lazar quickly moved to solidify his position. He turned to Rosa.

She was thirty-seven years of age, working long hours at the clinic, seeing no one, except during the weekly dinner at Lazar's house. She had become a hermit. Her beauty and intelligence were little cause for joy when it came to men in her life. She would have been better off not being the sister of the ''powerful Lazar Moiseyevich.'' Men—and women, too—simply kept her at a distance, mostly out of fear.

It was not the way to live, and she felt resentment. But she recognized that without her brother she would not be where she was. She, too, might be filling out the rest of her life in some mud stop like Kabany; perhaps she might have died at the side of a road, like her mother. No, she owed Lazar too much, and when he called for her, she had no hesitancy in rushing to him.

They met in Lazar's office at 2 Dzerzhinsky Square. He usually liked to see people there, especially those from whom he wanted something. It was always more official, more intimidating when you were forced to sit across the desk from him.

Rosa had become a woman of exceptional beauty, with large coal-black eyes, jet-black hair with what seemed to be violet highlights, and a handsome well-shaped nose. She was of medium height and, unlike most of the other women representing men in power, who Lazar said ''resembled beach balls with legs,'' Rosa was slender above the waist but had strong legs and an "admirable rear," as Lazar would fondly tell Maria.

She looked at people the way her brother did: how they might be useful to her. She had learned well, and whatever Lazar told her would have to be reevaluated in that way. She, too, understood the words of Uncle Levick: "Whatever is good for the Jews."

"He needs someone like you more than ever," Lazar said. He didn't have to explain who the "he" was. Rosa had been in the examining room when Stalin was brought in after his collapse. She had already heard the whisperings around the clinic. She knew that when it came to women, Stalin was in a vacuum. His first wife, Catherine, died of tuberculosis after only three years of marriage. Now his second wife had died after fifteen years of marriage, and under more tragic circumstances.

The whisperings continued to center on Stalin's need for lusty women, but on a part-time basis. He seemed to desire the company of men more.

She looked into her brother's eyes. They held few clues as to the thoughts behind them.

"What is his need?" she asked.

"Needs. Needs in the plural."

Lazar had seen what was happening at the Kremlin. The first symptoms of persecution mania had already appeared in Stalin just as they had appeared in Ivan the Terrible after the death of his wife. It was on this fact that Lazar must base his plan.

"First, he needs a physician and someone he can trust. He knows you. He got you accepted into the clinic, and he trusts me. Thus, he will trust you and your medical knowledge."

Rosa nodded.

"Agreed," she said. She had no choice. Personal physician to the Soviet leader meant being able to listen and encourage. She could do that.

"Second," Lazar held two fingers in front of her. "He needs a more stable family life. Svetlana is six. She needs a parent. Stalin is not that. We need to establish a family relationship for him."

Rosa nodded again, and Lazar could see the same determined mood and understanding that he had seen decades ago when Sasha would return to the house only to find that Moisev had given the dinner away. Sasha would set her jaw firmly, shake her head as if to accept the

170

inevitable, and then go out to barter something for the family's evening meal.

"Finally, you must be there as an anchor, not someone for him to argue with, not someone he can bully, but someone he will call and come to as almost a haven. You understand this is to be totally apolitical?"

Rosa listened intently. She would be given full latitude to do what she felt best, and perhaps this would also give more substance to her own life, which up to now had been mired in a past that was horrendous, a present that was barely passable, and a future that looked mundane.

Lazar studied her. He needed her badly. The opportunity was golden. He just had to seize it with the right people at the right moment. Rosa fit the bill perfectly. He had never liked her when she was small. Now he did. But, then again, back in Kabany, he never needed her.

She did more than she was told. Stalin's dacha at Gorinka was completely modernized. She brightened the colors, brought in new furniture, and began to entertain. Twice a week she held receptions there, receiving her friends from Nizhni Novgorod, first and foremost being Nadezhda Bulganin, a doctor like herself. Rosa had become a gracious hostess in a number of ways, and as the focal point of his life, Stalin found his most devoted disciples at the Gorinka dacha: Molotov, Bulganin, Mikoyan, Voroshilov, and, of course, Lazar.

But Lazar went an extra step. Recognizing Stalin's penchant for security, he had several buildings constructed near the dacha to house the fifty new members of his bodyguard. Machine guns were placed in turrets, and large Russian wolfhounds patrolled the grounds twenty-four hours a day. Even a signal system was installed along the road from the dacha to the Kremlin. The system wended its way along the Arbat and was used to inform the police of Stalin's car and guards constantly. Now Lazar could keep tabs on him with little effort.

No, Rosa had done what was expected and then some. Within a year, she was known as Rosa Stalin.

Lazar's seeds began to yield fruit rather quickly. As Stalin recovered, he was shown that there were many around him who were not his friends. Lazar would give reports indicating that as the hardships of industrialization and collectivization multiplied during the First Five-Year Plan, small opposition groups had formed within the party. He felt that they had to be watched carefully, for they apparently had

171

united into a loose anti-Stalin coalition. Others surrounding Stalin at the time said the same thing. Some on the Politburo were anxious about Stalin. Was he indeed the proper one to lead the country? Was he truly in command of his faculties? What had really happened to Nadezhda? A feeling that Stalin was incompetent emerged.

Lazar, too, realized that his own standing was in jeopardy. He was knee-deep now, and as Stalin went so would he. Like Rosa, he felt he had no choice.

But Stalin turned stubborn, He vowed to conduct a fight against all his enemies. Rosa had warned Lazar of this. She understood his mental state: He was acting as Ivan the Terrible had, even imitating the czar in his policies of state. Action was being met with too strong a reaction.

Stalin sensed danger; Lazar confirmed it, although he suggested restraint at the outset. They would tread lightly at first, with a routine reduction in the party to weed out members of "dubious" backgrounds. The result was the expulsion of some 800,000 persons from the party rolls.

No one was arrested. Their party cards were just lifted. It served its purpose, to throw a "scare" into the opposition leadership, whoever they might be.

Lazar knew this would not be enough. There were too many of those he called "disillusioned friends" around. Stronger medicine was needed. The question was when to administer it and in what dosage. Timing was the key. The following year, he found it.

In 1934, V. R. Menizhinsky, head of the OGPU, was replaced by G. G. Yagoda, of Polish descent, and with him came another change in the secret police's name, this time to the People's Commissariat for Internal Affairs, the NKVD.

Lazar liked Yagoda. He seemed a pleasant fellow and an extremely able strategist. His only problem was that he seemed too pleasant, too willing to help, almost obsequious in his dealings with Stalin. Unlike those around him, like Molotov, Voroshilov, and even Malenkov, who was rising rapidly through the ranks, Yagoda had difficulty handling Stalin's constant shift of moods and his habit of setting one person onto another. Lazar had seen that early on in his own relationship with Stalin. Actually, everybody did. He liked playing one of his associates off against another, enjoying the controversy, the tension it created. The newer and thinner-skinned individuals could not handle such machinations and quickly dropped by the wayside. The hardier ones who understood the games being played would survive. A sense of humor, albeit a perverse one, was needed.

Yagoda had a more serious nature. If Stalin told him something, even in jest, such as citing the defense minister as someone who slept with sheep instead of women, he took it as the gospel.

Stalin became more and more preoccupied about a possible revolution in the country. He saw it fermenting everywhere he went, but never as obvious as in Leningrad, where the party chief, Sergei Kirov, controlled the governing apparatus, and in fact the entire province, with an iron hand. Kirov, whose real name was Kostrikov, was a leading Bolshevik and had been a Politburo member for the past four years. He was ambitious and well liked, a deadly combination. He was also attractive, handsome was the word, in an almost boyish way. This appealed to the masses, as did his command of the language, which was so great that each speech became an eagerly awaited event. Such charisma had not been seen in the city since Lenin himself.

Stalin saw this firsthand. He was attending a ballet at the Mariinsky Theater, a magnificent, five-tiered gilt horseshoe—all plush and crystal with flying angels to top it off. The applause for his own presence when he entered the czar's box on the second tier was respectable yet restrained, but it was no match for the cries of *"Da, da, da*—'yes, yes, yes'" that he heard when Kirov stood to acknowledge his own introduction.

It was clear that Kirov was not one to be taken lightly. As soon as he returned to Moscow, Stalin presented these facts to Yagoda. Within hours, the NKVD chief had plans to neutralize Kirov. Stalin listened intently, the ever-present pipe fixed between his teeth. At the end of Yagoda's presentation, he simply left the room. He said nothing, but Lazar saw his eyes on his way out. They were sparkling.

Within forty-eight hours, Kirov was dead, assassinated by a man named Nikolayev.

At a huge Moscow trial that had all the trappings of a theatrical play, the murder was explained as part of a vast treasonous plot arranged by Stalin's rivals. Prominent men now publicly "confessed" to organizing the assassination. It sounded like a stage play. Nikolayev was the husband of Kirov's secretary, and he had been made to believe that Kirov was having an affair with his wife. It was all fabrication, but it became a great crime of passion, filled with intrigue, for the only witness to the murder died a few days afterward in an automobile accident. He was the sole person in the automobile to die, and he sat in the rear; the other four, including the driver and front-seat passenger, "coincidentally" lived.

The trial unearthed other matters as well. The confessing parties said they had planned to kill all the other top Soviet leaders and to sabotage USSR military power by destroying Soviet factories. It was all for the cause of "Trotskyism," and Trotsky was the true mastermind of such a high-level conspiracy. Accordingly, Trotsky was sentenced to death in absentia, the sentence eventually being fulfilled a few years later.

The court decisions came down exactly as planned. Most of the people indicted were executed, and 90 percent of Leningrad's party members were expelled. The tactic was a huge success. Kirov was gone, many of the dissidents were gone, and Stalin's control of the NKVD as well as other party apparatus was now unquestioned.

Stalin sat back. Yagoda and Lazar were now free to carry out any other ideas they had to solidify their leader's position and, more importantly, their own. Truly, the end results justified the means.

Lazar grabbed the reins with both hands. Another opportunity had presented itself, and he would make use of it fully and completely. This time, though, it went beyond his wildest dreams, for what was seen now in Russia was something known as "the Great Terror," mass purges that swept across the country like a deranged prehistoric animal. The purges went everywhere, taking on a momentum and frenzy never before seen. It was as if all Hell had broken loose.

Stalin's old rivals were executed, many without a trial. Relatives, office staffs, protégés, and friends were imprisoned. Anyone who had ever crossed the path of the "alleged criminals" was categorized as "under suspicion" and often purged. Every person of dubious political background was arrested: former czarist bourgeois, priests, kulaks, Russians with relatives abroad, foreigners who immigrated into the USSR and became Soviet citizens, even children if necessary. No one was safe. Millions of loyal Soviet citizens were demoted, arrested, imprisoned, or simply just killed.

Solutions were relatively simple. Lazar sat at his desk and dispensed judgments as if he were ordering a meal. Breakfast: Solution to the peasant problem? "Enforced famine; exile to Siberia." Lunch: Solution to political problems? "Execute opponents; exile suspects to labor camps." Dinner: Solution to foreign affairs problems? "Subversion."

The main section of 2 Dzerzhinsky Square, known as the Lubyanka, was made the prison of no return. People entered but never came out again.

The Soviet Union was plunged into a nightmare that would last until 1939. It affected all levels of the country, from the party's Politburo (three fourths of whose members were either executed or sent to labor camps) to the Red Army, whose leaders were purged, to the people in the streets, who found themselves arrested on prearranged charges by those they had trusted. No one was exempt . . . no one.

Religion was especially slandered. The original Soviet constitution of 1918 permitted "freedom of religious and antireligious propaganda." That was amended in 1936 to "freedom of religious worship and antireligious propaganda." The Church was thus deprived of its right to propagandize—to transmit its creed and values on a formal basis. The new provision meant no group study, no Sunday schools, no evangelism. On the other hand, the party was free, even obligated, to preach atheism.

Prisons were filled to capacity. People were simply stripped naked and flung into a cell to face absolute silence coupled with starvation. They would never be seen again. The average citizen would purposely walk on the other side of the street from any prison, eyes averting the steel doors in the rear that served as the entranceways.

No one was immune, even at the top layers of government. On one occasion, Bukharin (the party's theoretician) was summoned by Lazar, who had purposely arranged a confrontation between him and Grigory Sokolnikov in the presence of high-ranking Chekists. Sokolnikov talked about the "parallel rightist center" (parallel, in other words, to that of the Trotskyites) and about Bukharin's underground activity against the Stalin regime. Lazar conducted the interrogation aggressively, and when it was over, he ordered Sokolnikov to be "taken away." He then turned to Bukharin and in a friendly, almost sugary, tone said, "He lies through his teeth, the whore!" Bukharin was delighted, but two days later, Lazar handed a report to Stalin calling Bukharin a "Fascist hireling" and demanding that he be shot. The paper also bore Molotov's signature and agreement. It was evident that Lazar's task also involved the extermination of whatever party cadres he determined.

Trotsky became the devil incarnate. Every disaster at home, every setback abroad could be explained away by blaming the "Trotskyite-Fascist-wreckers."

On his trips around the country, Lazar would telegraph Stalin with wires such as: STUDY OF SITUATION SHOWS THAT TROTSKYITE-WRECK-ING HAS ASSUMED BROAD DIMENSIONS HERE—IN INDUSTRY, AGRICUL-TURE, SUPPLY, HEALTH CARE, TRADE, EDUCATION, AND POLITICAL WORK. APPARATY OF OBLAST ORGANIZATIONS AND PARTY OBKOM EX-CEPTIONALLY INFESTED.

There was no other explanation, clarification, or report made.

The reply from Stalin consisted of only one word: AGREED.

Lazar then proceeded to destroy that area's party structure. In just the first year, Lazar supervised the purge of nearly half a million people. More than 70 percent of the Moscow committees were expelled, and there seemed to be no end in sight. Nothing and no one could stop him. He had indeed become Stalin's true right-hand man. In fact, letters coming in from all over the country were addressed to "Com-rades Stalin and Kaganovich."

And yet, it was still not enough. He acquired positions like no other person. He watched over ideological events, ran the Central Committee Transport Commission, chaired the Party Control Commission, chaired the Central Committee New Agriculture Political Department, and chaired the Organizing Committee for the Seventeenth Party Congress, among other duties.

When Stalin went off to his Black Sea retreat, it was Lazar who took over in Moscow. Apart from Stalin himself, nobody else in the USSR held as many key posts in the party power structure as Lazar. And he wielded that power with determination. Nothing would or could be overlooked. He even took to falsifying the results of a secret ballot in the Central Committee, destroying some 300 voting slips on which Stalin's name had been crossed out and he tracked down those whom he believed were responsible for such deletions. He knew then that he controlled the fear of the people ("Fear has big eyes") and with fear came power, "and with power come the laurels."

From this time on, Lazar went about organizing everything he could. He practically reconstructed Moscow itself, but cared little about trying to preserve valuable monuments: The great church of Christ the Savior was demolished for a new Palace of Soviets, the Holy Week monastery was turned into a theater for use by party members, and the Iversk Gates and clocktower at Red Square were torn down notwithstanding protests from leading architects.

He even took over the transportation area. People began to take note that for the first time the percentage of car loadings daily had been increased. Under his leadership, Soviet railways loaded more than 90,000 cars every twenty-four hours. A year before, the railways loaded only 50,000 in one day. He knew how to accomplish what he wanted: fear. Lazar issued orders that in the event of any accidents, railway officials would be "personally responsible." They knew what those words meant: Lubyanka, and worse.

The papers were full of Lazar Moiseyevich Kaganovich. He was delighted when the staid *New York Times* once again spoke of him in long articles:

> The reputation of Lazar M. Kaganovich, for conceiving large-scale projects and accomplishing [sic] in Russia, almost overshadows that of Joseph Stalin himself. Mr. Kaganovich is credited with having originated the idea of machine-tractor stations, dominated by Commissar agents, for guiding the collectivized peasants, stimulating the agricultural output, and, in brief, consolidating the "agricultural revolution" effect by collectivization.
>
> To him also is attributed the liberalization of literature and the arts that has come about in Soviet Russia in the last few years. He holds the presidency of the Moscow Soviet, an important and difficult post, and is a member of the Communist Politbureau.
>
> The task he has now, of rehabilitating the Soviet railroads, is one that has baffled others who were (and still are) held in the greatest esteem by the Bolshevik rulers, but none of the others had quite so great a record of accomplishments as Mr. Kaganovich.

Along with this came continued purges. Other newspapers, such as *Vozrozhdenye*, a czarist exile publication, wrote about these. It celebrated the first purge of the trial of sixteen top officials with a poem:

> We thank thee, Stalin!
> Sixteen scoundrels,
> Sixteen butchers of the Fatherland
> Have been gathered to their forefathers.
> But why only Sixteen,
> Give us Forty,
> Give us Hundreds,
> Thousands.

> *Make a bridge across the Moscow River,*
> *a bridge without towers and beams*
> *a bridge of Soviet Carrion*
> *and Add thy carcass*
> *to the Rest!*

Lazar would. He would give them the forty, the hundreds, the thousands, the millions. He would give it to them in spades. And he did, turning people against people. Children reported on the activities of their parents, husbands on wives, wives on husbands, grandparents on children. No one was exempt. No one cared about anyone else. It was total involvement in the self. People whispered, even to themselves. Stores would be packed with shoppers, yet there was silence. Even comedy in the theaters was met with stifled chuckles. People were even afraid to laugh. It was as if a huge blanket had been dropped over their mouths. No one was safe; no one could be safe. It was glorious!*

He was destroying everything and everyone in his path. Whoever was against Stalin he termed "an enemy of the people," although even he began to wonder how many of the people would be left after he was finished.

He saw little of his family during those years. Like everyone else in the hierarchy, he spent his time in the Kremlin, constantly at Stalin's side, or he would be out visiting areas around the country. To Lazar, it was power beyond anything he could imagine, and he exercised it without the least reserve. It had seemed so quick, this success of his. He felt that it was only "yesterday" when he was being escorted out of one town to another, a fugitive on the run. He was powerless then, another harmless and ineffectual spoke on a giant wheel, going round and round, but with little control as to where he was being taken. He had been in his twenties at that time, that yesterday. Now, at age forty-two, he was the wheel itself. He had the control. He had the right to roll wherever he wanted and to crush whatever was in his way.

Although he continued to rip things down, to destroy what was, he was building. He turned his attention to countless projects to replace what was no more, to look for new achievements, new glories. He

---

*The human cost was enormously high. It has been estimated that between collectivization casualties and the labor-camp deaths, 20 million people lost their lives. This was approximately the total of the Soviet Union's military and civilian losses in World War II. In other words, a staggering figure of 40 million in a ten-year period.

found one in his position as commissar of transportation. He had discovered plans drawn years before—by American engineers for the construction of a subway—a Metro—to aid mass transportation in the rapidly growing capital.

The subway was patterned after those built in other countries, except that it would run on electricity. He noted that the first subway, built in 1863 in London, was operated by steam locomotives. All subsequent subways were built to run on electricity. Boston in the United States had the second system in 1898, then Paris in 1900, Berlin in 1902, New York in 1904, Madrid in 1919, and Tokyo in 1927.

With the world trying to find its way out of the depression, and the Soviet Union concentrating on industrialization and its own survival, Lazar drew plans for a massive subway network that would be second to none in the world. He disregarded the mass-transportation concept. That would simply be a by-product of something more splendid he had in mind. The real reason for such a project was the desire to construct, in record-breaking time, the best and most beautiful subway in the world. It would become a prize exhibit—a showcase—for foreign delegations, journalists, and tourists, a visible proof of the superiority of the socialist-planned economy over the free-enterprise system. Here at last would be concrete evidence that the first Communist state had already caught up with and surpassed the capitalists.

The architecture had to be both monumental and decorative to reflect, as Lazar termed it, "the greatness of socialist construction." It would give the populace a psychological lift as well, for it would offer them a symbol of a Communist future.

Lazar, of course, had no experience in this kind of venture. He knew it and Stalin knew it, but Lazar did have ability and persistence in solving problems, and in not shying away from the smallest detail. Stalin assigned the project to him, and Lazar began a self-inflicted schedule to finish the project in record time. He set an unprecedented course for his workers: 70,000 men and women would toil steadily in three shifts around the clock every day. He had never constructed tunnels under a crowded city. But, as he told Stalin, "There is always a first time."

He employed shrewdness and unlimited ruthlessness if a problem could not be solved by gentler means. He showed no mercy. He ignored the precautionary measures urgently recommended by experts and took it upon himself to issue orders that no responsible specialist would dare think of, let alone do. It resulted in countless deaths.

179

He devised an extraordinarily tight time schedule, which became known by the laborers as the "time schedule that grabbed us by the throat." He was hated with a vengeance. An excerpt from a speech delivered by Lazar around New Year's Eve, 1933, to construction managers and shop brigadiers sheds light on the working speed expected from them:

We must declare with the utmost sharpness that the present stand of the construction work cannot insure the completion of the first subway section by November 7, 1934. The main task is to speed up the construction tempo . . . In the shortest possible time we must increase the speed of the excavating five times and the speed of the tunnel building eight to nine times.

There was to be no discussion following this. It was an edict. It had to be done—or else.

Speed, speed, speed.

There were rumblings of discontent. References to Lazar could be heard every now and then.

"*On ni huya ni znayit*—'He doesn't know a fucking thing!' "

"*Ssat ya na nivo hat' el*—'Piss on him!' "

"*On id' ot pirdachim param*—'He's getting there propelled by fart steam.' "

They were stopped just as quickly as they started. His wide network of informers brought back the names of the sarcastic ones, the rebellious ones, the mischief-makers. A number were innocent, many were guilty. They were all shot.

Lazar assigned Khrushchev the job as foreman on the actual construction. He was charged with carrying out Lazar's decisions. Bulganin was appointed the superintendent of the project. He watched over Khrushchev. The three of them turned the city practically into an armed camp to finish the building by the May Day festivities in 1935.

Lazar left no stone unturned. He shanghaied people of all ages onto the project. Occasionally, he would have heart-to-heart talks with groups of workers to try and instill an incentive in what they were doing but more often to let them know how closely they were being watched. Once, he had spoken with a group of Komsomol (Young Communist League) members working on excavation. Some were as young as eleven years of age. One of them asked why the wages were so low.

His father had questioned him about this and insisted upon a "proper answer."

Lazar replied, "Well, it is possible that the rates are too low. But you should know that the rates are calculated on the assumption that the work will be done at shock speed."

The message was clear. In order to earn a living one had to work at the speed Lazar had set. The youth learned this; the father apparently not. The youth continued in the excavation process; the father was sent to Siberia.

Lazar stopped at nothing. For the sake of the subway and its lavishness, he expended the people's time, health, and, when necessary, their very lives.

In May 1935, though, the new subway opened. It was a magnificent structure, designed by Alexei Shchusev, the architect of Lenin's Mausoleum and the most celebrated Soviet architect of the time. The subway was built some 200 feet below ground. The stations, more ornamental than functional, were handsome works, decorated with classical busts and mosaics. Elegant ceilings rested on seventy-two marble columns, and chandeliers, lavish marble mosaics, and porphyry columns adorned the stations. Breathtaking was an understatement.

The trains were scheduled to run on the time tables and clocks posted on each platform. Lazar designated the first car of each train as reserved for women with children. He set the cost of a ride at two cents and had installed a ventilation system that forced a change in the air eight times every hour.

It was a master achievement, and Lazar knew it. He also made sure others knew it.

A parade was held in Moscow with more than half a million people cheering for the builders of this new Metro. In response, Lazar pronounced that "Russians work for the masses while other nations help the rich." He was greeted with tumultuous applause even from the workers, although most of them did not mean it.

He then proceeded to ride the subway with Maria, Maya, Khrushchev, and Bulganin at his side. The rest of the Politburo sheepishly followed. Stalin remained back at the Kremlin, his paranoia about security preventing him from venturing that far underground. He would see Lazar at the reviewing stand later.

Lazar's chest swelled, especially when Stalin decreed that the system would bear his name, which would be deeply incised in stone above the main entrance to each station. He felt his eyes moisten, something that had not happened to him since Rosa told him of the death of their parents. It had been a long time ago.

In ceremonies before the main terminal in Revolution Square, Stalin had taken an extra step. He had pinned onto Lazar's fine new suit a medal consisting of two orange ribbons with gold borders connected to an oval medallion with Lenin's likeness in the center surrounded by gold trim. There was a maroon star on one border and the hammer and sickle on another. At age forty-three, Lazar was now one of the first to be awarded the country's highest mark of distinction, the Order of Lenin.

He looked up at the blue Moscow sky. "*Where are you all now?*" he shouted to himself. "*Where are you, Papa, Mama, Uncle Levick, Morris? Where, where are you?*

It was the greatest day of his life, and he expected more just like it.

At a dinner that night given by the Moscow Soviet for the British and French engineers who had assisted in drafting plans for the subway, Lazar finished his speech with these words:

"This opening of a subway means more for us than the opening of a factory. It is a symbol of improvement in living conditions for Moscow people who have entrusted to us their future betterment. In Western countries, attention is chiefly paid to means of transport for the richer classes. Automobiles continue to improve in comfort, but popular transport remains a matter of secondary importance. We, on the contrary, are determined that our subway, which is a chief means of popular conveyance, shall be not only as comfortable as possible but as good-looking and artistically perfect as possible. We did not build the subway for profit but for the benefit and comfort of the Moscow masses."

Not everyone in the audience applauded.

It did not stop only with his name carved in stone. Now it became attached to towns. Stalin had issued the edict. Just as Tsaritsyn became Stalingrad and Petrograd became Leningrad, the order came down. The names of eight villages, including his birthplace of Kabany, were changed. They would forever more be known as the towns of Kaganovich.

Lazar would have preferred the change of name in Kabany earlier, when there were still inhabitants who remembered him as a boy. Now the inhabitants were all emigrants from the west, and they had neither heard of him nor did they care. Whether it was Kabany or Kaganovich was of little import to them.

Still, to Lazar, the accolade was there, as was his new nickname.

He now became known to the media as "the Iron Commissar." His role as the transportation chief had even then far-reaching effects, for he was now able, with Stalin's consent—which seemed to be open-ended—to move into other areas as well.

He handed over control of the Moscow city and Oblast party organization to Khrushchev by first appointing him to run the Bauman and Krasnaya Presnya party district committees and then promoting him to his own deputy in the Moscow organization. What Stalin was doing for him, Lazar was doing for Khrushchev.

The purges, though, continued under Lazar's watchful eye in every area of the economy. He even became the leading figure in the coal trust purge, in which he ousted twelve prominent leaders of that industry. It seemed again to foist his presence before the public. Once more, he could read about himself in the daily newspapers:

> Stalin's pinch hitter, Lazar Moiseyevich Kaganovich, who probably did more than anyone except Stalin himself to insure the success of the collective farm movement and who subsequently reorganized the rail transportation with marked success, was not long ago put in charge of heavy industry. He lost no time tackling one of the basic problems, local production, which had fallen considerably behind schedule. Today, he issued a formidable blast, discharging a dozen or so leading officials of the coal trust and introducing a number of reforms.

The papers, of course, were always light-years behind actuality. Lazar was now commissar of heavy industry, dealing with fuel, electricity, steel, pig iron, chemicals, and building materials. In effect, he had a stranglehold on the lifeblood of the country. The Estonian newspaper *Zalndustrials Zatiu* reported this, along with Lazar's biography:

> Mr. Kaganovich—a member of the all-powerful Political Bureau—is J. Stalin's prize pinch hitter. His first spectacular success was in building the Moscow subway when he was head of the Moscow Communist party organization. From that post, he

was drafted to take charge of the railroads, which three years ago were lagging so badly that they were holding up every department of Soviet economy. His methods have done hard-hitting wonders in that thankless job. Now he goes to the most important of all commissariats, the smooth operation of heavy industry, a prerequisite to every important Soviet economic undertaking.

At the same time, he was also making sure his flanks were protected. Rosa was watching Stalin, and Khrushchev was at his rear. Now he turned to one side and brought Mikhail into Moscow, making him deputy commissar of heavy industry. To spread the Kaganovich influence even more, he had the oldest brother appointed head of the main board of the aircraft industry. As a result, he became a member of the USSR Central Executive Committee, another vote in his favor.

Even Yuri was not overlooked. He, too, was transferred to Moscow to work in the People's Commissariat of Foreign Trade.

It was no secret that Moscow was quickly becoming a gathering place for the Kaganovich clan, and some members of the Politburo began to warn Stalin about possible subversion of his own position. It went nowhere. Stalin turned a deaf ear. He saw only success after success and the strengthening of his own post. Lazar would never turn on him. Stalinism was too much ingrained in him. He was devoted to him, a loyal servant. And those who questioned Stalin's authority would find themselves on the outside looking in. The purge applied to all: Yagoda spent only two years as head of the NKVD. He was ousted and then shot a year later on trumped-up charges as a subversive.

Lazar could only smile. He knew it all along. The man was just too, too pleasant.

N. I. Yezhov then succeeded at the NKVD, but he, too, served only two years and was shot the following year.

Even Stalin's good friend Yenukidze, who at one time had been secretary of the Central Executive Committee, found himself removed from his posts and expelled from the party. And Ordzhonikidze, who was a friend to all, showed them the only way out. He committed suicide, a final gesture of protest against what he saw was happening to the glorious revolution.

That death shocked everyone in the government. This was a man all remembered as good-natured, witty, a devoted Bolshevik, a friend.

As he carried the urn of ashes to the Kremlin wall, Lazar recalled those early days back in Petrograd at the Smolny Institute. Sergo was a fun fellow to have around, even if his jokes were downright unfunny. The snow swirled about him, the bitter wind whipping his face, adding to the wetness on his cheeks. It was a sad day for all Russia. He could see it on the faces of Stalin, Voroshilov, and Molotov, who walked beside him as the official pallbearers. Their friend was never a threat. Perhaps that was why he was considered a friend.

Now it was the four of them left, the most powerful men in this huge land. Lazar began to wonder where this would all lead: distrust upon distrust, agony upon agony, death upon death. But then the thought faded. There was still some good out of this. That much was apparent. After all, Krupskaya had died that year, too.

Other changes were happening. Lazar had seen the departure of Mikhail to the United States as the new commissar of defense industry. Stalin considered it worthwhile to send Mikhail to Washington to visit airplane factories and to learn about mass-production techniques. At the same time, he was asked to explore the possibilities of promoting Soviet flights over the Polar route to the United States. Stalin was reaching out to the American government, hoping for some recognition, perhaps even a trade agreement. The West was beginning to come out of the depression, and Stalin reasoned this was a propitious period to extract some favors.

Lazar had been totally supportive of such a trip. Stalin had asked him first, before Mikhail, but he had turned it down. He knew he would have trouble leaving the Soviet Union now. He was important at home, but he was not sure how far that extended. Perhaps the most telling reason was the one he inadvertently let slip to Maria the night before Mikhail left:

"I can't afford to leave here for even an instant. You can't be sure what Stalin will do. There are too many people trying to persuade him to forget what I have already done. I leave for America, and they will even have a new husband for you by the time I am halfway to Paris."

Yet, he was torn. He wanted to see Uncle Levick and to find out what he was doing. Was he even living? He would have to be well into his nineties by now. And he wanted to see Morris. "He's probably married and has kids older than I was when I last saw him in the dawn hours on the day I left Kabany," he said to Maria.

He was also sure that his own success outweighed theirs. After all, he was constantly in the news and had certainly been written about at length in *The New York Times* on a number of occasions. But that same paper mentioned nothing about an Uncle Levick or a Morris. That thought delighted him.

Mikhail departed with a delegation of fifteen people, including a few generals and, of course, the usual contingent of NKVD people, whose primary function was to see how much information they could extract that Washington did not want them to have.

Mikhail had specifically asked Lazar if he wanted him to look up the family when he was there. He would make a special trip to New York. Lazar knew that it was not so much his wanting to see what there was remaining of the family but rather the idea of going to New York. The city wasn't on the original agenda. His brother was obviously milking this for all it was worth. It was now his turn to shine, and he would do so to the hilt.

Mikhail had originally thought that as the oldest there would be no question but that he would lead his brothers. He had believed that when he succeeded so well in Arzamas and then again in Nizhni Novgorod. He suspected that Lazar would never succeed. Even Yuri would surpass the youngest. But now he realized that it had not turned out that way. Lazar had done well, too well, in fact, and it bothered him. Perhaps, though, he would be able to even it all up. He had the golden moment with this trip, and he would seize the opportunity for all it was worth.

No, he would go to New York. He would show the "beloved" Uncle Levick who was the stronger, the more important nephew. Maybe Lazar did have his name in the papers more, but Mikhail would be the one to visit. He was in America. He was the one able to travel where he wanted. He was the one meeting with American officials. He was the one truly representing the government.

He hadn't realized how deep these feelings ran. They were there, that was for sure, and it showed how restless and anxious he was. Only Yuri seemed content. He had his family around him, and that was enough. But not to Mikhail, and certainly not to Lazar.

Lazar waited the two weeks until his brother's return in a state of suspense. He had daily reports on his activities and knew exactly where he was and what he was doing. Mikhail had spent the first few days dealing with U.S. officials and had taken side trips to air bases in and around the U.S. capital. Then he had gone to New York. He was going to try to see the family.

The people Lazar had sent to accompany Mikhail had done well in reporting back his movements, even down to an excursion to a place called the Bronx, which seemed to be outside New York City. It was narrowed to a place called Tremont Avenue near something known as 166th Street and the Grand Concourse. A review of the telephone book showed no Kaganovich in such an area. The reports stopped there. No one seemed to know who Mikhail had visited. Lazar would just have to wait until his return.

Lazar was more excited than usual waiting for Mikhail. He didn't realize how much anxiety he had accumulated, or why. He snapped at almost everyone until it was apparent that retaliation was essential. Even the normally staid Molotov found it necessary to throw in a few barbs, and Stalin himself, who could be a downright practical joker when he wanted, enjoyed himself at Lazar's expense. They sent him cans of American-made food, they folded up a copy of a New York newspaper in his briefing packet at Central Committee meetings (this had less impact than they thought as Lazar could not read English), and they even went so far as arranging for a U.S. attaché to subject Lazar to a personal speech lasting one hour on the environs known as the Bronx.

The more anxious he appeared, the more fun the others had.

Finally, Mikhail returned, and Lazar could scarcely contain himself. He hadn't realized what effect this trip had. He had visions that Uncle Levick, Morris, and all the others would be sending him flowery regards, inviting him to the United States, pleading with him to consent to a visit, in awe of him, complimenting him on his success, and telling everyone in New York about him as only a family could. For a fleeting moment, Lazar wished that Sasha and Moisev could be alive to join in the adoration. He had proven himself beyond any of their wildest dreams, and he so much wanted to revel in it with them.

"So, Mikhail, you had a pretty good trip, eh?"

He pretended to be reserved, almost blasé about the matter. Mikhail had not been back long enough to hear about the state Lazar had been in or the countless practical jokes that had been played on him.

"The trip was most successful," answered Mikhail, and then proceeded to detail all the data he had learned from the Americans on air travel, planes, armaments, and the numerous other matters he had "garnered from the capitalists."

Mikhail was a good party member, or at least he was good at spouting the party line. Lazar sat back and heard the words, but he was not listening. His mind was beyond that. He wanted to hear the news, the real news. Yet, he couldn't just come out and demand it. That would show eagerness in a misplaced way. No, he had to wait for Mikhail to get to that part himself. He couldn't let on as to his real interest.

Mikhail spoke for almost two hours, recalling his many meetings, his visits at air force bases, even discussing what the American generals wore and what was served at the luncheons. Mikhail had obviously enjoyed himself.

"Would you believe that they served us blini at one meal? Blini and *ikra*-caviar. They had mountains of the stuff, as if this were something we ate all the time. And then, some thin, watery soup they dared to call red beet borscht. I swear, Lazar, it must have come out of a jar. The only good part was the bread—pumpernickel was their word. That was good, although sliced too thinly for me. For dessert, they offered dried fruit that they called a compote. A compote of dried fruit? Can you imagine what Mama would say? It was funny, very funny. I liked it better when they didn't try and imitate us. Their own food was good enough, especially their chicken, and their meat is superb. Nothing like we have. Theirs is thick, not stringy, and almost veinless."

Mikhail was off on something else, and Lazar shifted uneasily in his chair. Finally, he could contain himself no longer.

"And how was New York? I understand you went to something called the Bronx?"

Mikhail looked surprised. He knew that his activities were monitored. Everyone's were, but he didn't realize how detailed it had been. He decided now to talk about his trip to New York, and Lazar sighed and sank back into his chair. He wanted to lean forward in order to pepper his brother with a myriad of questions he had formulated in his mind, but he didn't want to appear too interested. That would be a sign of weakness.

Mikhail took his time, as he had with the Washington visit. As was his wont, he liked to feel his own self-importance, and he spent another half hour in his preface remarks, setting the stage, as it were.

"You know, New York is a curious place. There are so many people and so many things to do. It is like watching perpetual motion. Quite different from Washington. That's a very conservative city. There only seemed to be one activity there, the government. Nothing else. But New York is filled with different activities. For example . . ."

And he was off again on the foundation-building. Lazar reaffirmed in his own mind that Mikhail got as far as he did only through his efforts. Without his help, he would remain a lowly *apparatchik* in a city far from the seat of power. His brother was a nitpicker. He reveled in the minuscule. He could never get to the heart of a matter, cut quickly to the bone, and those who could do so were the only kind of people Stalin wanted around him.

"And your trip to the Bronx?" Lazar edged in again.

Finally, Mikhail turned to what Lazar wanted.

"Most curious, and I don't know why. There is no Kaganovich in the phone books. Oh, there were some Kaganovs, but most of them had nothing to do with our family, and I saw a few Kagans. Actually, I couldn't reach any of our people and in particular Uncle Levick."

Lazar's heart sank.

"No, he reached me."

Lazar looked perplexed. Mikhail picked up on it immediately.

"Yes, a man called where I was staying and told the attaché who he was and to pass the number along. It was Uncle Levick, and he gave me an address at which I could meet him. Lazar, it was so strange. It was as if he didn't want me to find him unless he decided differently."

Lazar hunched forward in his chair. He felt as though he were now part of a dramatic story, out of Dostoevsky or Tolstoy.

"I went to this apartment house in the Bronx, and I saw Uncle Levick. There was no one else there except for another man who I did not know. I don't even remember being introduced to him."

"How did Uncle Levick look?" Lazar interjected.

"Actually, he looked quite well. He still has the same goatee we remember, but now it is all white. In fact, all his hair is white. He also seems shorter than I remember. Maybe it's his age. They say you lose inches as you get older. You know, he's ninety-three now, and I tell you he acts like he's forty-three. He still talks very quietly, almost a calming effect, but he's certainly in charge of all his faculties. He seems to know exactly where he is and what he's doing . . . and he knows about you."

Lazar's ears perked up even more.

"He reads all the papers, and he has followed your every move."

Mikhail was saying this all grudgingly. Lazar waited for him to explain that last part more, to hear how proud Uncle Levick was of him, how glad he was for his success, how he approved of it. He felt almost like a child in his eagerness to learn more. But Mikhail was somewhere else.

"He explained why he was not in the phone book. I think we forgot that when our Russian name is transposed into English, the letters are changed. What is a G to us becomes an H to them and what is a V becomes a W. In any event, their name is now Kahanowitz. It wouldn't have mattered anyway, because they're still not listed."

Lazar frowned. Kahanowitz? What kind of a name was that?

"But not everyone has that name. The family has scattered. Some have shortened it or dropped letters, and only Uncle Levick remains in New York because of his business. He's doing something with ladies' dresses. I think he has a factory and makes them. Typical capitalism. I wasn't sure what he was saying, but most of the family has gone off to other cities. He didn't say which ones. They're also into other businesses. He didn't explain that either."

"And you saw Morris?"

"No, he, too, was gone. Somewhere else. All I know is that the engagement to that Hannah Gutman in Mozyr that we heard about was his. He's even got children, and grandchildren. Would you believe Uncle Levick is now a great-*zayda*?"

"But where is everybody else, and why don't we have more details?"

Mikhail studied Lazar. There was still more to tell, and it would be information that would be difficult to get Lazar to understand.

"This may be hard for you," said Mikhail, "but he doesn't want you to know, specifically you. Let me explain."

Mikhail sighed.

"There is a great fear of you, Lazar, a fear that because of you, they will all be lifted up and brought back here and then sent to Siberia. Uncle Levick seems to know more about what is truly going on in this country than the average American. I think this applies to all Russians living there. Information comes through a pipeline reaching right back to Moscow and every other area. I don't know who or what, just that it exists. So, the family has dropped their name and moved to other parts of the United States, taking jobs where no one knows what they are doing."

Lazar frowned.

"You see, they work for themselves. No one files any papers for the government—tax forms and the like. They don't want anyone to know what they are doing or where. I guess taxes are never paid, but they are afraid—petrified is the word—of being forced back.''

"The U.S. government would do that?" Lazar asked naively.

"No, you would do it. They are afraid of you, but to the point of paranoia. Morris, who is now the titular head, so to speak, has laid down an edict that no one in the family is to travel abroad, that no one is to take out a passport or visa, that no one is to communicate with the old country, as they call it. And, whatever they have to say to each other cannot be done by post or by phone. It must be in person, in the home, away from windows and behind locked doors.''

Mikhail paused to catch his breath.

"And Uncle Levick, how come he contacts you?" Lazar asked.

Mikhail laughed.

"You know Uncle Levick. He listens to nobody, let alone Morris, who is always thought of as a little old lady anyway. He figures, 'Eh, what will they do with a ninety-three year old man? Give him a droshky and send him to Siberia to haul ice back to Moscow?''"

Lazar smiled. Good old Uncle Levick. Thank God for his sense of humor.

"Tell me about Morris."

"All I know is that Morris lives elsewhere. He has, or had, four children. One died. And there are two grandchildren. That's all I know about him other than he is petrified of you. The names he calls you are not complimentary. He seems to know everything that is going on. Everything. I don't know how, but he does.''

"Would he really think that I would hurt him? Would he really think I would hurt or come to hurt anyone in the family? Uncle Levick knows this. Why can't Morris?''

Lazar looked despondent. He reached for his worry beads and twirled them around his hands, tighter and tighter.

"Mikhail, don't they understand us at all? We are still family. Isn't that above anything else?''

He looked at the ceiling for a while. Then his eyes dropped, and he caught Rosa standing in the doorway. She had heard Mikhail had returned and had come over to see him. Lazar didn't know how long she had been there, but from the look on her face, it appeared to be for quite some time.

"At least we are safe, eh?" he chuckled nervously. "At least they know we are surviving, eh?''

He looked at his brother and sister.

"But they don't trust us, right?"

Mikhail and Rosa looked at each other. The word *us* formed on her lips, and she shook her head from side to side.

Mikhail's report had an almost perverse effect on Lazar. He began to throw himself into his work more than ever before, injecting his opinions in every part of the country. He even pushed Stalin hard to give Mikhail a medal for his successful trip to the United States as if to show those in America that he was not what they thought. Lazar's actions were not always grounded in logic.

On his fiftieth birthday, Mikhail was awarded the Red Banner of Labor for merits and achievements in organizing the aviation industry of the USSR and for the promulgation of the nonstop flight from Moscow to Nikolayevsk-na-Amure.

The announcement was accompanied by formal congratulations from the Communist party leaders and a letter signed by Commander Loktyanov of the Red Army Air Force and other famous Soviet aviators, which said, in part: "Your leadership of the aviation industry has won great successes in the organization of production, the installation of new technology, and the newest types of planes."

Mikhail seemed eternally grateful, and Lazar hoped that somehow the information would be forwarded to the Bronx for distribution.

But other changes were appearing in the country that also would find their way around the world. By April 1938, Lazar was already considered as the number-three man in the Soviet hierarchy, ahead of Voroshilov and behind Yezhov and Stalin.

Lazar was involving himself in a plethora of areas. Since the death of Ordzhonikidze, he had become the driving force in heavy industry, taking over control of even the fuel and oil industries. Thus, coupled with transportation, he had the perfect opportunity to venture into the defense and foreign affairs waters.

"We know the significance of transportation in defense," he said to a congress of 2,500 Stakhanovists. "We must be ready to defend the Soviet Union; the Red Army will do this. Transport's role in any wartime is very vital. We transport workers say, 'Rest assured we will not fail the Red Army and the Soviet motherland, and will repel the enemy.'

"It is our Soviet policy to mobilize all antiwar forces in foreign lands—workers and intellectuals alike—and at the same time, to help any revolutionary movement, which is the only serious force opposing imperialistic schemes. But the struggle for peace is the best means of strengthening our Red Army.''

Four months later, another change took place. Yezhov was gone, replaced by a man named Lavrenti Beria, a Georgian like Stalin. Lazar had no say whatsoever in Beria's appointment. All he knew about him was that during the 1920s, he had worked as an underground leader and member of the secret police in the Caucasus Mountains. Stalin now called him to Moscow to head the country's secret police.

Lazar disliked him intensely. He had heard stories about him, how he was perverse with women and would have them beaten and disfigured if his favors were not met. Lazar characterized him as a ''sneaky, suspicious, tight-lipped, bald mountaineer.'' Of course, the characterization was never made within Stalin's ears.

On August 23 of that same year, *The New York Times* reported a bombshell: ''L. M. Kaganovich is Vice Premier in Rearranged Cabinet.''

Lazar had been named vice president of the Council of Commissars and chairman of the Politburo. Apparently, his opinion of Beria had not mattered, for Lazar was now second only to Stalin.

He now spoke about anything and everything. He was free to discuss his thoughts and express his opinions, all of which were in tune with the party line and with Stalin's own desires. It had paid to keep the path straight and narrow.

At the reopening of Moscow's Park of Culture and Rest, he said:

''We have started many new factories while in Germany, for example, all the old factories have been closed down. This is because the Germans pay indemnities and old debts. If we had to pay the czar's old debts of many thousand millions, canceled by the Great October Revolution, it would take a hundred million gold rubles every year, and our taxes would be spent, not on building factories but in paying interest on those old debts.

''We fight for peace as no other government does. We know that capitalism is going to perish by the hands of its own workers. But we have to defend our land and we say: 'Know that our hands are no longer empty. Our factories are building bigger and bigger tanks, capable of striking at our enemies. We have small airplanes but also big airplanes of two and three engines which are capable of reaching the enemy on his own territory if he attempts to raid our Socialist Motherland. Our relations with Japan constantly grow worse. We must expect to be attacked any day now. Remember how in 1904 the Japanese negotiated with the czar's diplomats and then suddenly attacked the czar's warships in Port Arthur? That was in 1904, when the czar's government was a fool's government. Now they have got to deal with the Soviet government, and they will not catch us napping. If Japanese generals try to force our frontiers, they will get a taste of our Red Army's strength.

"Now all countries in the world will have to take our country into consideration because it has become a powerful force, with our great and victorious Red Army armed with all modern weapons—tanks, guns and chemicals."

Lazar had learned his history well. To succeed, you had to have the support of the military. He wanted to succeed even more, and he wanted to make sure that the support was there.

At the same time, Lazar pushed hard for a Soviet Germany. "We, too, struggled underground for a long time. We, too, were arrested. Our people, too, were whipped during the czarist regime. But we fought back and we won."

He reminded people what had happened in 1923 when the German Social-Democrat government deliberately encouraged inflation as an excuse for not paying reparations to the Allies as they agreed to do under the 1919 Versailles Treaty.

"In fact, the exchange rate was two hundred marks to the American dollar. That was in January of 1922, and by November of 1923 it was 4.2 billion marks to the dollar."

But Lazar was also aware that although the German masses had been desperate in 1923, the Comintern officials in Moscow had not given clear orders to the German Communist party. Lenin was then ill, and uprisings had occurred in Saxony, Thuringia, and Hamburg; without leaders, however, or even objectives, the party had been defeated. On November 8, 1923, an unknown named Adolf Hitler had staged his Munich beer-hall putsch.

Six years later, the "crisis" suddenly hit the capitalist world with the crash on Wall Street. Lazar heard that some capitalists committed suicide rather than live in poverty. Mass unemployment hit country after country. In Germany, 6 million workers were unemployed. The Social Democrat party president resigned. The rickety foundations of the Weimar Republic were about to collapse. Hitler's Nazi party had obtained 800,000 votes the year before. A year later on September 14, 1930, the figure jumped to 6.5 million. And although in this same period the German Communist party increased its vote from 3 million to 4.5 million, its attitude toward Hitler was one of complacency. Ernst Thaelmann, the Communist leader in the German Reichstag, saw no reason to panic over Hitler. Stalin agreed. His order to Thaelmann was that he should refuse a Communist-Socialist alliance at all costs.

"Social Democrats are nothing more than social-fascists," he said. "And it is against them, not Hitler, that our fire will be concentrated."

In retrospect, Thaelmann wrote: "We stated soberly and seriously that 14 September 1930 was in a sense Hitler's best day, after which there would be no better, but only worse days."

The German Communist party refused a united front with the socialist organization, and in 1933 Hitler came to power.

The Seventh Congress of the Communist International met in 1935. Its delegates were unaware that this was to be the last Comintern meeting. The Bulgarian leader Dimitrov placed the defeat of the German working class squarely on the shoulders of the German Communist party. The Popular Front was announced, conceived as an alliance between the Communist parties and the "democratic bourgeoisie" to defend democracy.

In France, the strikes of May to June 1936 burst suddenly upon the country with a new problem—the occupation of the factories. Léon Blum, a socialist, was in power with both the Popular Front support of Communists and the bourgeois Radical party. Blum promised a slew of social reforms, including paid holidays and nationalization of industries. The French Communist party, under instruction from Moscow, ended the strikes and factory occupations.

In Spain, moderate Republicans and left parties had formed another Popular Front, which drove the conservatives out of office in the elections of February 1936. On July 17, 1936, civil war began as a number of generals led by Francisco Franco provoked revolts against the Republican government in a number of cities as well as in Spanish Morocco. Franco was supported by the church, the nobility, the military, and the Spanish fascists.

The Popular Front government in France—following Britain's lead—adopted a policy of "nonintervention," which meant no help for the Spanish Republic.

Hitler in Germany and Mussolini in Italy didn't care about nonintervention. They immediately sent arms and troops to help Franco. Stalin, after a few months of strict nonintervention, began sending help in 1936. Demoralization and aid did their work. Spain fell to Franco in the spring of 1939. The handwriting was on the wall and something had to be done—and quickly.

August 23, 1939, 10:00 A.M: Lazar stood on the edge of the tarpaulin at Sheremetyevo Airport on the outskirts of Moscow. This land previously had belonged to one of imperial Russia's wealthiest families. At that time, white-suited gardeners had fussed over the flowers, bushes, and lawns, while stable boys in brown knickers and yellow tops exercised quarter horses on the small cinder track that encircled a large barn.

Now the entire area was ringed with green-hatted militiamen. There were no more gardeners and stable boys. Instead, a group of schoolchildren moved about anxiously, shuffling their feet and patting down their hair: twenty-five children, each carrying a bouquet of flowers. They were unhappy being here, but they also realized it was better than grinding away in the classroom on a hot summer day.

Lazar looked up at the blue Moscow sky. It was crystal clear, as Moscow skies usually are in August. At first it was quiet. He scanned the horizon to the west. Two enormous JU-88 planes could be seen. They were right on schedule. The Germans were indeed punctual. Whatever their faults, at least they were prompt. Lazar admired that quality. He wished more Russians were like that. He also wished he knew whether this venture of Stalin's would be successful. An exchange of telegrams with Hitler had produced this visit by the German foreign minister. The idea was to negotiate a nonaggression pact between the Soviet Union and Germany, an arrangement that, it was hoped, would keep the Nazis from Russian soil. In addition, the pact would divide Poland and allocate Estonia, Latvia, and Bessarabia to the USSR, while Lithuania would go to Germany.

On the surface it seemed like a good idea. The world was restless. Hitler's Germany was definitely marching, and it would continue to do so. Stalin was adamant about striking a bargain with the Nazi regime. He needed a period in which Russia could arm itself. It was a typical Russian maneuver: gain time in order to prepare militarily, and pick up a few territories in the same breath.

Two giant planes landed, one slightly ahead of the other. The second plane moved past the first on the apron and taxied to a stop a few feet from the line of waiting dignitaries.

Heading the contingent was Molotov, his bald head shining in the hot August sun, his light-gray suit blending with the bluish hue of the runway. Molotov stood ramrod straight, thrusting his full five-foot four-inch frame as high as it could go, the supreme example of Russian stoicism. He was the cold gentleman—to the extreme.

Just a few months earlier, Molotov had replaced Litvinov as commissar for foreign affairs. Litvinov's independence and his proclivity for deviating from the party line were too much for Stalin. He turned now to Molotov, who was simply tossed into the breach. He would do what Stalin ordered with no resistance.

The door of the plane swung open, and a long line of men came scurrying down the steps. There were at least thirty of them, all in the light and tan garb of Hitler's elite troops. They formed an aisle, fifteen on each side, and stood at rigid attention. The last one out was a tall, thin, fair-haired man carrying an umbrella in one hand and a bowler in the other. He was dressed in a dark blue suit, the only person not in uniform. He held his head erect, his chin forward. It was Joachim von Ribbentrop, Adolf Hitler's top diplomatic agent.

Lazar smiled. He knew quite a lot about this man. Beria's dossier left little unsaid.

He was the same age as Lazar, born in Wesel, Germany. He had studied in France, worked for a while in the United States and Canada, and after World War I had become a champagne merchant, earning quite a lot of money. He joined the National Socialist party in 1932 and so impressed Hitler with his knowledge of foreign languages and countries that he quickly became his foreign policy expert, setting up his own office, which often superseded the foreign office of the Third Reich. At the same time, he was designated Germany's ambassador-at-large. In 1935, he negotiated a naval treaty with England that gave Germany equality in submarines. In 1936, he was influential in the formation of the Rome-Berlin Axis, and in 1938, he succeeded Constantin Neurath as foreign minister.

One of the fascinating attributes of Ribbentrop was his memory. He never used notes, he never wrote anything down, and he could recall the most minute piece of information in an instant. He had a reputation for being unnerving at any negotiating table, always alert, always probing, a distinguished, courteous gentleman fluent in Russian and with a mind like a steel trap.

The next week saw banquet after banquet, meeting after meeting.

197

It was Lazar's first foray into international waters, and he decided to stay on the sidelines as an observer, listening, watching, trying to learn how the give-and-take of diplomacy worked. Ribbentrop was indeed a master at this, and Lazar decided he would not try to compete with him but would keep within his own subject matters, offering advice when asked. Most of the discussions centered either around territories, about which he had scant knowledge of what was really happening on the borders, and the question of anti-Fascist propaganda within the Soviet Union. It was strictly Molotov's show, but he was running a poor second to Ribbentrop.

The German foreign minister sat in the center of the long rectangular table with his aides to his left and right. He didn't really need them, for almost 100 percent of the time others spoke directly to Ribbentrop and he spoke directly to them. His aides rarely said anything. It was quite obvious that he never referred to them in public and probably not in private, either, and he seemed to be annointed with the unquestioned power to make his own decisions.

On the Soviet side, Molotov led the talks, but it was also quite apparent that he did not enjoy the same status as his German counterpart. Everything had to be referred back to a committee in one fashion or another. There seemed to be one committee meeting on top of another. Lazar noticed how the government was beginning more than ever to congeal into a small group with each member's view being given almost equal weight. Stalin, though, was above the group. The reign of terror had served dual purposes in not only neutralizing whatever anti-Stalin factions remained in the general populace but also in frightening sufficiently the members of the ruling body itself. They were all reduced to the simplest and oft-quoted term that older soldiers in the army regurgitated from the civil war of some two decades earlier: "Red or Dead!"

The other telling aspect was that Stalin never appeared during the entire week of talks. It was as if he and Hitler had already agreed to what would happen, and they had then turned the matter over to their appointees to minister the agreement. Stalin attended only his own Central Committee meetings, where he was briefed on the matters discussed that day. Everyone was in full agreement to cooperate with the Germans. Stalin, Molotov, and Voroshilov ignored the enormous number of facts that the NKVD submitted, testifying to Hitler's preparations for an eventual invasion of the USSR.

Only Beria, the newest member of the committee, seemed uneasy about what he heard. He even went so far as to make a rather lengthy and impassioned speech about Hitler's real intentions. Lazar was surprised. He hadn't seen such a performance by a junior member since his outburst against Krupskaya, which seemed to have taken place centuries ago.

Lazar sat back and watched Beria at work. He admired his aggressiveness, but he also knew then that Beria was somebody to be reckoned with, somebody to be handled very carefully, like a viper.

Lazar had his own plans, too, and he had fewer than four years (before he reached fifty) to make them operative. He would not be upstaged. Beria might be right. Yet, Lazar was counting on it.

On August 31, the Supreme Soviet ratified the nonaggression pact between the Soviet Union and Germany, a pact that even included a secret protocol calling for the prohibition on Soviet territory of anti-Fascist and anti-Hitler propaganda.

That night, the German-Russian treaty was celebrated in a "Frontiers of Friendship" banquet given at the Kremlin in honor of Ribbentrop and his entourage, but only he sat at the table with Stalin, Molotov, Voroshilov, Lazar, Mikoyan, and Beria. It was an evening of eating, drinking, and frivolity. Hundreds of bottles of vodka were consumed in the giving of toasts.

The party ended at 3:00 A.M. An hour and fifty minutes later, the Germans invaded Poland. World War II had begun.

5

At midnight on June 21, 1941, the commander of the Kiev district, Colonel M. P. Kirponos, reported that a German soldier had been captured. The soldier said he was from the 222nd Infantry Regiment of the 74th Infantry Division. He had swum across the river and presented himself to the Russian frontier guards at Ternopol, advising them that German forces were going to mount an offensive within four hours.

Colonel Kirponos called for a status alert and notified Moscow. At 3:17 A.M. Marshal Georgi Zhukov received a call from Admiral F. S. Oktyabrsky, commander of the Black Sea fleet: "The fleet's aircraft warning system reports the approach from the sea of large numbers of unidentified aircraft. The fleet has been alerted. I request instructions."

At 3:30 A.M., the chief of staff of the Western district reported that an air raid had begun on a number of villages in Byelorussia. Calls were made to Stalin. No answer. To Lazar. He picked up the phone. It was Zhukov who apprised him of the situation. He asked for permission to start an immediate retaliation. There was silence.

"Do you understand me?" Zhukov repeated.

Silence again.

201

"Do you understand what is happening?"

Lazar was shocked. He tried to compose himself to ask a question, any question.

"Where is the commissar for defense?"

"Talking with the Kiev district."

"Go to the Kremlin immediately. I will advise Stalin."

By 4:30 A.M., all of the Politburo members were in their seats. Stalin, his face ashen, his eyes bloodshot, sat at the end of the table cradling a pipe in his hand. No one spoke. All turned to Stalin. After some time, he said, "We must immediately phone the German embassy."

He nodded to Molotov, who rose and left the room. In a few minutes he returned.

"The embassy replies that Ambassador Count von der Schulenburg is anxious to deliver an urgent message."

Stalin nodded again. Once more Molotov left the room. He had been authorized to receive the German ambassador.

Everyone sat at the table, looking from one face to another. It was quiet, each member wrapped in his own thoughts. It seemed impossible, a nightmare. Only Beria had a different expression. He stared at the ceiling, a slight smile forming on his thin lips. He had known.

Meanwhile, word had come in that a strong artillery barrage on several sectors in the northwestern and western regions had begun. German land forces were on the move. In twenty minutes, Molotov returned. He addressed only Stalin.

"The German government has declared war on us."

Stalin's head dropped onto his chest. Zhukov rose. He spoke rapidly, as if he had been preparing his remarks for quite some time.

"We are facing combat experience on the side of Hitler. He has been fighting for a long period. The initiative is also on his side since his attack is predatory. The quantity and quality of troops and matériel are his, too. The entire war potential of Europe is now in his hands."

From the Arctic Ocean to the Black Sea, some 260 German divisions began to cross the long Soviet frontier, their destinations the major cities of Moscow, Leningrad, and Kiev. The reports from agents began flooding in. Some six months prior, on December 18, 1940, Hitler had signed Directive No. 21, otherwise known as Operation Barbarossa, which defined the strategic goals of a military campaign against the USSR. Operation Barbarossa was named for a medieval German emperor who had been militarily successful in the East.

Under the plan devised, the large number of Nazi troops and their allies deployed on the borders of the Soviet Union were to be divided into three main groups: Army Group North, Army Group Center, and Army Group South. They were to advance in the directions of Leningrad, Moscow, and Kiev respectively. Barbarossa's objective was to occupy Soviet territory and to destroy the Red Army. Hitler had figured that within eight weeks he could capture the three areas. He wanted no prisoners, especially Soviet officials. Orders were specifically given that all captured officials were to be shot.

Great importance, however, was attached to seizing Kiev, thus building a bridgehead on the left bank of the Dnieper River for a swift drive deep inside the USSR. The intention was obvious: a breakthrough to the industrial south of the Ukraine as quickly as possible. From there they would proceed to the Caucasus in order to confiscate grain, coal, and oil desperately needed to continue the war.

According to Warlimont, deputy chief of the general staff of the Third Reich, instructions to draw "the plan of operations in the East" were given by Hitler for the first time in the spring of 1940—even before France was invaded or approximately six months after the Soviet-German nonaggression pact had been signed. Hitler considered the campaign in France as an opening move to a later assault on the Soviet Union. His aim was to destroy Russia quickly and decisively.

Stalin, though, had relied on a codicil to the ten-year nonaggression pact that provided for the division of Poland and Bessarabia to the USSR and of Lithuania to Germany. The purpose was twofold: gain time in order to make any long-range military preparations and to secure a few territorial advantages. In fact, beyond Bessarabia, the Balkans looked promising. But Hitler knew this, too.

On June 30, 1940, a week after France fell, General Halder (chief of staff of the Wehrmacht's ground forces) informed Deputy Minister of Foreign Affairs Weizsaecker that the fuhrer's "eyes" were indeed "fixed on the East." Hitler wanted to "crush Russia."

"If Russia is vanquished, Britain will lose its last hope. Then Germany will dominate in Europe and in the Balkans. Hence, Russia should be liquidated."

On June 22, Molotov went before the nation in a radio address. His high-pitched monotone voice was not exactly inspiring. His speech ended with, "The government appeals to you, citizens of the Soviet Union, to rally your ranks even closer around our glorious Bolshevik party and our Soviet government. Our course is just. The enemy will be defeated. Victory will be ours."

It seemed almost silly, at least to those in the government. Stalin had no plans to counter such an offensive. The Soviet regime simply disbelieved all the warnings. As a result, the onslaught was greeted with shock and dismay; the Germans smashed the Red Army at its own borders.

Germany's advance was three-pronged. The first push was toward Leningrad from Finland and from Europe, targeting along the way the cities of Novgorod and Tikhvin. The second was aimed at Moscow, taking in Minsk, Smolensk, and Kiev. The third came from Rumania, which had joined Germany to recover territories taken by the Soviets. They headed also for Kiev, the capital of the Ukraine, Kharkov, the industrial center of the area, Odessa, and Rostov, with a view toward Stalingrad.

On July 3, Stalin spoke to the nation. His was a stronger voice, and it shifted the focus:

"Comrades! Comrades! Brothers and sisters. Fighting men of our army and navy. I am addressing myself to you, my friends."

It was a dramatic change from the way Stalin usually addressed the people. Now he was talking to them as "brothers and sisters and friends."

"We must immediately put all our work on a war footing, subordinating to the needs of the front and to the task of routing the enemy. The peoples of the Soviet Union see now that German fascism is implacable in its mad fury and its hatred of our motherland, which assures free labor and prosperity to all workers. The peoples of the Soviet Union must rise up in defense of their rights and their soil against the enemy."

His speech ended with "All the strength of the nation—for the rout of the enemy. Forward, to our victory!"

Lazar, with his intimate knowledge of the Ukraine, was dispatched to Kiev to supervise the coordination of transportation, fuel, and matériel. But he was not prepared for what met him. He learned all too quickly that many Russians along the border welcomed the Germans as friends, "friends who have come to free us from Stalinist oppression." Reports came in that they were giving the Nazis food, clothing, and shelter and proclaiming them "liberators." The invading army accepted what was offered them, but it took even more. The Germans considered the Russians *untermenschen*—"subhumans"—fit only for slave labor. It seemed inconceivable that this would happen; yet Lazar could only accept it and smile.

Hitler had ordered a completely ruthless campaign against the defeated people. He decided to strip them of all human rights. Acts of brutality, such as tossing babies—infants—into bonfires, were commonplace.

Hitler had succeeded in turning the initial good will to hate.

Upon hearing of this, Stalin, at Lazar's insistence, ordered the evacuation of all people from the borders; in particular, the Jews who made up most of the area. Stalin had no love for the Jews, but his order to them was to burn their houses, kill their livestock, and emigrate to the interior of Russia. Many in the Politburo could not understand this. Everyone knew that Stalin detested those people. And everyone knew that Lazar, too, a Jew, had little patience with his own as well. But it was Lazar's influence that swayed Stalin's mind to issue the order. There was no choice. In order to save Russia, everything and everyone had to be subordinate to the nation. Individual preferences were put aside. It was far better to have the Jews come to the backside of Russia, leaving behind nothing for Hitler, than to leave working slaves, livestock, food supplies, and other materials for him to collect.

The Nazis had established extermination camps in Germany and Poland and now in Babi-Yar, a camp on the outskirts of Kiev, where more than 100,000 Jewish prisoners of war were tortured and killed. Jews were in a panic. They would do anything to escape Hitler, anything, including whatever Stalin wanted.

Lazar mobilized 200,000 people in Kiev. Regular soldiers were supported by special detachments of the home guard, which numbered another 30,000. The headquarters for the Kiev defense was set up on July 6, and the city was turned into a veritable fortress. Hedgehogs were planted in the streets, barricades with slots for machine guns were built at every intersection, and the entire population, mostly women, as the men were at the front, spared no effort, around the clock, in preparing positions for guns and mortars. They dug antitank ditches, they planted mines, and they put up barbed wire fences. Every house was fortified, readied for the onrushing Germans.

All this only delayed the inevitable. Kiev eventually fell, and more than 300,000 people were sent to slave camps in Germany. Lazar, however, escaped and went back to Moscow. The Nazi juggernaut was rolling, and it was heading toward the capital.

When Lazar returned, the city was not the same. It was costumed in camouflage. Buildings that could be identified from an airplane were now draped with huge scenic curtains depicting woodland villages. Open areas were painted to give the impression of a rural countryside. Army vehicles were made to look like farm trucks. Whatever tanks were in the city were hidden from view.

The Muscovites set up four defense lines: one well beyond the city limits, a second on the city's border, and two on the inner and outer boulevard rings within Moscow.

What surprised Lazar, as it surprised many others in the hierarchy, was that Stalin had taken absolute control. He created a Command of the Rear of the Red Army to assume logistical support and an Army of the Interior to maintain absolute security. And he had a plethora of other ideas in mind. It was as if he had never let go of his position in the first place. Lazar now saw the Stalin he remembered when he first came to Moscow. The energy and strength had returned, almost as if they had never left, as if he had only been taking a catnap, letting everyone around him do what they wanted but only for a limited period of time. That time had come to an end. Stalin was dishing out the orders, and specific assignments were constantly flowing out of the Kremlin.

Even Yuri, who had been working slavishly in foreign trade in the capital, was sent to Mongolia as a trade delegate. He was to help with the further implementation of Lazar's plans for the Urals. They would reconstruct a new war industry beyond the reach of the Nazis.

Stalin especially liked the idea of producing armaments, primarily tanks. The T-34 was said to be superior to the German tank. That was welcomed. Lazar had convinced Stalin to build factories and industry behind the Ural Mountains, out of the world's eyesight. The Germans were bombing most of the factories on the European side of the Urals; they wouldn't know about industries on the Siberian side. Besides, most of the population lived in the European sector, and most of the commerce was with Europe. The concept would work; it had to.

Stalin also realized that he had to change the people in charge.

"Politically dependent incompetents will not win this war," he said. "Steps must be taken to encourage initiative."

The military had always supported mediocrity. Since the 1937 purge only a handful of generals had surfaced who showed initiative. Fear and subsequent inaction had spread through all levels of command. No one wanted success, for Stalin was too good at this game; he cut off every head that appeared above his.

Only one commander, Marshal Timoshenko on the central front, possessed any real ability. In the south, Marshal Budenny was considered incompetent. However, Stalin thought him politically reliable. But that too would change. Marshal Voroshilov was another one of rather limited talents; he eventually was replaced by Marshal Zhukov, a man of enormous ability.

Stalin also knew he had to rally the people. Building armaments was one thing; replacing old, inefficient generals with those better qualified was another. Now he had to do something with the Russians themselves. The Nazi ravaging of towns, the torture and execution of whole populations, had all combined to turn against the invaders a people who had been inclined at first to accept the enemy as relief from the harsh Stalinist tactics. But it had changed, and with Stalin's scorched-earth policy, starting with the Jews, partisan bands were formed in the encircled areas at the German rear. It was typical Russian strategy: Trade space for time.

"The future is his who knows how to wait."

By October 20, when German troops were only 40 miles outside of Moscow, he had no choice but to move his ministries to Kuibyshev, a town 550 miles to the southeast on the Volga. Everyone in the government, or close to it, was ordered there. Rosa went, as did Maria and Maya and all the other families of the Politburo members. His chief lieutenants, though, including Mikhail, who was now commissar of aviation, remained in the Kremlin.

The city was in a panic. Trucks and buses laden down with old men, women, and children joined deserting bureaucrats in the journey eastward. Roads were jammed, and every inch of platform at railroad stations and on track sidings was littered with families carrying whatever they could. It looked like World War I all over again, except much worse. Now, bands of youths roamed the city, looting food and other stores, even breaking into abandoned houses. And to make matters worse, it began to snow again.

Within a two-week period, some 2 million people had either been shifted from the capital by government order or had somehow managed to flee. Russia's moment of truth was fast approaching. A communiqué from the Red Army admitted, "During the night of October 14, the position of the western front became worse. The German-Fascist troops hurled against our troops large quantities of tanks and motorized infantry, and in one sector broke through our defenses. We have little left to hold them."

Nazi patrols had come so close that they were able to see the Khimke water tower in Moscow. The USSR had indeed reached bottom.

Stalin took complete and unchallenged control. He sent Timoshenko to relieve Semyon Budenny on the southern front, where the German Rundstedt was now approaching the Caucasus. Timoshenko was replaced with Zhukov, who now decided to wait for his major ally, known as "General Winter."

Stalin turned again to the people. He had to make them understand the concept that they were fighting for their homeland. Even with the Germans banging at the gates of Moscow, on the evening of November 6, he held a party dedicated to the twenty-fourth anniversary of the October Revolution in the entranceway to the Mayakovsky Street station of the Kaganovich Subway. On the following day, he watched the traditional military parade in Red Square. Stalin, in his beige uniform with the long coat and cap with the red star, appealed to the people to rally in the name of the country. He urged them to fight for their "Motherland"—for *Rodina*—"Mother Russia." He termed it "the Great Patriotic War" and saw his country as a land of continuous heroes who had defeated one barbarian invader after another. This was just one more. He succeeded in making it almost a crusade, a war to be waged in patriotic terms rather than as a defense of Communism.

It seemed to Lazar that whatever paranoia Stalin had prior to the war appeared to be gone. He had taken the wheel of leadership firmly, and Lazar realized he had underestimated him all along. This was the same formidable individual he recalled from his first days in the party. He knew that when the war ended, he would have more than his work cut out for him.

When the parade was over, the soldiers went straight to the front. The event served a clear purpose: It strengthened the morale of the army and of the Soviet people. The confidence of the government in the inevitable rout of the invaders was trumpeted. They would not fail.

The people retaliated by sabotaging German troop trains, poisoning water wells, and even murdering soldiers. At first, their acts were scattered, but as Nazi repressive measures grew worse, the resistance began to take on organization. Soon, the partisans behind the lines were playing a vital role on behalf of their country.

In Moscow, snow, sleet, rain, ice and mud slowed the Germans. Hitler's generals urged him to stop for the winter, but he refused. On December 5, they did indeed stop. They could go no farther. The cold of winter prevented them from moving. It was subfreezing weather, and the German army was immobile.

On December 6, Zhukov gave the order: "We both cannot move because of the weather. Now is the time to attack."

The Russians moved to the offensive. Zhukov brought in 105 divisions for a counterattack. Included were the Red Army's Siberian troops—hard fighters, well-trained, and inured to the cold. Stalin had originally delayed in bringing them west for fear Japan might then attack Siberia. But now he had no choice. The Russians moved swiftly and aggressively. The Nazi lines dissolved.

"The myth of the invincibility of the German army is broken," Zhukov wrote.

The Germans were no match. Even their dark uniforms were a handicap compared to the white ski suits of the Red Army, which not only camouflaged the Russians in the snow but were lined with a warm quilt. The Germans were desperately trying to keep warm by stuffing their summer denim overalls with paper.

When it was over, thousands of Nazi soldiers were now prisoners, and photographs of them were published in the newspapers showing them wearing women's undergarments to protect them against the cold. Cold was an understatement. The weather was savage. Everything was frozen. Dead horses were found all over, their eyes pecked clean by ravens. The intestines of dead soldiers were strewn on the snow like pieces of rubber tubing. All in all, the Germans left at the doorstep of Moscow more than 155,000 of their army, 800 tanks, 500 guns, and 1,500 aircraft.

Now, Zhukov set the tone of Russian behavior toward the enemy:

"Soviet cities are to be converted into natural fortresses, defended to the last block and house. German troops waste time destroying Soviet towns inch by inch. We will not make that mistake. When encircled by German tank columns, we will continue fighting even if we have to stop the tanks by the force of our numbers alone. Or, we will melt into the forests to become guerillas. Everyone will be a guerilla, no matter what the age. Even the cute little peasant boy who German officers give candy to and pat on the head will report Nazi gun positions to Soviet scouts.

"When we sweep on the offensive, we will not waste time besieging cities. Towns will be bypassed. Our objective is to rush on and catch the main Nazi forces. As shock troops, we will use men whose families

209

have been killed by the Germans. They are under orders not to take prisoners. They will probably not want to anyway. Early enemy capitulators will be shot so that our army's advance is not slowed.''

The thought behind the speech was apparent. Zhukov wanted to trigger something in the Russians that would never be forgotten, an anger that would be manifested in many ways and would raise its ugly head even after the war.

As millions of men were drafted into the army, the shortage of industrial labor became acute. Lazar instituted a new law in early 1942 that mobilized all able-bodied men from sixteen to fifty-five and all healthy women from sixteen to fifty who were not already employed. The sole exceptions were students under sixteen and mothers caring for small children. Those trying to avoid this mobilization were sentenced to a year of forced labor in their own town.

In 1942, Stalingrad became a primary focus of attention. The name itself had special meaning to Hitler as, of course, it did to Stalin. The six-month battle of Stalingrad eventually became the turning point in the Nazi-Soviet war.

During the summer of that year, the Germans began their last major offensive in Russia, driving for the Caucasus and the lower Volga River. Hitler's objective was to capture the vast oil fields, or at least to halt aid from coming north to the Red Army via Volga tankers. The lower Volga bended westward at Stalingrad, which except for those in the Urals, contained Russia's largest tank factory. The city was like a long, narrow ribbon, stretched for miles along the west bank of the river.

The Wehrmacht aimed at Stalingrad. It had already taken Sevastopol and Rostov-na-Donu. Hitler was throwing 1 million men into an operation targeted at the oil fields of the Caucasus. Marshal Alexander M. Vasilievsky, chief of the general staff of the Red Army, had said that ''the Caucasus was seen as the goal of the Germans' 'main operation.' In order to secure the left flank of the troops intended to achieve this goal and to assist them in a rapid forward advance, the German High Command decided to deal a heavy blow in the Stalingrad sector.''

In the original German directive No. 41, the objective was spelled out: ''to attempt to reach Stalingrad and at least to subject it to the influence of heavy guns so that it would lose its importance as a center of war industry and as a communications nucleus.''

By August, a Russian army of half a million men retreated into the city, defending it, street by street, house by house.

Stalin had already conferred with Britain's Churchill in Moscow, asking for a second front in Europe to relieve the pressure, but Churchill advised that North Africa had been chosen for such a front instead because a cross-Channel attack was not yet a feasible operation. Stalin realized that he would have to go it alone. And he did. Despite three months of deadly assaults, the Germans could not capture the city.

Foolishly, the Wehrmacht had placed soldiers of its weak allies— Italy, Hungary, and Rumania—to the north and south of the city to guard the German flanks. That was precisely what the Red Army wanted. A huge Russian assault force massed across the Volga, waiting for the river to form ice thick enough to support the heavy artillery, trucks, and tanks. There was no river bridge.

In November 1942, the river froze solid, and Russian troops immediately crossed the ice exactly north and south of Stalingrad, slashing through the inefficient Axis troops and striking inland for sixty miles. They then joined with other Russian armies in a pincer movement, and the main German army of 300,000 men, commanded by Colonel General Von Paulus, was trapped.

The Russians used every conceivable means at hand to defeat the Germans: Soldiers without guns simply threw themselves into the tank treads to stop the vehicles; hardy Siberian ponies, able to withstand zero-degree temperatures, were used to transport matériel, since trucks stalled in the snow. Everyone fought, even without equipment. Cavalry units charged without helmets, wearing only their medals. The fighting was violent. It was all for Mother Russia and the Germans soon realized it.

A German ditty that escaped the battle expresses the Germans' plight:

> *Russians ahead,*
> *Russians behind,*
> *And in between*
> *Shooting*

The German generals realized then that Hitler was unprepared for a winter war. He had planned to conquer Russia during the summer and autumn months but when winter hit, the German tanks and trucks stalled. They always had used ersatz lubricants that froze solid when Russian temperatures plummeted. In fact, Nazi steam locomotives blew up because they lacked a special cold-weather valve that was usually found on Soviet engines.

In addition, the Wehrmacht didn't have the soldiers needed to hold the huge expanse of the USSR. After all, Russia occupied a quarter of all European soil. This created supply problems. The line was just too long.

Even war tactics were questionable. The German artillery fired fast and furious at the start of a battle for psychological effect, then eased off to save ammunition. Stalin, however, constantly surrounded the Germans with fresh troops and armaments manufactured in those factories on the Siberian side of the Urals.

The battle was a violent, furious one, but the Germans began to withdraw in westerly and southwesterly directions through the Kalmyk Steppe at the same time as the siege at Leningrad was lifted. The Germans had lost 210,000 men from the Sixth Army and what was left of the city became known as the Gerai Gorod—the "Hero City."

Lazar went to see Stalingrad, and he was shocked beyond all belief. It was in rubble. Near the town of Kourman, he could see the remnants of Nazi war matériel: cannons, trucks, tanks, mortars, weapon carriers, machine guns, airplane bodies, command cars, motorcycles, bulldozers, locomotives, and hundreds of boxcars marked DEUTSCHE REICHSBAHN. Altogether at Stalingrad, the Red Army had collected an enormous array of trophies: 750 planes, 1,550 tanks, 670 large guns, 1,462 mortars, 8,135 machine guns, 90,000 rifles, 61,102 automobiles and trucks, 7,369 motorcycles, 480 traction engines and transporters, 320 radio installations, 3 armored trains, and 235 dumpsters of arms, ammunition, and supplies.

Lazar confiscated and used everything he could. The railways were more than overloaded with having to transport huge volumes of military equipment and personnel to all parts of the country, not to mention the evacuation of people who had been fleeing before the onrushing Germans.

Despite the occupation of the Ukraine, the siege of Leningrad, and the battles for Moscow and Stalingrad, most Soviet industrial centers had escaped the German attack and continued active throughout the war. In and beyond the Urals, on much of the Volga in the Caucasus, and in Central Asia, factories continued in full operation around the clock. New industry was established using raw material deposits: coal near Kuibyshev, copper at Orsk, iron at Sverdlovsk, zinc at Begovat, and tin at Barnaul. Every resource in every area of the country was being tapped.

The Germans knew about these resources, too, even before the war began. In fact, word had filtered back that in the months prior to the German invasion, the Nazi ideologist Alfred Rosenberg had drawn up plans for the future of the conquered territories. His vision was to secure grain from the Ukraine, oil from the Caucasus, raw materials from the Urals, and coal and cotton from Turkestan.

Lazar never forgot Stalingrad. He had seen and heard the truth. One German officer had written, "The street is no longer measured by meters but by corpses. It is no longer alive. By day it is an enormous cloud of burning, blinding smoke, a vast furnace lit by the reflection of the flames. At night, it is a terror. Animals flee this hell. Perhaps only men can endure it."

Now he could hear the Russian infantry in the distance, trudging forward, large cannons bringing up the rear. Rifle shots continually rattled through the woods, in a staccato effect. There was little more to fire at in the city; there was nothing left of it. Over 900 buildings were destroyed, the bridges were all gone, as was the railroad terminal. All the supply systems were wrecked, and there were no more transportation or public facilities.

Lazar had turned fifty. He saw in the mirror what he witnessed at Stalingrad, that he, too, had changed. There were marked physical differences, things lost that could never be replaced, only reconstructed in another way. He, like the city that once was, would never look the same or act the same again. A sadness crept in along with the realization that told him Stalingrad could be rebuilt, perhaps not like before, but rebuilt anyway, to stand possibly for centuries more.

He, on the other hand, could not enjoy such favor. His existence was limited. He knew that he must take advantage of it before it escaped. Stalingrad could die many times and still be given a rebirth. He would die only once.

His progress continued during the war as it had before. He became vice chairman of the Transport Committee for the coordination of railroad, sea, and river transport and was also a member of the State Defense Council. As a member of the Supreme State Council for Defense, he concentrated on the defense of the Caucasus along with General Tulyenev.

By the end of 1943, Rostov and Kharkov were recaptured, climaxing a 375-mile drive from Stalingrad. Smolensk and then Kiev fell back into Russian hands. Lazar could return once more to Moscow.

In February of the following year, Stalin decided to hold a lavish reception in the Spiradonivha Palace to celebrate the twenty-sixth anniversary of the Red Army. Diplomats, army generals, navy admirals, and other dignitaries from all over the world attended. The host and hostess were the Molotovs, who stood under an immense crystal chandelier greeting everyone. It seemed as though the czar's court were back in session. After cocktails, there was a concert by Russian singers and musicians.

Then there was a buffet of extraordinary proportions. A dozen dining rooms displayed an incredible variety of food: sturgeon, caviar, roast beef, chicken, wild pheasant, crepes suzette, ice cream, and champagne. Nothing had been seen like this in Moscow for decades. In the Grand Ballroom, there was dancing with songs by Kozlovsky and Baturin, the most popular singers of the day.

Toasts were made in many languages, but most of them were in either Russian or English in deference to the party's theme, which was Anglo-American-Soviet friendship. The U.S. ambassador, Averell Harriman, was there in a long, double-breasted business suit, topped by a stiff collar. The British ambassador, Sir Archibald Clark Kerr, wore tails. For the Russians, Andrei Vishinsky, the foreign office vice commissar, was in a new dark-blue formal foreign office uniform.

After considerable toasting, many guests started gathering around Lazar. He was wearing a uniform, too, with a long tunic to hide much of the added weight he had accumulated. His mustache had become thick and was now the same size as Stalin's. He drank a lot of vodka, more than usual, and spoke at great length. He had an audience, and he intended to use it.

"Compared with the assistance that the Soviet Union renders you allies by deflecting upon herself the main forces of the German-Fascist troops, your assistance to the Soviet Union is of little effect. The only way to extend and improve this assistance is for the allies to undertake a complete and timely carrying out of their obligations."

He wouldn't stop.

"You have a misconception," he told reporters also standing around.

"You think that allied aid enabled us to turn back the Nazis at Moscow? Nothing could be further from the truth. The supplies from the United States and Britain were extremely slow in starting and only

214

a mere two percent—two percent—of what we needed arrived in time for the pivotal battle of Moscow. We were on our own and won it on our own. This war shows you clearly the elemental strength of the Russian people.''

Mikhail came to his side and took him by the arm. Lazar shook it off. He pointed a finger at Clark Kerr.

"We ought to run this war like I run my railroads. We work all the time, all together. There are three eight-hour shifts working day and night. We work under bombs, under shells, under all conditions. We never stop. But how are you running this war? Only one full-time shift. The Red Army is working its shift. But the British and Americans are only working part time.''

Clark Kerr protested, trying to explain the North African strategy and the Italian campaign. Lazar would have none of it. Instead, he came back with figures about the number of Allied troops and equipment in England and "other nonactive bases.''

"What you need are pile drivers,'' he said, hammering a huge fist first into his hand and then against the wall. "Pile drivers. They get things done. We can't beat the Nazis with only one shift working. What you need are pile drivers.'' He was shouting.

Mikhail now literally twisted his arm behind him. Lazar, though much stronger, didn't resist. He was put into his coat and fur hat and escorted out, all the while screaming about pile drivers.

The Red Army continued to push the Germans back. Novgorod was evacuated by the Nazis, then Estonia was entered by the Russians. Nikopol, an important manganese center, was recaptured, as were Tarnopol, Odessa, Simferopol, and Sevastopol.

On June 26, Stalin called for the firing of Moscow's 224 guns to mark the first great victory of the summer offensive, as Vitebsk fell to the Russians. Minsk was back, then Grodno was taken. By the end of the summer, the Russian troops had entered Bucharest.

The Germans had ruled western Russia for two years, but now the Russian army began the liberation of the conquered territories. Starting with a front over 1,500 miles long, they advanced in the south over 600 miles from Taganrog to the Carpathians. In the north, after the siege of Leningrad was lifted, the Red Army offensive swept the Germans before them, killing most of their prisoners as they advanced.

In October 1944, when the Polish Ukraine was reoccupied by the Soviet army, Lazar came from Moscow to take over from Khrushchev.

Only 504 collective farms had been set up, and in the next ten months the tempo was accelerated in a startling way. Another 1,150 collectives were organized. Lazar's appointment to the Ukraine was only partly connected with nationalism. Stalin felt that, as a Jew, Lazar would be more ruthless in eliminating Ukrainian national tendencies. He would be the strongest arm possible in putting down any sign of disturbances. Stalin was not disappointed. After all, Lazar was now the vice president of the Council of People's Commissars. And he was considered the most colorful and energetic member of the Politburo. He was not named "the Iron Commissar" for nothing.

Stalin's self-confidence, like Lazar's, began to return with the victory at Stalingrad. Churchill's acknowledgment of Soviet interests in eastern Europe that fall was taken by Stalin as a Western agreement to his having a free hand in this sphere of influence. He would now have political and economic friends on his western and southern flanks.

On December 21, 1944, Stalin turned sixty-five years of age. His birthdays had not been publicly celebrated, or even noted in the press, for the previous five years. But everyone realized that Stalin was not getting any younger. The possibility of his death was being raised, and the inevitable question "Who will succeed him?" arose.

Many names floated about: Molotov and Mikoyan, who handled foreign relations; A. S. Shcherbakov, secretary of the Moscow party and chief of propaganda; Zhukov, the deputy supreme commander in chief; Malenkov (only forty-four), Stalin's private secretary; Andreyev (forty-nine), another secretary; and Andrei Zhdanov (forty-five), former secretary of the Leningrad party, president of the Russian Republic, and a colonel general in the Red Army. And, of course, there were Beria, Lazar, and the new man, Vishinsky, who some were saying would be the heir apparent. He was a lawyer who rose to fame as chief state prosecutor and was now a first vice commissar of foreign affairs.

Lazar knew that things would continue to change as they did. And he knew he had to wait until the end of the war, when the dust settled both militarily and politically, to do what he had to. It didn't take long.

At 3:00 P.M., Berlin time, on April 30, 1945, a telephone call brought such an end: "There is a red banner flying on the Reichstag. Hurrah!"

On May 1, only the Tiergarten was still in German hands. This was where the Chancellery of the Third Reich stood.

216

By 3:50 P.M. on that day, Georgi Zhukov received the chief of the general staff of the German land forces, Hans Krebs. He advised that he was authorized to establish direct contact with the Red Army's Supreme High Command in order to discuss an armistice. Ten minutes later, Zhukov received a telephone call from General Chuikov that Hitler had committed suicide. Krebs said that the suicide had taken place two days earlier. Chuikov then read the contents of a letter signed by Goebbels:

"In accordance with the will of the führer who has left us, we authorize General Krebs as follows: To inform the leader of the Soviet people that today, at 15 hours 30 minutes, the führer has voluntarily departed this life. Based on his legal right, the führer in the will he left behind has handed over all power to Doenitz, Bormann, and myself. I have authorized Bormann to establish contact with the leader of the Soviet people. This contact is necessary for peace negotiations between the States which have the greatest losses. Goebbels."

Hitler's will was attached to the letter with a list of the new leaders of the Reich. It was signed and dated: 4 A.M., April 29, 1945.

On May 7, the Germans signed a declaration of unconditional surrender at Reims. On May 9, it was repeated at Karlshorst, on the outskirts of Berlin, for the benefit of the USSR.

The European war that brought death to 6 million Jews, and 3 million Russian civilians, and 7 million Russian soldiers was now over.

World War II had come to an end, and as far as Lazar was concerned, it also brought with it an end to many other things, and other people as well. It happened almost immediately with the surrender of Germany.

Previously, news had traveled eastward of the death of the American president. To Lazar the news meant little. He had not met the man nor had he even been a party to any of the conferences with him. In fact, he knew little about the foreign leaders, what they looked like, or even how they spoke. For example, the conference at Yalta was attended by Stalin, Molotov, Vishinsky, Gromyko, Ivan Gusev, and Maisky. Lazar didn't go nor was he even invited. At the time, he thought this was a typical Stalin ploy to keep him off-balance, but as Molotov quickly pointed out, Lazar had more than his work cut out for him at home with trying to reconstruct the transportation facilities both in the countryside and the cities.

"Besides," said Molotov, "Who needs to meet with two tired old men [Churchill and Roosevelt]? We already know what we will get before we even sit down with them. They have no choice but to give us what we want. They wouldn't know differently anyway.''

Stalin's primary concern was security. The Russian liberation of eastern Europe was followed almost immediately by the establishment of a number of Communist regimes, and an iron curtain descended from the Baltic to the Adriatic. Communist rule, of course, brought with it subservience to Russian policy and the subordination of all personal liberties, exactly what Stalin was able to extract from the Western bloc. Even the cities of Berlin and Vienna were divided into separate sectors: American, British, French, and Russian.

At home, the Russian ruling party had changed to deal with the postwar world. It had been streamlined considerably from the war days. No longer was it an amalgam of people with department heads tripping over department heads, with commissars being appointed for every little task. Now there were fourteen men who worked as a board of directors: Stalin, Kaganovich, Molotov, Beria, Malenkov, Zhdanov, Voroshilov, Khrushchev, Andreyev, Mikoyan, Shvernik, Voznesensky, Bulganin, and Kosygin. They, and nobody else, ran the Soviet Union. They made up the Politburo, the directing brain. These men held the key jobs controlling every strand of the country's administration. Nothing could be done without their approval. So strong was their position that their lithographed portraits adorned millions of homes, schools, and offices. Billboards along the streets and highways sang out praises to them. Their names were everywhere, from towns to buildings. They were the epicenter of all information, welcome and unwelcome.

It seemed to Lazar that everything filtered through him, both governmental and personal, and sometimes the lightning struck twice in the same day.

It was a hot Sunday morning in August when Mikhail showed up at Lazar's apartment. He had come unannounced, which he had never done before. His face was a study in grief.

"I don't have good news," he said.

A call at home usually meant someone in the family was ill.

"Rosa? Yuri? Anya, your wife?"

Mikhail shook his head. "No, much closer."

They stood silently in the foyer to the apartment. Lazar frowned. He nodded for more information.

"I just heard from Fiegelson," Mikhail said gravely.

He looked around as if he wanted to find a place to hide. Lazar raised his eyebrows.

"Fiegelson? Who's Fiegelson?"

Mikhail realized that he hadn't told Lazar what he had found out. He didn't know why.

"The man I saw in the Bronx New York. Remember, the man I told you was with Uncle Levick? I didn't know who he was at the time. I learned later his name is Fiegelson."

"So, Fiegelson? Why do I care about him? I don't know him anyway."

Lazar was prepared to dismiss the entire matter. He started to turn away, but Mikhail reached out and put a hand on his wrist.

"It's not Fiegelson. He's just the one who told me. It's Uncle Levick."

Lazar faced his brother. He picked Mikhail's hand up and removed it from his wrist. He said nothing but stared hard. He was waiting for the explanation, the explanation he somehow deep down already knew and feared.

"Uncle Levick got up last week ago on a Thursday morning. He was getting dressed. He bent over to tie his shoelaces, closed his eyes and . . . and . . ."

Mikhail did not have to explain further. He closed his eyes. Tears were forming. Lazar stared at him for a long while.

"Lazar, he was over a hundred. I think some said one-o-two. He had never been sick a day in his life. He had a good life. And he simply bent over to tie his shoelaces and was gone. No pain, no nothing, as if he went back to sleep. I understand it was peaceful. It is the only way to go, wouldn't you agree?"

He could only nod to Mikhail. It was obvious he didn't want to talk further or even to have Mikhail stay longer.

"You will excuse me, I am sure," he said, his chest swelling as he brought himself up to full height, standing erect, his shoulders back, his chin raised, towering over his older brother.

Mikhail did not resist. He could not resist. He had known this about Lazar from the first moment he was able to communicate. He would not show emotion. He could not show it. He would talk but that was about all. And he would not reach out to anyone. Whatever he felt would remain inside him, if there was anything at all.

Mikhail left. Lazar waited a few minutes and then went down to the street. He had to be in the outdoors where there might be people, where the bright glare of the sun would keep the emotions under control. He had to breathe. He had to walk the streets of Moscow even if he wasn't supposed to. Security was always uppermost in the minds of the members of the hierarchy. No one in the Politburo would think of venturing forth alone among the throngs of citizens. Everyone used a chauffered car to get around, traveling from home to the office to appointments to social events. Others, like wives and secretaries, took care of whatever shopping was required—whether it be food, clothing, or similar necessities. One couldn't "risk" the populace.

But this was a Sunday, and there were few people on the streets. Sunday was a quiet day in Moscow. It was the only time for rest, and tourists were still not a part of the daily scene. No one would recognize him. He felt sure of that.

He donned a white, wide-brimmed hat and kept his head down as he wandered through the empty streets. Within a little while, he found himself walking along Bogdan Khmelnitsky to Old Moscow, the Kitai-Gorod, or Chinese City, as it was called. It was here that the scholars and merchants lived, and it was also where Ivan Fyodorov produced the first books in Russian. In fact, the first Russian newspaper, published under Peter the Great, was printed in these narrow streets.

Lazar smiled for an instant when he thought about the area's name. Although it was referred to as the Chinese City, China actually had nothing to do with it. *Kitai* was a Mongol word meaning "central." Thus, Kitai-Gorod meant "central city," which seemed reasonable enough since the district was located adjacent to the Kremlin itself. "Sometimes we embed ourselves in silliness," he muttered under his breath. The area was once surrounded by brick walls, but Lazar had had much of that removed some ten years before.

He stopped at the corner of Razin Street and Nogin Square, contemplating whether he wanted to go into his Kremlin office via the secret tunnels under the warehouses that lined the street. Instead, he turned right and continued to Rybny Pereulok—the "Fish Lane"—to look at the building he first occupied when he came to Moscow so, so many years before.

A brisk wind caught him off guard and forced him to the side of a building. He thrust his hands deep within his pockets. The right one felt paper. He lifted it out. It was an envelope, pure white, with only his name on the front, written in a script that was vaguely familiar. He didn't know where it had come from. Mikhail? Had Mikhail slipped it into his pocket when he gripped his wrist? He would have felt that. But maybe not. It was curious.

He turned the envelope over and over. There was something crinkly inside. Carefully, almost ponderously, he slid his forefinger along the seam and opened the envelope. He withdrew a thin sheet of paper—onionskin—and stepped into the sunlight to read the faint handwriting. It was dated a week ago; in fact, a day after Uncle Levick's death. It had the word *Philadelphia* written beneath the date. There was no salutation. Lazar read what was written:

Yitgadel veyitkadash shemei raba bealma divera chireutei, vey-anmlich malchutei bechayeichon uveyomeichon uvechayei dechol beit Yisraeil, baagala uvizeman kariv, veimeru: amein.

There was no signature, but the handwriting was unmistakable even after all these years. It was Morris's.

Lazar read and reread the words. There was a familiarity to them, and he reached back as far as he could. He strained desperately to remember where he had heard these words before. It was deep somewhere within him, dormant all these years, but now ready to surface.

He looked up at the sky, stared into the sun until he could bear it no longer. He closed his eyes, the heat beginning to make them tear, and then it struck him as if his brain had been pressed by a hand somewhere. He remembered at last.

Let the glory of God be extolled, let His great name be hallowed in the world whose creation He willed. May His kingdom soon prevail, in our own day, our own lives, and the life of all Israel, and let us say: Amen.

Let His great name be blessed for ever and ever.

Let the name of the Holy One, blessed is He, be glorified, exalted, and honored, though He is beyond all the praises, songs, and adorations that we can utter, and let us say: Amen.

For us and for all Israel, may the blessing of peace and the promise of life come true, and let us say: Amen.

221

*May the One who causes peace to reign in the high heavens, let
peace descend on us, on all Israel, and all the world, and let us
say: Amen.*

*May the Source of peace send peace to all who mourn, and
comfort to all who are bereaved. Amen.*

It was from the Mourner's Kaddish, the Gates of Repentance, from
the Kol Nidre service on Yom Kippur, the holiest day to the Jews.

He no longer had to look at the writing. It had come back to him,
words that he had shunned, words that he had cast aside, words that
for decades had meant little to him. But Uncle Levick was now gone,
and he could feel something tumbling from his lips, cascading forth,
and he kept repeating them:

"May the source of peace send peace to all who mourn, and comfort
to all who are bereaved. Amen. May the source of peace send . . ."

Lazar didn't return to the apartment until late afternoon. Maria and
Maya were already out, probably in the park meeting Paulina Molotov
and her children, something they liked to do on Sundays. It was rare
that they could ever spend the day with their husbands. There seemed
to be no time when their men were not on call—the price for being
in positions of power. Stalin especially would call them at any hour
of the day or night. Lazar already saw a message taped to the telephone.
Stalin had indeed called from his dacha at Gorinka. Lazar dialed the
private number. Stalin answered almost immediately.

"Comrade," he said in his usual quick speech. "I have been trying
to get you all morning on a matter of utmost concern to you." He
emphasized the last word.

Lazar simply listened. Stalin didn't need to hear any questions. He
would get straight to the point with little fanfare.

"I am holding a document here in which Mikhail Moiseyevich
Kaganovich has been charged with being a German spy planted by
Hitler to form a puppet Russian government after the Germans captured
Moscow. Mikhail would become vice president of the new fascist
government."

This time Lazar could not contain himself,

"What?" he exploded. It was at the top of his lungs, and he could
picture Stalin pulling the receiver away from his ear. Lazar didn't
bother to apologize. He just couldn't believe what he had heard.

"Do you want me to repeat what I have just said, Comrade?" Stalin asked. This time Lazar's voice dropped in volume considerably. He almost whispered, "No, Comrade, no. I have heard it clearly."

Stalin continued. His tone became conciliatory as if he were trying to sympathize with what was obviously going through Lazar's head.

"I have instructed Comrade Mikoyan to conduct a hearing, to obtain testimony as to precisely what these charges consist of. I understand that Mikhail deliberately ordered the construction of airplane facilities near the Ukrainian border before the war so that the Germans might capture them more easily. At least, that apparently constitutes more of the claim."

Lazar could feel his head simply nod. He had been struck by a thunderbolt. It was the last thing he had expected. He had always prided himself on expecting the unexpected, but this totally unnerved him. He had seen his brother only a few hours before and had seen nothing in his face or manner that would indicate trouble of this magnitude.

"Comrade leader," he said. "Does Mikhail know anything about this?"

"No. It was decided to contact you first. Only Anastas [Mikoyan] knows, as I have already given him the job of gathering the testimony." He paused. "I do have one question for you, Comrade, and I will be guided by your opinion."

Stalin was letting it be known that Lazar would be making this decision.

"Yes, of course."

"We must determine whether Mikhail is to be arrested based solely on the charges we have received. Generally, it is thought that one is brought in if there are any connections with fascists."

Lazar didn't hesitate. He saw no other answer. Once more Stalin was giving him the opportunity of deciding his own fate by his determination as to how to proceed.

"Well, so what?" he said. "If it's necessary, arrest him."

"As you wish, Comrade Kaganovich. As you wish."

Lazar replaced the receiver and began pacing the apartment, going from one room to another. Uncle Levick's death now seemed far away, as if it had taken place years and years ago. But wasn't this always the way it went, one problem on top of another, a second tragedy following the first? It seemed incredible that this had happened. How

223

could he have not known about it? He had to know what was going on. It was part of his job, part of the system.

He stopped his meandering and settled into a large easy chair in the living room of the small apartment. Maybe it is not true, he said to himself. Maybe this is all a figment of someone's imagination. Or perhaps it is Stalin up to his old tricks of trying to disrupt the Politburo. It might even be someone bent on derailing "the Kaganovich Express," as Bulganin once said jokingly to him. Mentally, he began to list the people who would take part in such a scheme: Beria, yes, Mikoyan, no, Bulganin, no, Zhdanov, yes, Khrushchev, no. Then he stopped quickly.

It was getting away from him. He would have to think carefully. He could not let panic dictate, for with it came illogical thoughts. No, if there was to be an indictment with the purpose of ridding the Soviet Union of him, then there could be other and better ways of doing it than simply to concoct a story about Mikhail. He emphasized the word story. It seemed so far-fetched, outside the realm of feasibility, that Lazar began to realize that only if it were true would it make sense.

Mikhail had traveled outside the country on many occasions. He had even met with Hitler's chief of staff for air operations at one point following the signing of the nonaggression pact. It was no secret that he had many friends within Germany, and it was no secret, for whatever it was worth, that Mikhail's German was quite good.

The more he replayed the possibilities in his mind, the more he became convinced that the charges might be true. Mikhail had never been an opportunist like himself. He had no feel for it. One had to make sure by a full 100 percent who would win before any deal could be struck. But Mikhail was trying too much to move his career forward, and he probably had bit off more than he could chew. Lazar had sensed this about his brother when he returned from his trip to the United States. He tried to do too much and completely underestimated those around him.

It was years later that the true results of Mikhail's trip to the United States became known. Mikhail had boasted to all who would listen about how he extracted top secrets from the "unknowing Americans." The truth was that Washington had fed him unimportant information about U.S. military capabilities. It was typical Mikhail. He was best left to party functionary roles like disseminating the Communist party line to new recruits and staying out of the limelight. It was obvious, and always was, that he had no feel for foreign or even domestic affairs.

Lazar wondered why he pushed his brother so much. Whose was the responsibility for Mikhail's predicament? He was the one who had convinced Stalin to give him more difficult tasks. No, it wasn't his problem. After all, he had simply made it possible for Mikhail to grab the banner of success. The rest had been up to him. He had just given him the opening. That was all he could do, nothing more. Mikhail had to fill it.

Lazar shook his head. It was clear that Mikhail could do something very foolish, and this was the height of foolishness. He leaned back in his chair and reviewed what he had just heard himself saying. He realized that he was condemning Mikhail just as quickly as he tried to point the finger of blame elsewhere. He also knew that in the relatively short span of time he had been thinking about this after hanging up the phone with Stalin, the order had already gone out for Mikhail's arrest. Chances are he would be detained at Dzherzhinsky Square, perhaps not in the prison downstairs but in rooms on the second floor facing the courtyard in the rear. That much they would give him. He wouldn't be treated like a common criminal yet; besides, they had to keep him away from the general populace. Rumors could fly too quickly. It would not look good for the government to have its commissar of aviation thought of as a traitor, especially when Russia had lost 20 million of her sons in the Great Patriotic War.

He also had to think about contacting Mikoyan. If he did, he had to be careful so as not to give the appearance of interferring with the process of depositions or, of course, of trying to exert influence over what Mikoyan was to do. That would not sit well with Stalin. It would go back to him too fast and perhaps even implicate himself in what Mikhail may or may have not done.

He didn't wait any longer. He called Mikoyan at home where he knew he would be.

One thing about Anastas, he rarely went to his office on Sunday no matter what. Lazar could never understand how he was able to do this. Everybody else on the Politburo did as Stalin beckoned, but for some unexplained reason, Mikoyan was able to preserve his one day with his family.

The conversation yielded nothing. Anastas had not yet heard the testimony. All he knew was that Stalin asked him to preside over the taking of the depositions and to make sure that the entire matter was kept well within the walls of the Kremlin. He especially did not want any leaks to the foreign press, members of which, under the openness of the postwar victory, were coming in and out of Moscow with increasing regularity.

Anastas did invite Lazar to the hearings, which were scheduled for Tuesday. It was a courteous gesture, and Lazar realized why Stalin selected the Armenian to supervise the proceedings. Mikoyan was a gentleman, one considered beyond reproach. He would be objective and even more so, for Stalin knew that he and Mikhail had been friends going back to their early days in Nizhni Novgorod. Mikoyan would have to be inscrutably fair.

It was fast approaching the end of the day, and Maria and Maya would soon be home. Also, Mikhail would have been picked up by now, so he could expect to receive a call from Anya, Mikhail's wife. It would be best to go immediately and stay overnight at his office in the Kremlin. He would leave the usual note for Maria. He probably didn't have to; she was already used to the fact that if he hadn't returned by early Sunday evening, she would not see him again for another twenty-four hours.

He was certainly right about Anya. She was there Sunday night pouring her heart out to Maria. Lazar knew it would have little effect. Maria had no stomach for politics. She also knew that nothing could dissuade her husband once his mind was made up. The most she could do was to forward the note Anya left for him. One of his assistants delivered it to him late that evening.

Lazar had never read anything from Anya, and it took him a few minutes to understand exactly who had written the note and what it was about. It was a plea to save Mikhail, a plea for him to save his own brother. And it ended, "He is the son of Moisev, as you are."

Lazar studied the words carefully: *brother, son, Moisev*. It was as if he had just seen those words for the first time. And then he pulled out the letter from Morris and laid the two side by side on the desk. His eyes leaped from one to the other. It seemed incredible: two in one day. One has died, and one is about to die.

He reached for paper and pen. He would answer Anya, and he would answer Morris through her. He only wrote one sentence on the paper. That was all he would do, or wanted to do. He stared long and hard at what he had written.

"I have only one brother—Joseph Stalin—and forget about the voice of blood."

A chill rose up his back.

He got out of his chair and brought the letter to his secretary. It was to be taken by messenger to Anya. He saw on the desk messages already there from Mikhail. He wanted to see Lazar, to "explain these charges," the secretary said.

Lazar knew that whatever action he took would be reported back to Stalin. He could not see Mikhail. There was little he could do but wait and keep his eyes and ears open for any rumors or indications of a change in policy—to him. Stalin obviously knew the seriousness of the charges, and he obviously had made up his own mind as to their veracity. He could trust only that Mikoyan would see that they were presented in their "proper" light.

Lazar had heard the talk around the Kremlin halls. There was considerable sentiment that the accusations were not trumped-up by his adversaries but were true. Even Beria, who was universally disliked among the Politburo, was deemed free of any blame for the attack on Mikhail. As far as everyone was concerned, Mikhail was already "buried." There was nothing Lazar could do about it, and any attempt to alter the course of his brother's destiny would only work against Lazar's own interests.

He remained in his office overnight, sleeping on the green-leather couch as he usually did. He would appear at the hearing in Mikoyan's office the next morning at Dzherzhinsky Square. It would be better to do it this way than go home and risk hearing more protestations from Maria or even having to encounter Anya. No, much better to stay here and decrease the chances of family conflicts. He wanted to deal with only one thing, Mikhail, and to decide what he wanted to do about him. He knew he had it in his power to make that decision.

There were a half dozen people in Mikoyan's office the next morning at ten. Anastas sat behind his huge desk, almost swallowed up by the immensity of it. He was a short, thin man who seemed lost in such a spacious room. He was somber in his dark suit and dark tie, which blended perfectly with his brownish skin and now heavy black mustache. He was a study in coldness, yet the large brown eyes were gentle and unassuming. Lazar instantly knew that Anastas detested his task but was determined to hear all sides fairly and evenly.

Mikhail sat to the side of the room in a comfortable leather chair.

227

He looked like an observer to the proceedings rather than the focal point of them.

There were only four other people present. One was a stenographer to take down all comments. Nothing anyone said would go unrecorded. She sat to the right of Mikoyan's desk.

Standing by the door was a representative from state security who functioned as Mikhail's guard. Next to him but seated was a small man, also dressed in black, who Lazar recognized as belonging to the translation section of the OGPU, obviously one proficient in German.

The sixth person in the room was Mikoyan's secretary, an older, gray-haired man who had come with him from Armenia and who some said rode with Lenin when he returned to St. Petersburg from Finland. He had just given his superior a sheath of papers bound in a light manila folder. It was clear from the thickness of the packet that the testimony involved more than one person; from an upside-down look, Lazar could see that many of the papers were in German, thus the reason for the translator.

Lazar caught Mikoyan's eye as he entered. Anastas nodded and dropped his head to the papers. There was no question that he would keep his contact with Lazar to a minimum. Stalin's eyes and ears were everywhere in that room: the OGPU representative, the translator, and the stenographer.

Lazar looked quickly toward Mikhail. His brother was visibly shaking. He kept puffing on cigarettes, lighting a new one with the end of a half-smoked one. He was pale, and his eyes registered absolute fear. They bore in on Lazar. The tongue in his mouth did not seem to work even if he wanted to say something.

Lazar turned away sharply and looked out the window onto the courtyard below. He watched the movement of trucks in and out of the large cobblestoned square. Men were taken off one truck, some in chains, and escorted rather forcefully to the prison area known as Lubyanka at the end of the yard. It seemed that only full trucks came in. Lazar noted that no one ever came out, and all the trucks left completely empty. He watched this activity for most of the morning, never turning back to the room and listening only halfheartedly.

He heard Mikoyan's voice drone on about the testimony he had been given to the effect that Mikhail had deliberately built airplane facilities near the Ukrainian border prior to the war so that the Germans might capture them without too much difficulty. There were attesting statements made by German workers, including the foremen at the sites. One in particular said he objected to Mikhail's instructions but was shunted aside by his supervisor.

Lazar grimaced at this accusation. Was there no rebuttal? For all anyone knew, Mikhail could have been building such facilities for Russia's defense or as a springboard for its own invasion of Germany. He failed to see how this tactic implicated his brother, no matter what the construction workers thought.

But then he heard allegations that Mikhail would become vice president of the new fascist government. He was ready to dismiss this as well, but then corroboration was read by a high-ranking German, someone Lazar knew. He looked over at the OGPU translator, who nodded his head. The document was authentic. There was no question about it. And there would be no reason for fabrication.

Lazar turned back to his brother. He wanted to ask him whether it was true, but he could see only the agony in his face. *Why? Why? Is this true? Is it not true?* He tried to find an answer but couldn't. He could only guess.

He stared down at the courtyard. Mikoyan continued the reading of more testimony for another twenty minutes. Then there was silence. Lazar heard someone rise and he heard Mikhail whisper something to Mikoyan. He had asked permission to go to the toilet. There was one that adjoined Mikoyan's office. He said his stomach was on fire.

"*Da*," Anastas said. "*Kaneshna*—of course."

Lazar felt Mikhail's presence behind him. He could hear his voice, weak and pleading.

"My brother, *moi brat*, you can't let this happen to me. It is wrong. It is wrong for us, for our family, for our country. We are related. The same sun dries our rags. Don't hang all yours on one nail. Don't. Don't."

There was a sob to his words. Lazar turned and faced him. He could see the eyes were bloodshot, so similar to what they were a day before when he came to tell him about Uncle Levick. Here was his own brother, his own flesh and blood, the oldest in the family, the one who always had had little time for him, who would simply slip a letter from Morris into his pocket but would not have the guts to comfort him when it was opened. Now he was begging for all he was worth. He was crawling to him, and Lazar was repulsed by the sight. He hated weakness. He would never do this to himself. He would never stoop so low.

He looked into Mikhail's eyes, which were set deep in their sockets.

229

They had begun to take on the appearance of the dead. And Lazar knew he had to do something, anything that would help.

He slipped his hand into his right pocket and lifted the object out, hiding it with his other hand so that no one else in the room could see. Silently and smoothly, he slid the object into Mikhail's pocket. He nodded to his brother. It was the right thing to do, his eyes said. It was the only thing to do. He turned back to the window. He heard the adjoining door open and close. He listened for the rush of water as all in the room did. It took only a minute and a shot shook the room. The hearing was over.

Mikhail's "suicide" was hushed up. As far as anyone knew, he came and he went. One day he was here, the next day he was not. He rose to his position rapidly, and he left it just as fast. He was gone—quick and simple—almost as if he never existed. That was the way things were done in Russia. In fact, Lazar had not even seen Anya or the children. They left Moscow right after Mikhail's funeral, which Lazar did not attend. Word passed back that Yuri, too, was absent, something about his being ill with a high fever at the time. Only Rosa attended. It didn't matter anyway. Lazar had proved something for all to see. He had shown his final and most dramatic allegiance to Stalin. There could be no doubt as to his place in the hierarchy. He had solidified it. But he also knew what his actions meant and what the others around him saw. He had only a few steps left to tread, and he knew precisely in what direction they must go. So did everyone else in the Politburo, and if they knew, he wondered whether Stalin did, too.

One thing was certain. He could read Stalin like a book. He understood how the man thought and what he needed. It was simply a matter of tapping it at the right time. He estimated that while the country was still trying to work its way from beneath the ravages of war, he could strike again, when members of the ruling echelon were still off center, still disorganized. He had once consolidated his and Stalin's power after the death of Lenin. Two decades later, it would be time to do the same thing all over again, but this time on a grander scale.

Stalin was now closing the door of the country in order to restore life to what it had been before the Germans invaded, happy and content in the knowledge that he had political and economic friends on his western and southern flanks. The hatches were clamped down. He had seen to that in his discussions with the Western powers. A wave of Soviet culture flooded the nation. Non-Russian culture was rejected.

Lazar saw the iron curtain drop. He was delighted with it. And inside Russia, another curtain was just coming up: the opening of the expunction of the Jews.

Lazar knew that Stalin distrusted all religions, as they were not considered Russian. Moslems and Christians seemed to him to be people of another race, "centrifugal forces," as he called them, and therefore "dangerous elements." He treated them as such, too. They were confined to detention camps. The Baptists also went to rot in the same camps. As for the Jews, it didn't matter whether they practiced their religion or not. The Jews had always been persecuted, and they would continue to be. They would be the victims of the coming purges, once again the sacrifical lambs for the coming winter.

The work that he had mapped out for himself began almost immediately. His desk felt the weight of what was coming in. It was as if Stalin had lifted a temporary blockade. Things began to flow more freely now.

Lazar looked at the mounds of paper. It seemed that the piles were endless. His secretary had divided them into categories: reports and statistics to the left, letters to be signed in the center, incoming correspondence at the top, and details of plans to the right. Where to begin? Where?

His decision was made for him when Rosa appeared at his office. He hadn't heard from her since Mikhail's "difficulties." And he didn't think he would.

He was shocked at her reaction. She herself was surprised. She had always deferred to her brother, to the fact that it was he who had taken her completely under his wing after Moisev died. Without him, it was recognized that she would never have risen to such a high position. To her, Lazar had stepped into the shoes vacated by one father and had given her two fathers instead, himself and Stalin. She had to struggle with herself, with her very being, to be able to confront Lazar. She was torn between her sense of right and wrong, her humanity as a physician against the allegiance to her brother, and all of this was shadowed by overriding guilt. She knew too well that it was only through Lazar that she had been given the opportunity to get as far as she had. Lazar had entered her life at the most influential and vulnerable time. But now she had grown and was no longer a naive, inexperienced

231

girl. She had become a woman with responsibilities, respected in her profession and feared in her position. She summoned all her courage to face her formidable brother with whatever verbal weapons she had. She would be direct, no matter how accusatory the words. There was no greeting.

"Why did you do it?"

Lazar sensed the tone immediately. He would answer all questions with questions. It was always a good tactic.

"Do what?"

"This is not a guessing game. You killed Mikhail. Why?"

"I pulled the trigger?"

"You made him pull the trigger."

He waved a hand in the air, ready to dismiss her as he would a secretary.

"You talk gibberish."

"Mikhail was your brother, your flesh and blood. And, no, don't tell me about Stalin. I know what you wrote Anya. That's disgusting. How could you? She thinks you are a wicked, vindictive man whose love for mankind is very questionable."

Lazar chuckled.

"I never said I had a love for mankind."

"But for your own?" she said. She began to pace the room, waving her arms about. "But for your own? Where is your loyalty? Where is your decency? We are not talking about pieces of paper. We are talking about your own blood, your own family, your own people. My God, Lazar, what kind of a Jew are you anyway?"

Lazar slammed his hand onto the desk. The room trembled. His eyes flashed. His voice boomed.

"The Jews? The Jews? *Yob tvoyu mat'*—'I don't give a fuck!' *Bros' dumat' zhopoi*—Quit thinking with your ass!' They do nothing to help themselves. They sit back and they take. They take. No questions asked. Just like our beloved father. And to let those people decide my fate? Never! Never! Why should I live in fear? Fear leads to vulnerability and that is destruction. No, Rosa, don't tell me about religion. Do I need to remind you of what we are doing? Do I need to remind you of the words? 'All religion is an anachronistic and potentially dangerous brake on social development.' You remember, eh? I am interested in only one thing and one thing only: survival. I will fight against anything for it: family, religion, even country. No, don't tell me about any of it. You have survived because I have seen to that, and Mikhail did not survive because . . . because . . . I had to.''

He paused. ''I am scared not to.''

He was breathing heavily now, and Rosa stared back in amazement. She could not believe what she had just heard. It was the first time she felt there was truth coming from her brother's lips. She waited until his breathing was normal again, until the color came back into his cheeks.

''And that is your position, your side of the story?''

Lazar smiled. He was calm again. He walked over to his sister and put one of his enormous arms around her. It may also have been the first time he had ever done that.

''You remember what our mother said? I do, very well. She said, 'Lazar, there are always three sides to any story: your side, my side, and the true side. And no one will ever know the true side.''

He began to walk her to the door. ''You know, half the lies they tell about me aren't true.''

He tried to get her to laugh, even crack a smile. He squeezed her shoulder. His voice dropped to a whisper.

''We have much to do, Rosa, so much to do, and I need you. I really need you. We all need you, more than you realize. See you tonight for dinner. We will talk, eh? We will talk like we never did before. You will see. We need you.''

When she left, he returned to his desk. He reviewed the piles of paper. He would begin with the most important and took the one awaiting his signature. He studied the top sheet. It was a deportation order. A factory worker was being sent to Irkutsk in Siberia. He was accused of anti-Soviet remarks. He was seventy-three years old, a Jew, with a wife of seventy. She was an invalid. They had no children, no grandchildren.

Lazar picked up his pen, hesitated for an instant, and then signed the paper. *Survival*. That was the key word. This old man does not know how. *Survival*. This fifty-five-year old bureaucrat does know how.

Lazar would continue talking to Rosa. He would keep her at bay, close enough to use her yet with enough distance to protect her. He knew that he would need Rosa's help, but the time was not ripe. Until it was, he would do everything possible to keep her on an even keel,

233

just as he had done all these years. He would keep her fires of dissent low. If he had to placate her, then he would. What he planned was too important. Rosa had to be under control.

Stalin was feeling immense power by the last days of the war, and Lazar realized he could ill afford any chinks in his own defense. Molotov, Bulganin, and Khrushchev were aligned with Lazar. Even Malenkov (the new bright spirit) withdrew from pandering to Stalin's every wish. Only Beria seemed eager to extol his master's virtues, especially in Stalin's presence. But behind Beria's back, the talk was as disgusting as it could be, completely normal with a man who was an expert in perverse, womanizing tactics. Even twelve-year-old girls were not too young for his known sadistic tendencies. Many a mother was saved from exile to Siberia and almost sudden death by turning over her six-year-old to Beria for the night. Lazar was known as a monster to many, but even he was sickened and repulsed by Lavrenti's crudeness. Stalin, however, saw nothing or, at least, seemed to occupy himself in more productive areas.

He concentrated on those political advantages he could gain after the war. He made sure that the Soviet Union was the first to enter Berlin. He also ordered the army to solidify Soviet domination in Hungary, Czechoslovakia, and other surrounding countries. By the same token, the Red Army was to pull Poland into its sphere of influence; accordingly, he did not take Warsaw until the Polish underground had been crushed. He could take no chances in losing men or engaging in a conflict he might not win.

The same tactic applied to the Far East. He would not throw Soviet troops into the fray until he was positive that Japan's defeat was imminent. Stalin's master spy, Richard Sorge, had operated from Tokyo for years. He had sent back all the bargaining chips Stalin would ever need. He had told him when Pearl Harbor would be bombed; Stalin had kept the information to himself. He never told the United States. Why should he? Any war that kept American troops divided in two different parts of the world would be to his benefit in Europe.

By 1945, Sorge had given him the most crucial information of all, that Japan was looking for a way out of the war and would entertain talks with Truman and Churchill. Again, Stalin kept this to himself. He knew about the A-bomb and decided it would be better to have a neighbor, like Japan, weakened by the loss of a few million people than it would be to have an armistice signed that would do little to diminish Japan's growing population.

Mikhail Kaganovich when he was Soviet aviation commissar in 1938

Lazar Kaganovich in a formal photograph as vice premier in the 1940s

Yuri Kaganovich in the 1940s

From left: Khrushchev, Kaganovich, and the Ukrainian Foreign Minister Manuilsky in the Ukraine in 1946

May Day, 1952, at Lenin's Tomb. Stalin is in the center in uniform. To his left are Malenkov, Beria, Molotov, Mikoyan, Kaganovich, Andreyev, and Khrushchev.

Stalin's bier in the Hall of Columns in March 1953. Front row from left: Molotov, Kaganovich, Bulganin, Voroshilov, Beria, and Malenkov.

Standing watch at Stalin's bier (March 1953). Kaganovich is on the right, flanked by Khrushchev and Mikoyan.

UPI/BETTMANN NEWSPHOTO

Kaganovich as commissar for railways in 1935

AP/WIDE WORLD PHOTO

First Deputy Premier Kaganovich at a reception with Mrs. Charles E. Bohlen, wife of the U.S. ambassador to Moscow in 1955

Lazar Kaganovich and Joseph Stalin in 1935 S. KAHAN FILES

*Carrying Stalin's coffin. From left: Shvernik, Kaganovich,
Bulganin, Molotov, Vasily Stalin, Malenkov, and Beria.*

*Stalin's funeral procession, Red Square, March 9, 1953. Following di-
rectly behind the coffin is Kaganovich, flanked by Bulganin and Voroshilov.*

The apartment building in which Lazar Kaganovich lives

*The Moscow subway
originally was called the
Kaganovich subway.*

*Stuart and Jack Kahan
in Leningrad in 1981*

"If only they would drop the damn bomb on Tokyo," he said to Lazar and Molotov. "Then that would wipe out more of them. Damn that Truman. Why doesn't he do it the right way!"

Stalin also knew how to deal with China. He brought Mao Tse-tung to Moscow to sign a new Sino-Soviet Pact. Stalin wanted to control all of Siberia as well as Mongolia. He especially desired bases in Manchuria and North Korea. Although Mao balked at such demands, he had no cards to play. It also didn't help to learn that one of his most trusted advisers, Kao Kung, had aligned himself with Stalin, hoping to sign the pact if Mao refused. Mao had only one choice: he could do what Stalin demanded; otherwise, he would find himself a man without a country.

Stalin was making sure that he was protected on all sides with proper buffers. No more would the motherland have to endure invasions from without. No more would it have to see the likes of Attila, Napoleon, or Hitler.

By March 1947, Stalin was getting everything into shape. His work patterns were back-breaking to all.

He would spend hours studying reports radioed in from all over the Soviet Union. He would operate from his office in the Kremlin, where he worked and slept. It was a large room with familiar portraits of Marx, Engels, Lenin, and, of course, Stalin, hanging on one wall. Elsewhere in the room were paintings of Alexander Nevsky, the thirteenth-century prince who was granted sainthood by the Orthodox Church and was one of the great Russian military leaders; and various czarist field marshals, like Suvorov, who took Warsaw in 1794, and Kutuzov, who defeated Napoleon in 1812 at Smolensk.

Stalin kept his staff of secretaries busy taking dictation and making out reports all day and well into the night. He never seemed to tire. About three in the afternoon he lunched at his desk, and except for an occasional glass of green tea this would last him until ten at night, when he had supper. The meal always took from one to three hours, and that was the time he would discuss party, governmental, and military problems with members of the Politburo, the general staff, or both.

Stalin ate heartily, although he drank moderately. Yet, at large state banquets, he had been known to increase his consumption of alcohol with as many as thirty *stakanchiki*, or little glasses of vodka. It had no effect on him except to increase his amiability.

Everyone else followed Stalin's regimen. The average workday of a high Soviet official began at 11 A.M. He worked through steadily until after midnight, with a brief recess at four and again at eight for something to eat. Reception hours at most government offices and ministries ran from 11:00 P.M. to 1:00 A.M. During this period, the official had to be available in case Stalin telephoned. Such an official generally returned home around two in the morning, at which time he ate dinner and went to bed.

For most government workers, it was a six-day workweek. The Politburo members, like Stalin, went one better: They worked the full seven days.

One of the most sensitive areas in the country was, as always, the Ukraine. For the past few years, Khrushchev had been put in charge, but Stalin was beginning to feel more and more uneasy about the short, bald man.

"I don't trust him," he said to Lazar. "There is something unappetizing about him. He always seems to look past you when he speaks. Nothing is taken seriously. He has this obsequious manner, constantly with a 'Yes, sir, Comrade, and No, sir, Comrade,' as if he was trying to please your every whim. But I don't really think that's the intention at all."

Lazar needed no further explanation. There was only one option available.

"Then I will relieve him," he answered quickly. "As simple as that." He paused and then added for his own protection, "Naturally, it should be for a limited period of time. We have too much to do here. And too many people to watch."

Stalin's eyebrows went up. Lazar loved to play with the paranoia switches in Stalin just as much as Stalin liked to foist one of his trusted men onto another. For a while during the war, it had seemed that Stalin had successfully rid himself of constantly looking over his shoulder. He appeared to be in full control, fearing no one. Now there might be a soft spot in the armor. Perhaps Stalin was reverting to form, to the suspicious, neurotic, crazed man Lazar had known and liked so well prior to the war. Lazar could only hope for such a return. He needed it.

In the meantime, he would take over the Ukrainian party apparatus in Kiev. In some respects, it would work to his advantage.

"He'll be the real boss of the country," said *The New York Times*, a source that Lazar looked upon as the barometer of his success. He also liked the term "the Iron Commissar," which was coined during his days as commissar of building and materials. But now he had relinquished such a post to take over more demanding work for the Supreme Soviet. Of course, with it came companion spoils. As vice chairman of the Council of Ministers (corresponding, as all knew, to vice premier of the Soviet cabinet), he now had all the luxuries he could want, beginning with an apartment at 26 Kutuzovzky Prospekt, an eight-story building overlooking the Moscow River. It was the largest apartment he had ever lived in. A short hall to the left upon entering led to the bathroom and wide center corridor. Down the corridor on the right was a large dining room, and on the left was a kitchen. Farther down the hall, on the right and left, were two bedrooms. At the end was an enormous living room furnished with a sofa, two wing chairs, a piano, a large radio, and in the middle a round table sitting atop an oriental rug of many colors. A cupboard served as a bar, and there were shelves filled with books, a number of them in French and German and even a few in English, although Lazar could not read them.

Then there was the dacha in the rolling countryside of Uspenskoye, west of Moscow. It was filled with every modern convenience available from the Western world: a refrigerator from Sweden, a toaster from Italy, and a radio from England.

He also had an office in the Kremlin that had paneled walls, carpeting, green velvet cloths on the desks and tables, and a cathedral ceiling. Finally, he was given a new apartment on the top floor of the best building in the most fashionable section of Kiev. And with it went another title, this time first secretary of the Communist party of the Ukraine.

Lazar was to concentrate on two areas to help improve the situation: agriculture and nationalism.

For the Ukrainian peasant, winter wheat was amore traditional and reliable crop than spring wheat. Spring wheat was customarily sown mainly as a reserve in case the winter crop was damaged by bad weather.

The Ukraine was quite different as far as Soviet agriculture was concerned. In this area, winter wheat gave an average of one and one half to two times a higher yield than at any other time of the year. Winter wheat sown in early autumn managed to grow sizable grass vegetative mass. In spring, it quickly shifted to reproductive growth, maturing in mid summer.

Therefore, with this kind of cycle, a summer drought, which was common in the southern regions, would have little effect on the yield. In other words, from autumn to the middle of the following summer a greater number of reproductive stems grew from a single seed. Accordingly, the result was a higher yield per amount of seed grown.

The drawback in spring wheat was that it was sown when its reproductive development had begun in mid summer; therefore, maturation would start with summer's end. A drought at that time of the year, even a mild one, decreased the yields dramatically, and a severe drought ruined the crops entirely. For this reason, expanding the production of spring wheat in the Ukraine was considered extremely risky and was not a popular undertaking. Everyone advised against it. One noted economist who was in favor of winter sowings only asked Lazar, "What else can I do to help?"

He was told sharply, "Take your fucking hands off the fucking economy."

Lazar had no time to waste. He insisted on the rapid expansion of spring sowings. He wanted a hard grain with a higher protein content. He had no trouble in getting his way. The Ukraine party apparatus was already saturated with his own supporters.

Fortunately, there was an excellent harvest because of spring rains. He had guessed right again.

With this quickly behind, Lazar was able to shift from agriculture, which was no longer a problem, at least for now, to the international scene and the rekindling of the spirit of nationalism.

His emphasis first was on those outside the country. In an election speech in Tashkent, he reiterated Moscow's recent declaration on the international authority of the Soviet Union and added that the Soviet Union was not without enemies:

"We must always remember that our country continues to be within a capitalist encirclement. Therefore, there is no place for complacency. We should not relax but strengthen Bolshevik vigilance."

It was clear that he meant military preparedness. "The world is still the enemy." He would try to get the army on his side, too.

Stalin was moving on many different fronts. He had commenced another purge of the Jews. It began as early as 1946, with the persecution of writers, composers, and drama critics. A series of speeches by Zhdanov resulted in the expulsion of Mikhail Zoshchenko and Anna Akhmatova from the Union of Writers. The arrests soon followed.

Nowhere, though, was the persecution felt more than in the Ukraine. Lazar had seen to that. He spent only nine months there in 1947, but by the time he left the Ukrainian people were calling those months "the Black Days."

Lazar insulted, denounced, and terrorized just about everyone. His attack wasn't relegated solely to the Jews. He made a shambles of the party structure, ousting practically all the officials. Without justification, he accused these officials of Ukrainian nationalism and working against the Soviet Union and the Communist party. He mounted an ugly campaign against what he called "cosmopolitanism" and "worship of things foreign." He also meant the Ukraine in those "things foreign."

No one was immune. Even military personalities were targets, including Marshal Vasilievsky, the minister of war and one of the heroes of Stalingrad, Marshal Konev, one of the conquerers of Berlin, and Marshal Govorov, a well-established and respected admiral.

Lazar's broom swept into every Soviet home. To be Jewish in the Ukraine or even to be Ukrainian meant instant persecution. Of course, Lazar saw to it that anti-Semitism in particular following the war would have its strongest roots in the Ukraine, more so than anywhere else. If Stalin wanted a new purge, Lazar would make sure he got the credit for it.

But all this was only the tip of the iceberg. There would be much more to come, and Lazar had to be in the thick of it. He knew it was important to his long-range plan, which was becoming shorter each day. He also knew that he didn't need the Jews. They could never be counted on, especially with what he had in mind. He had to dissociate himself from them in every way possible. His ultimate success or failure would be measured on that basis. The Jews and his own Jewishness through birth were the final stumbling blocks as far as the eyes of Russia were concerned. He had to orchestrate what he wanted to do in the proper way, particularly now with what was going on in the world.

By the end of the year, he had returned to Moscow, leaving his usual mound of debris behind. His parting act at Kiev seemed to inscribe his name on the household doors of every Jew left in the area. When the religious people begged him to save their oldest and most famous synagogue from being converted to a warehouse, Lazar's decision was swift and sure: "Close up. Use for storage."

Russia in 1948 was seething in activity. All sorts of things were happening. The Soviets blockaded all land and water communications between West Berlin and West Germany, and the United States undertook to supply the beleaguered city by a large-scale airlift through three air "corridors." It had little effect on the Kremlin leaders. They knew what they were doing. Their actions would be wide and sweeping. They would set the Western nations on the edges of their seats whenever they could, and they would steal anything they could get their hands on, exploiting the open, capitalist system in every way possible. The Kremlin recalled Lenin's words all over again: the West was comprised of "useful idiots."

Agents from State Security were sent in droves to America to enlist scientists, teachers, and others in relinquishing every secret the United States had. Plans for all sorts of weaponry and technology flooded back to Moscow, atomic secrets being of the highest priority. This was the only way to do it. The West had captured most of the best Germans involved in Hitler's rocketry section. What the Soviet Union had obtained were not the real top-level scientists. Therefore, it had to make up the difference. The Kremlin knew they could always count on capitalist greed. Lazar laughed at the good fortune being acquired by Russia.

"Is everyone in America selling us material?"

Not satisfied with simply accumulating information, Stalin also sent people like Lazar and Molotov into foreign waters whenever feasible to see how much influence the Communist party could have on the rest of the world. No stone was left unturned. Even supposed adversaries were exploited, friends one moment, enemies the next; whatever would serve the political, economic, and military purposes of the Soviet Union. Everybody did this. Why not Russia?

The USSR was now a charter member of the United Nations, and Stalin saw to it that his country would be treated as a world power, even if it meant temporarily voting against its own interests. One was the state of Israel.

To many Jews throughout the world, a Jewish nation in Palestine seemed the best escape from the religious persecution they faced in other lands. During the late 1800s, in the hope of establishing such a

248

nation, Jewish immigrants began arriving in Palestine. They worked the land as never before: drained swamps, irrigated deserts, and planted trees. Farm settlements appeared overnight and once useless land became rich and fertile.

In August 1947, the United Nations announced a partition plan. The Jews accepted it. The Arabs did not. Egypt, Jordan, Syria, Iraq, Saudi Arabia, and Yemen vowed a war of extermination. However, in November of that year, by a vote of thirty-three to thirteen, aided by the behind-the-scenes diplomacy of Andrei Gromyko, the Soviet Union's delegate, the UN voted to end British control of Palestine and to divide the country into two: One was a Jewish state and the other an Arab state. The Jews quickly agreed to the UN plan, but the Arabs wanted all of Palestine.

U.S. President Truman sent Undersecretary of State Dean Acheson to Moscow to meet with Molotov regarding the new state of Israel, which Truman intended to recognize. Lazar, the sole Jew in the hierarchy, attempted to influence Acheson in holding back on such recognition, or at least delaying it for a while. For the moment, it seemed to be against Stalin's wishes.

"I was born a Jew," Lazar told Acheson, "and I am against it. What good will it do to have a Jewish state in the Middle East? The country is desolate. Nothing grows there. It will contribute little. There is no oil to speak of. And the most important aspect of all is that the Arab countries do not like it. We need to understand the economic ramifications. If the Arab world blames us for this, what happens to the oil? You, least of all, can afford to be without it. We have plenty of our own, but look at your situation. Do you really mean to say in this day and age that there is a similarity between oil and people?"

It was an argument that seemed specious at best, and Lazar knew it. But he could leave nothing to chance. He believed that a state of Jews would serve no purpose. He knew where Truman stood. He had no choice. After all, 6 million Jews had been destroyed in the last war. Somebody had to make reparations somewhere. Isn't it better to give them a piece of desert land and call it even?

Hitler had tried to rid the world of these people, and Stalin, too, was trying to do something as well, except that he wanted the Jews to stay within the Soviet Union. "Their minds must be tapped, and nothing more. It is essential, absolutely essential, to keep these people under strict control."

But Acheson would have no part of it. Truman was adamant. Israel came into existence on May 14, 1948, and the United States gave it de facto recognition the same day. Stalin saw the pattern clearly. Three days later the Soviet Union became the first major power to grant Israel de jure status.

Stalin was also a realist. As long as he went that route, he decided to go the extra step and invited Golda Meir, Israel's new ambassador, to Moscow for talks. It seemed like the only sensible approach. Perhaps more could be accomplished by allying the Soviet Union with Israel initially and then picking her apart later. Lazar and Molotov both saw no advantage to the visit. Stalin was stubborn. Meir's arrival in the Soviet capital brought with it a welcome far beyond anything contemplated. Soviet Jews poured out into the streets of Moscow. They surrounded her hotel day and night. Her very appearance brought thunderous roars of approbation.

Stalin was in shock. It was the most lavish reception ever given a representative of a foreign government, especially by a minority of the population, and it completely overshadowed anything he had experienced from the majority of the populace.

Stalin called an emergency meeting of his closest advisers, even dragging one away from a meeting with Meir herself. He could not contain himself.

"This is what we get for trying to be legal in the world's eyes," Stalin screamed at the Politburo, his face now bright red instead of its customary yellow. "This is our thanks. The Jews? The Jews have still not been able to adapt themselves or become acclimatized like other minorities. Only very few can—or want to."

He looked directly at Lazar. "They constitute an ever-present danger. Every Muscovite Jew has foreign connections. We are threatened by the danger of Zionism."

Lazar stared back. Stalin was waiting for a signal, the usual signal. Lazar nodded. Stalin smiled. That was all it took. Stalin would unleash his "apparatus of terror" again, and Lazar would once more play the part of a vicious dog ready to tear limb-from-limb any group that Stalin set him against.

Lazar would do what was required, except that it would be on an even grander scale. The purges, as in the 1930s, were all under his orchestration, and he relished it. No one doubted his sincerity, his honesty in dealing with the Jews, his faithfulness and loyalty to the state. He had proven it over and over. And he didn't disappoint. He drove the spikes into almost every part of Soviet life.

The Jewish Anti-Fascist Committee, which was considered to have done excellent work during the war, was now dissolved, and its leaders were arrested. The charges were too easy. They were deemed to be working against the state. All Jewish cultural institutions, like the Moscow Jewish Theater, were liquidated. The Communist party apparatus and the ministries at all levels were purged of Jewish personnel. In colleges, in scientific institutes, even in many factories, a quota system was introduced. The number of Jews was reduced to a minimum; in some instances this number was set at zero.

Lazar's intention was simple. He would quietly wipe out all the victories of the revolution. He would rob the Jews of their dignity and turn them once more into second-class citizens, perhaps even less. In effect, he stopped just short of extermination.

Important Jewish figures were hustled off to detention camps for "redevelopment and reorientation"—if they survived. Prisons became filled to capacity. In Lubyanka, each cell contained one Russian and five Jews.

The level of sadism ran deep this time and touched every aspect of society, even those who had previously received the state's blessing. S. M. Mikhoels was a truly gifted actor who had been invited to give private performances of Shakespearean roles for Stalin. He had been a favorite, and each time he performed Stalin thanked him publicly and praised his acting. But in 1949 Mikhoels was shot to death in Minsk during a performance of *King Lear*. The order had been given by Lazar with Stalin's approval. After all, Mikhoels had been labeled as a spy for Anglo-American intelligence. This was his only "escape."

Those who had managed to escape the German slaughters in the Ukraine and Byelorussia now found themselves the subjects of another mass repression, but more grotesque than ever before.

For the next two years, the average citizen's life in the Soviet Union progressively worsened. Turmoil seemed right around the corner, and although Stalin formed an eleven-man special committee to "draft a new basic program for the Communist party to be founded on [his own] new economic theses," the committee basically did nothing. All one knew was that agriculture, industry, and consumer goods should be increased, much like what was happening in West Berlin, and even in Tokyo, but there were no concrete suggestions from Stalin as to how he wanted to accomplish this. Accordingly, no one could determine precisely what these new economic theses were. Besides which, Stalin's paranoia was deepening. He trusted only himself and spent an extraordinary period of time locked in his office. The committee, of which Lazar was a part, managed to construct a Presidium with twenty-five full members and eleven candidates that it hoped would replace the Politburo and thereby dilute Stalin's stranglehold on the country. It also formed a ten-man Central Committee Secretariat to replace the five-man Secretariat.

The efforts had little effect because the same men, led by Stalin, continued to control the Soviet Union. Any attempt to introduce new elements was shunted to the side. For Lazar, it meant that Stalin's grip on the leadership had tightened. More and more distance could be seen between the premier and his constituency. Politically, it was not a favorable situation.

Things were changing on Lazar's personal front as well. Maya was now a full-grown woman and out of the house. She was an architect and had taken a dacha not too far from his own. She seemed happy there, among her books, and Maria visited with her every day. It seemed that Lazar saw even less of his family than he had before.

The year 1951 also brought with it another death. This time it was Yuri. Word had come back to Maria from Anya that Yuri had died of lung cancer in Nizhni Novgorod. Apparently, he had contracted it many years before. Actually, the illness that prevented him from coming to Mikhail's funeral was the beginning of the long-suffering years of the disease. Yuri had been a chain smoker, and according to what Maria learned, the doctors found his lungs the color of coal.

This latest death of a family member had little impact on Lazar. He had neither seen nor heard from Yuri in at least six years. Even if he had, he had never considered Yuri to be close. He was termed a "squeezed-in brother," someone who was born and lived between the oldest (Mikhail) and the youngest (Lazar). It was as if he were a nonperson. Of course, the fact that he was extremely shy and at times subservient didn't help matters either. "*Mukhi ne obidit*," Lazar would say about Yuri. "He wouldn't hurt a fly." There was no question in Lazar's mind that Yuri would be forgotten even faster than Mikhail. He was, too, for Lazar's head was being turned rapidly by other developments in the country.

Late on the night of August 12, 1952, twenty-four of the leading cultural figures in the Soviet Union were rounded up by the MGB and shot to death in the basement of Lubyanka prison. That same night, 217 Yiddish writers and poets, 108 actors, 87 painters and sculptors, and 19 musicians disappeared as well. Most were sent to the camps of the Gulag in Siberia as slave laborers. It was akin to death; many would not return. Among the twenty-four murdered was Peter Markish, considered the best Yiddish poet of the time, whose wife, Esther, a writer and translator of many French authors, was a personal friend of Maria's. Also killed were the poet Itzhik Feffer, a friend of Lazar's, and the writer David Bergelson, who was a friend of Paulina Molotov's.

Lazar was aghast. He had not known anything about this: neither had Molotov, nor, in fact, had most of the inner circle. Stalin had issued the orders on his own. He had consulted with no one except Beria.

Lazar, however, found buried in the reports two little words: "*i drugiye*—'and others.'" Obviously, there was much more to come, and he began to have an uneasy feeling in the pit of his stomach. It was the first time that he felt genuine fear. It was too close, much too close.

Most anti-Jewish measures were not given any publicity whatsoever. And they certainly were not made the subject of written reports. Usually, they were carried out on oral instructions. Who needed a paper trail? But now what was thought to be a secret started to have ominous overtones. Everything indicated that Stalin had something more sinister in mind.

A few months later, another shoe dropped.

Lidiya Timashuk, a radiologist in the Kremlin hospital, wrote Stalin saying that she had observed a number of eminent doctors applying inappropriate methods of treatment. It was well-known that the Moscow polyclinics were considered gloomy dispensaries where the sick were received with something termed "haughty indolence." The profession of medicine itself did not enjoy a high priority in the land of Stalin. The medical corps, for the most part, consisted of a few ranking specialists, such as those who had been the subject of the letter, and poor, underpaid, underprivileged women. A doctor in the Soviet Union was graduated from school now in four years, and there seemed to be little dedication. As a result, most Russians turned away from doctors and instead treated themselves with home remedies, such as medicinal herbs and vodka massages.

Abakumov, the minister of state security, ordered Ryumkin, the head of the investigation department, to "misplace" the letter. He even arrested him to make sure it was not found. Stalin caught wind of this and ordered Ryumkin's release. But he didn't stop there. He dismissed Abakumov and appointed a flunky named S. D. Ignatev as the new minister. Stalin would personally take charge of the investigation, and he told Ignatev, "If you don't get the necessary confessions, you'll lose your head, too."

Timashuk, who, it was subsequently discovered, was actually an agent for the MGB put into her post by Beria with Stalin's approval, charged that the Jewish doctors of the Kremlin polyclinic had promulgated "a scheme for assassinating Stalin and some generals of the Soviet army by medical means."

It needed little substantiation. Politburo members Zhdanov and Shcherbakov were offered up as human cadavers, "all murdered by these same doctors," said the report. The intention was clear. Of the fifteen doctors arrested, only six were Jewish (Vasilenko, Zelenin, Preobrazhensky, Popova, Zakusov, and Shereshevsky), but interestingly enough, none of them had treated the two Politburo members.

Thanks to the Stalin-worded official communiqué, this minority became a top-heavy majority. Tass reported only nine names of what they called the "infamous doctors plot," of which six were Jewish. The communiqué had tremendous impact. Hysterical patients refused to take their medicine, and some even physically fought with the hospital staff. Outbreaks at clinics became commonplace.

The communiqué did not stop with the doctors. It went on to other areas. "The majority of the terrorist group was connected with the international Jewish bourgeois nationalist organization, the Joint Board, created by so-called American intelligence organizations, to provide material aid to the Jews of other countries."

Israel, for one, was quick to react. It denounced the entire affair as "typical Soviet anti-Semitism." Stalin was even quicker and more graphic. He had a bomb exploded in the Soviet legation at Tel Aviv. It proved fruitful for it gave Moscow the opportunity to sever all diplomatic relations with Israel. By carrying the anti-Semitic campaign to its highest pitch, Stalin had shown, without the slightest doubt, that he now had aligned himself with the Arabs, something he had wanted from the very beginning. It was a typical Stalin maneuver: Kill two birds with one stone.

He was moving on many different fronts now. Next would be the intelligentsia, considered a special target of attack. A few days after the affair of the men in white, Esther Markish was deported to Central Asia together with her two children. The reason? "Member of a family of traitors to the country."

At the Kremlin, talk centered around the rules of behavior and the restrictions that would be introduced with respect to the Jews. These restrictions went almost as far as the laws that had applied to them under the Czars. The handwriting was on the wall. Everything indicated that Stalin was secretly making preparations for a mass deportation of Jews to remote districts of the USSR. And he meant all Jews.

Toward the end of 1952, Stalin succeeded in deporting several hundred Jewish intellectuals, writers, actors, and others he termed "undesirables." He also banned the Jewish press and closed the Jewish theaters throughout Soviet Russia. Lazar knew that time was running out, but when Paulina Semyonovna Zhumchuzhina, known as Paulina Molotov, Vyacheslav's wife, was facing imminent deportation, that was the final catalyst.

Paulina was Jewish, and during the 1930s she held responsible positions in the Council of People's Commissars. In addition, she was deputy people's commissar for food production, people's commissar for fisheries, and head of the Cosmetics Industry Board. Her importance had grown, and at the Eighteenth Party Congress, she was elected a candidate member of the Central Committee. However, it was also discovered that Golda Meir and Paulina were fairly good friends, and Paulina even had a sister who had emigrated to Palestine; she had corresponded with her until 1939.

As a result of all this, Paulina was arrested and accused of "possible treason against the Motherland," through her links with international Zionism. It was treated as a house arrest, and, therefore, no further punishment was meted out because of her husband's position—at least, not until now.

But word came down that she was to be banished to eastern Russia. This was reflected in another way at the Nineteenth Party Congress, when Stalin proposed the appointment of a Bureau of the Presidium, directing a list of nine people to serve. Molotov was not included.

It was a double-barreled approach: Paulina was being deported, and Vyacheslav was being forced from Stalin's inner circle. This meant he was also to be excluded from the midnight drinking parties at Stalin's dacha at Gorinka, a key indicator of who was or was not in the premier's favor.

It was evident to all in the administration what was happening. Stalin was about to launch a new terrorist campaign against the party's higher-ranking members, and it appeared that no one was safe, least of all those with Jewish connections. They would be the targets for the upcoming purges.

Besides Molotov, Voroshilov had married a woman of Jewish extraction, Beria's mother was half-Jewish, Khrushchev's son-in-law was of Jewish origin, and Lazar himself was a Jew. Even Bulganin was suspect; he had been strongly in favor of the recognition of Israel. There was no question what had to be done.

Bulganin, Molotov, Voroshilov, and Lazar left Stalin's dacha late one night, actually at 2:00 A.M. They had been discussing certain aspects of the new Presidium, in particular whether the foreign ministry should be supervised by this body or by the Central Committee, and Stalin directed them to have a report with suggestions ready for him by nine that morning. It was exactly what they needed, opportunity.

They ordered their chauffeurs to drive them to Voroshilov's dacha at Zhukovka. It was the perfect place to meet, and, obviously, such a meeting was expected of them. One could not take chances with Stalin. His eyes and ears were everywhere. Every meeting, no matter how small, was reported back to him. Not even chauffeurs could be trusted. Everyone was a spy. The tiniest conversation between Politburo members reached Stalin's ears.

Voroshilov's home was ideal. He had no children, didn't believe in keeping servants or even guards around, and his wife was away visiting her mother for a few days. Anyone questioning such a meeting would be dismissed rather quickly, for Stalin had instructed them to prepare a report that very morning. The only question that might arise would be why certain members of the Politburo were not present.

It was Voroshilov who opened the discussion:

"I know exactly what is really going on in Koba's mind," He was one of the few remaining members who still addressed Stalin by his nickname of some forty years ago. "It is what I have seen in Hitler's. The Nazi leader was also a pathological hater. Those anti-Semitic slogans in Germany were simply a tactic for whipping up the instincts of the masses. Stalin, you see, is now doing the same. The Soviet people are frightened—he is frightened—and it is always a good idea to give them a scapegoat and, more precisely, the scapegoat to which they have long been exposed.''

Bulganin spoke. His wife was a physician, and Nikolai liked to throw his acquired medical knowledge around whenever he could.

''It is obvious that Stalin is suffering from a persecution mania in an acute form. In his conversations with me, I heard him assert, not too openly or blatantly, but enough to understand, that he thinks you three are conspiring to murder him.''

Lazar's head shot up. ''Me? He thinks me?''

Bulganin nodded. ''He knows that you feel the Jewish deportation matter would make a disastrous impression abroad.''

''That's all I feel? Just abroad? What about us?''

Molotov began to pace the room. He was weary. Late night conferences had already taken their toll. He never liked to stay up around the clock. He did not have a strong constitution anyway and was exhausted from spending too many sleepless nights knowing Paulina was in prison.

''He knows, Lazar. He knows it all. The eyes are everywhere. They always were, but now it is more than ever. I don't think there is any question what is happening. He will exterminate all the Jews in the country, every last one, just as he promised Hitler, including those who have had any contact with them whatsoever. Do I have to remind you who that includes? What was past is long gone. He doesn't remember what you did for him a day ago let alone a decade ago.''

Molotov parted the drapes slightly with one finger and peered out the window. The sun was beginning to rise.

Bulganin spoke again, ''Stalin is making preparations for a veritable massacre, the almost total extermination of the Central Committee. This much I know, and I know we must stop him.''

He turned again to Lazar. ''You are aware of this as well. Rosa must have said something.''

Lazar's eyes flashed. ''Rosa says nothing. She barely sees him. He keeps totally to himself. He doesn't even acknowledge her anymore. I fear for her, too, and may just get her out of there as quickly as possible. The days of the Gorinka parties are long gone now, Nikolai. All she does is simply administer his medicine, and that is looked upon suspiciously.''

Lazar paused. All eyes were on him. He stared back. Everyone knew what the other was thinking. There was not a sound heard. They had to trust one another. It was the only way. They had to understand it and accept it completely and unequivocally.

It was Molotov who finally summoned up enough courage to approach the subject.

"What do you mean by 'medicine?' "

The moment had arrived. Lazar knew that part of his plan had been flushed out. But he also realized that the times had changed. Opportunity was no longer his alone, nor could it be.

He looked around the room: Molotov, Bulganin, Voroshilov, all old friends, all trusted, all good men who loved their country and, of course, their positions.

Voroshilov had been removed from his military post in the midst of the great war. It was no secret that Stalin kept him in the hierarchy only because he was an old political ally, the one who still called him Koba. It was a strange relationship, as if Stalin were indebted to him. But Stalin could afford to be magnanimous. He could show a trace of loyalty, for Voroshilov was no longer a threat; in fact, he had never been a threat.

Lazar's eyes moved to Bulganin. Nikolai was another of the old guards. He had been there from the beginning. Lazar noted that his twinkling blue eyes and white goatee gave him a distinguished air, as if he were the true ruler of the country, but he, too, offered little resistance to the power and hunger that were all Stalin's.

Molotov had seen what that power and hunger could do. He had lost his wife and would soon lose his own position. He had been beaten down badly, embarrassed, closed out, humiliated.

And then there was himself, the long-time, loyal right-hand who did the dictator's bidding at every turn. But now it wasn't a question of simply protecting a position; survival had always been uppermost in his mind. However, he needed to go the extra step. The time was at hand. He had to move forward.

Separately, each of them could not do what had to be done. Collectively, in the spirit of the revolution, they could now do the necessary, the essential, for with them would rest the fate of all Russia.

Lazar sighed and looked at the ceiling. They would have to know. They would have to join in.

They would have to understand completely the ramifications of all that he said. He had spoken to Rosa, many times in fact, but it was also important to him that she not attend a meeting such as this. She had to be protected at all costs.

Voroshilov raised his hand. He usually did that to signify he wanted to say something, no matter how many people were in the room, one or a dozen.

"It seems quite clear to me what we have to do. A small dose of a drug slipped into his wine, which now is usually not pretasted, would render him into a coma, and with his weak heart, his death would be speeded up. But, it would not be poison in the purest sense, but rather a drug to aid in death, a helper."

He sounded almost professorial. All eyes now turned to Lazar. He had specifically suggested this meeting.

"Almost, but not quite. Let me detail for you what we know."

He took out a sheet of paper from his pocket, unfolded it, and held it in one hand, not to read it but for reference purposes.

"I have here the report from Kuperin, head of the health service. Stalin has had strokes, cerebral strokes. Nothing disabling. These are caused by cholesterol added to the blood, which combines into a clot in the brain. He has not had to take medication for his heart. Two reasons: One, if there were a weakness in the heartbeat, he would have been prescribed digitalis, but there is, according to Kuperin, no blood test to measure the dosage and effects of the medication. Thus, two, Stalin is opposed to any medication for which testing is not absolute. Fortunately for him, and perhaps unfortunately for us, he has not had to need a drug like digitalis."

He looked down at the paper again. There were pencil notes in the margin. Obviously, Lazar had had the diagnosis explained to him in layman's terms, and the notes were made to facilitate the presentation to the group.

"Thus, his physicians are against such uses. They have been led, of course, to this conclusion by Stalin himself. Also, they have been questioning using a drug simply to combat the particular stroke Stalin has had and which can be tested.

"We then come to the drug dicoumarol. This is an organic compound, a white crystalline powder that is intended to retard the clotting of the blood."

Molotov was quick to react.

"I know the substance. It's rat poison."

"Precisely," Lazar answered, half-smiling. He realized that Molotov had not meant the comment facetiously.

"But in its proper dosage, it is an anticoagulant. It makes the blood thinner and as a result retards the coagulation of the blood. In effect, it liquefies and dissolves such a clot. This is what Stalin now takes, with two and one half milligrams in the morning and the same at night."

"He's taking something without testing?" Bulganin asked.

"No, of course not," Lazar replied. He referred again to his notes.

"Stalin has taken prothrombin time tests from the moment of the stroke. He started out with daily testing and then twice a week to determine the proper dosage of dicoumarol. It's as simple as that. And now, with the dosage so established, the tests are given once a month."

"So?" said Bulganin, who was beginning not only to get impatient but uneasy about what he was hearing.

"So," answered Lazar. "I am not a doctor, but I have been told that the dosage is no longer monitored like before."

"What form is the medication in?" Molotov interjected. He was beginning to see where this was all heading.

"White tablets. They are unmarked. This is another reason why Stalin keeps a close tab on his medicine cabinet. He is obviously afraid of someone sneaking in and replacing the pills with something that will kill him."

"Just as you are suggesting?" Voroshilov said.

"No, we are replacing the pills he is taking with more of the same."

Molotov frowned.

Lazar continued, again looking to his notes for guidance.

"The dosage can be increased to twenty milligrams instead of five. The tablets are unscored. It will be the same white, unmarked tablet. Stalin could never tell the difference."

"The result?" Molotov asked, but it seemed that he already knew the answer.

"The increased dosage will not necessarily kill him. But it will make the blood thinner, and Stalin will be more apt to hemorrhage. In other words, we are increasing the chances of another stroke."

"How good are those chances?" Bulganin asked.

"Quite good, based on his past history."

Voroshilov raised his hand again.

"Traceable?"

"Highly unlikely," answered Lazar. "And to who, the pharmacist?"

"Who will administer?" asked Molotov.

"Stalin. Know of any one better?"

Molotov walked around the room a few times, his hands behind his back, deep in thought. All eyes followed him.

"Will Rosa make the prescription?"

There was silence. Lazar breathed deeply.

"She doesn't have to. What we have here is enough—obviously."

"Can it work?" Bulganin said.

"It has to. What other choice is there?"

"Where are all the medications now?"

"The medicines are kept in the cabinet in his office. We all know he guards them jealously. The cabinet is always locked. They are prescribed by Rosa, although Stalin himself tends to his own needs."

Lazar turned to Molotov, "I need to have her leave the country when the time is appropriate. You can arrange that, I am sure. You know enough people, right?"

Molotov stared back, his gray eyes piercing into Lazar's.

"Canada?" he asked.

Lazar nodded.

"The others?" Voroshilov said.

Bulganin smiled. "What others? Only Georgi [Malenkov] and Anastas [Mikoyan] have sense. But they also have sense enough to keep out of a spotlight. They will neither support nor condone any of what we are talking about. But keep in mind that their very silence will suffice."

"Then," Lazar said, not quite believing that his entire life was coming down to this, "Then . . ." He glanced around. All three looked back at him. They looked at one another. It was settled.

Stalin heard of the late-night meeting, but it was not questioned because the report he had asked for was on his desk at nine that morning, although he did not show up at the Kremlin office until well past two in the afternoon. He didn't even question why only four members of the Presidium attended the meeting. This was indicative of Stalin's thought processes. They had become quite erratic. You could never be sure where his mind would be at any given time. From that evening on, in the December of Stalin's seventy-third year, there started to be a separation between leader and follower. Stalin kept his penchant for privacy intact, and he increased the security guards around him. He would see no one, and if he did, he tried to see only one person at a time with Poskrebyshev, his loyal secretary, in attendance. He refused to see groups of people, no matter who.

On the other hand Lazar, Bulganin, Voroshilov, Molotov, and even Malenkov would see Stalin, provided others of the hierarchy were present. They did not want to see him alone. Stalin's power was still too great. It would take more than one, as Lazar realized, to bring him down.

On February 17, 1953, Stalin had the last visit of someone from outside the Kremlin. K.P.S. Menon, the Indian ambassador to Moscow, met with the Soviet leader to wish him a belated birthday and to discuss the possibility of a closer contact between their two countries. India was being pressured to join the Southeast Asia Treaty Organization; however, it wanted to retain its neutrality in fear of involvement in international struggles. In fact, India and Pakistan were still embroiled over Kashmir, where most of the people were Moslems. The visit to Stalin was to see what the country, independent from Britain for only five years, could do about developing its resources and improving its standard of living.

As was his custom during conversations of late, Stalin took to doodling with a pencil and pad, and produced sketches of whatever was uppermost in his thoughts at the moment. On this particular day, as in all the days that followed, the sketches were the same: wolves in various postures.

"You like wolves?" Menon asked. He couldn't help but notice that Stalin's mind kept wandering from the issue at hand. He was intent on his sketches.

"Stalin is a very simple man but a very wise man. When the wolf attacks him, he does not attempt to teach it morals, but tries to kill it. And the wolf knows this and behaves accordingly."

"How do you know this?" Menon questioned.

Stalin laughed. "Make yourself into a sheep and you'll meet a wolf nearby."

"You, Mr. Premier, a sheep?"

Stalin continued laughing.

"Do not be deceived, Mr. Ambassador. Look around you when you leave. See what I mean. When a wolf shows his teeth, he isn't laughing."

Had he become senile? Was it being helped from the bottles in the medicine cabinet? People all around him, like Menon, shook their heads. Something was definitely wrong, but they didn't know what.

The country was still functioning, but it was doing so in spite of its leader. Stalin's course did not alter. He was concerned with continuing to deport and kill Jews. It became an obsession. Orders poured out from behind the locked doors of the Kremlin office and from the dachas. No one could get near him. Even Poskrebyshev had to keep his distance. He wouldn't let anyone in. In fact, Stalin would neither eat nor drink anything unless it was pretasted, and right in front of him.

But this security phobia also kept everyone else away from him. Lazar could not get to see him for weeks on end. He and the others were being restrained to such an extent that it seemed unconscionable for those entrusted with running the country. Lazar could hope only that Rosa was able to do what was necessary. It would be a long process, but it was the only possible avenue of escape from what had turned into a nightmare of gigantic proportions.

Stalin's condition continually worsened. Paranoia had reached its apex.

"They are out to get me," he would mumble to himself. "They will do anything to bring me harm." He was convinced of that, but finally he had no choice. The "they" all insisted on seeing him at the risk of releasing adverse information about his health and state of mind to the peoples of the Soviet Union. He did not fear them. He would take them all on.

Late in the evening of Sunday, March 1, 1953, the members of the new Presidium met in Stalin's office at the Kremlin. This was a typical time for a meeting with Stalin. As usual, all the lights blazed on the third floor. The intention was to show any Muscovite wandering by Red Square at any hour of the night that his leader was working away for the benefit of all Russians. This was done whether or not Stalin was on the premises. The Russian would see the lights and feel safe, secure his head of state, this leader, this "father to all," was awake and guarding his interests. He was watching over him.

But on this night, there would have been little comfort for a Muscovite capable of seeing beyond the windows and into the room. The members circled Stalin's desk. The premier leaned back in his chair, as if to protect himself from the germs on the breaths of those around him. Lazar got right to the point. He proposed that a committee be appointed to study the case of the doctors who had been arrested and charged with "this so-called plot."

"There has been no evidence offered against them, and they have been languishing in prison these past couple of months."

Stalin, who previously had taken control of the matter, still had not set a trial date or determined exactly what he wanted to do with them.

That was only part of the two-pronged attack. Lazar also demanded that Stalin immediately revoke his orders on the deportation and killing of Soviet Jews.

Stalin was shocked. He bolted upright in his chair, his eyes wide, disbelieving what he had heard. Lazar didn't hesitate. He quickly called for a vote. One by one right hands were raised around the desk. Only Beria and Khrushchev stepped back. They would have no part in such a decision. Lazar looked at his onetime protégé. The short, bald man averted his gaze and instead stared at Stalin.

Stalin's face turned beet red. He rose from his chair and slammed his right fist onto the desk.

"*Huyisosy*"—'cocksuckers,' he screamed at the top of his lungs. "*Huyisosy. Uyobvay*"—'Get the fuck out!' "*Pasasis huy*"—'Suck a prick!' He was ranting.

The members backed up. Only Lazar held his ground.

"If we do not leave your office freely, the Red Army will occupy the Kremlin."

Stalin shot a glance at Beria. Lavrenti cowered in a corner. His hand was upturned, his head shook from side to side.

Stalin came around to the front of the desk. He was shaking visibly now. Spittle appeared at the corners of his mouth. He poked a finger hard into Lazar's chest. "*At yibis at mina*—'Get the fuck away from me.' *At yibis at mina. Kurva*—'whore'—*kurva, kurva.*"

He turned to reach for the button to summon the guards, but Mikoyan and Molotov pushed his hand away. Stalin fell backward, tripping on the edge of the carpet. He collapsed like a sack of potatoes, his head hitting the side of the desk. He lay motionless, his eyes riveted to the ceiling, saliva dripping into his mustache. The others in the room were paralyzed, looking in horror at their master, who was crumpled up at their feet. Stalin began to groan.

Bulganin rushed to him. Molotov wheeled toward the medicine cabinet. Lazar picked up the lead crystal paperweight from the desk and hurled it against the glass door of the cabinet. It shattered. Voroshilov stood by the door to deter anyone from leaving or entering. Only Beria wanted to escape.

Lazar reached in for a bottle, gripped the one with the clear liquid, and slapped it into Molotov's hand. Bulganin cradled Stalin's head in the crook of his arm. His eyes were fixed straight ahead as if he were in a catatonic state. Molotov held the bottle to Stalin's lips. Bulganin squeezed the leader's cheeks. His mouth opened and Molotov poured the liquid in.

Stalin drank from the bottle automatically. There were only two swallows left. He finished and closed his eyes. Bulganin continued to hold his leader's head in his arms. He was rocking him gently. Stalin's breathing started to return to normal. The redness in his face faded.

Each one in the room looked at the other. Some had tears in their eyes. No a single word was spoken. It was nearly over.

6

March 5, 1953

The tension for the average citizen was over. The five, shiny black sedans had flashed by, and the Arbat was returning to normal. Bystanders exchanged nods. *"Hozyain proekhal*—'There goes the boss' " was heard up and down the thoroughfare.

Lazar thought he heard it, too. He settled back in the deep cushion of one of the cars and twirled the beads around his massive hands.

"Yes, that's true," he said out loud. "Here indeed goes the boss." This would be the day that would finally decide it.

He peered out the window and saw the city streets give way to country roads. It took only a few more minutes and the heavily curtained cars were rolling through a charming countryside. It looked like an enchanted land straight out of a Russian fairy tale. Dachas in this part of the Soviet Union all had an air of enchantment with their white walls, chimney stacks, and gabled roofs. Of course, one could see the houses only in the winter. In spring and summer, dark foliage concealed them, while in the fall, the green became bright red and yellow.

Lazar liked the winter, especially when the snow was stark white and untouched. There was a purity about it. The trees were all bare, and the dachas seemed to reflect themselves in the white-covered land. He had seen the change in seasons for many years now, yet it felt like only yesterday since he first came to Moscow. He knew it was some forty years ago. Forty years. A lifetime to many. He had just turned sixty this past November. Another milestone. But as quickly as the forty years had gone, the four days since the encounter in Stalin's office were like an eternity.

Stalin had suffered another stroke. There was no question about that, and there was no question that it had been triggered by what had taken place, an event that touched on everyone present in one way or another.

There was nothing that could have been done to prevent the reaction. He distinctly remembered the expression on Stalin's face when he confronted him with his demand to revoke the order for the deportation of Jews. He looked stunned.

"Did Stalin really think I was so concerned about the Jews?" he mumbled to himself. "Did he think I had now done an about-face, a reversal? Now I was a Jew lover? Is that what he thought?"

Lazar frowned. "Did he think that blood was thicker than anything else?" What had Uncle Levick once said to him: "Your blood is your blood is your blood."

He shook his head. He couldn't believe that. It was a question of his own survival, not that of the Jews. Yet, wasn't he a Jew? Wasn't he still considered, after all these years, after all these purges, still a Jew? Was it that simplistic? By saving himself, wasn't he also saving all the Jews?

He stared at the light in the ceiling of the car. Can a Jew ever succeed here? Had he been deluding himself all these years? If Stalin would not accept him after all his work—and groveling—after all these years of loyalty, after all these commitments, would the Russian people do anything different? Could they ever accept a Jew?

He grimaced. The questions had come in a torrent. They made him uncomfortable. He put his head against the window. "Is that what you think, Uncle Levick?" he said under his breath. "Is that what you really think?"

His mind replayed what had followed, particularly Stalin's attempt to summon help. He saw Mikoyan also pushing Stalin's hand away from the buzzer. Mikoyan. Why him of all people?

He wondered about that. Anastas always kept a low profile. He actively sought to keep his distance from controversy, to stay out of the middle of any trouble. Yet, here he was, neck-deep in the grossest act of all.

Lazar understood what was happening the following day when Mikoyan told him that he was on Stalin's death list. It seemed almost implausible, but the reasons were quite clear. First, Anastas had inside knowledge about the real cause of the death of Mikhail Kaganovich. Apparently, Anastas questioned Stalin before Mikhail was arrested. He was suspicious of the validity of the evidence being presented.

Was this now a trumped-up case? Lazar had believed the charges, particularly when he saw his brother's face at the hearing and listened to the hitches in his voice. But now, in retrospect, perhaps Mikhail was telling the truth. If so, then his original doubts about Stalin's motives toward him were well founded.

Second, Anastas knew too much about Stalin's earlier days. Supposedly, Stalin had been a spy for the Cheka and, in fact, had been in the czar's privately paid employ to report on the activities of Lenin. Needless to say, that would be more than enough to rid the world of Mikoyan, and Stalin, suffering from a full-blown persecution mania that was gathering momentum each day, had no options left but to purge the entire hierarchy in order to survive.

Survive. For the past three days Stalin had been doing just that, lapsing in and out of consciousness. Leading doctors from all over the country were called in for consultation after being screened first by the Politburo. One couldn't afford to have a physician who did not "understand."

It seemed that Stalin was recovering rather well, although one doctor said this was the "classic improvement before the end." The members would have their work cut out for them.

There could be no announcements to the public until it was known for sure whether Stalin was living or dead. It was the same procedure that had been followed with Lenin. Everything must be in order first. The Politburo must have the successor picked. There could be no break in the transition. There must not be any opportunity for another faction to enter the arena. This was the only way to prevent an outbreak of violence, a civil war, or another negative change in control. Continuity must be maintained to ensure the survival of the party and of the positions the party members held.

Lazar looked at his watch. He would be there soon. Calls to the homes of the leading members of the hierarchy had been made not from Stalin or even from the attending physicians but rather from the officer of the guard. Where was Poskrebyshev or even his personal bodyguard? It was clear that something was wrong. The caller had said that he waited three hours, not daring to enter the inner sanctum of Stalin's bedroom. Everyone else had vanished. The door was bolted, and there was no answer to repeated knocks. He said he found one doctor, but he wouldn't take it upon himself to break down the door. No one would risk the penalty of death by choosing to violate Stalin's privacy.

The big Chaika, its bright yellow headlights sweeping the path in front of it and exposing the pines and white birches that lined the road, came to a stop at the wooden gate that led to the main driveway of the dacha. Lazar peered out the window. There was more activity than usual.

The number of guards at the gate had already been tripled, but now he could see red patches on the collars of their uniforms. This told him that the MGB people were here. Furthermore, it told him that Beria had arrived.

The gate opened, and as the Chaika lurched forward onto the path that would take him to the dacha itself, Lazar saw his route lined with trucks containing the MGB's elite troops. They were armed with automatic weapons. Beria again. He was sure Molotov and Voroshilov had seen this display. It wouldn't have surprised Lazar to find Red Square now ringed with tanks. He knew that this was all Lavrenti could muster with his own delusions of grandeur.

"No matter," he murmured. "We have other plans for you."

Lazar found that he was actually one of the last to arrive. Most of his colleagues were already in the main living room. A fireplace was lit in one corner; all the lights were on.

The first one he saw was Malenkov, who was looking grim yet calm. Georgi always seemed to have that demeanor. His lumpish, middle-aged face gave him the appearance of serenity and this was not betrayed by his soft and soothing voice. He was huddled with Beria, who was listening to what Malenkov was saying but whose eyes were darting everywhere. It was obvious that Lavrenti was trying desperately to keep his emotions until control.

Bulganin saw Lazar and quickly came over to him.

"We have a locksmith who has just come in. Georgi called him.

Lavrenti wanted to bash down the door. We had to remind him it was steel, the ass. Georgi is trying to keep him down. He's already got the Kremlin surrounded with tanks.''

Lazar smiled. It was exactly what he thought. Did Beria really think he would succeed Stalin? He was indeed an ass.

"What about the commandant? Did he report this activity?" Lazar asked.

"Commandant? What commandant? He's vanished. And so has Poskrebyshev. Gone. No one knows where."

Molotov walked over. He gripped Lazar by the arm. He had heard what had been said.

"The entire household is gone. Servants, guards." He stared hard into Lazar's eyes. There was only one question coming back to him.

"Canada?"

Molotov nodded. Lazar sighed.

Voroshilov came from the hallway leading to Stalin's bedroom.

"There's a locksmith working on the door, and Konovalov, Tretyakov, and Kuperin are there," he said, referring to three of the medical experts treating Stalin.

He looked at Bulganin. "Secure?"

Bulganin turned to the sole guard at the door.

"No one comes in for any reason, do you understand?"

The guard snapped to attention.

"Make sure the door is locked."

He then turned to the officer who had telephoned the Politburo members.

"You are to do nothing without clearance from Comrade Malenkov or myself. And you see and hear nothing. That is clear, right?"

"Yes, Comrade Commissar." He, too, stood at attention.

No information would come from either of those two. Discussions had already been held about what would happen if Stalin did not survive. Tass had just released a communiqué announcing Stalin's illness and that the "highest medical authorities" had been selected to undertake treatment. It also served to assuage the feelings of insecurity in the populace by advising that "the Central Committee and the Council of Ministers have taken into consideration, with all necessary seriousness, the direction of the party and the country, and all the circumstances relating to the provisional withdrawal of Comrade Stalin from the activities of the direction of the party and the state."

The groundwork was being laid.

The past four days had been a merry-go-round of meetings. Up to then, any kind of discussion centering on succession had to be done in secret because of the presence of Stalin's spies everywhere. One could not risk having any meaningful conversation of more than one other Politburo member without Stalin knowing about it.

But since the second stroke, there was little risk in the members getting together. They had no other option. The government still had to function, and with Stalin spending most of the time unconscious, plans had to be solidified. Besides, there wasn't anyone who felt Stalin would last for more than a few days. Even if he were to recover, it would be only temporary. The prognosis was that he would be much like Lenin in his waning days: almost incompetent, with hardly the strength, both physically and mentally, to hold onto the ship's tiller.

The discussions favored Malenkov to succeed. He was considered Stalin's favorite now, and he had begun to control the party machine as secretary of the Central Committee. He also was close friends with Beria, which gave him the support of the MGB and state security forces if push became shove in the leadership struggle.

Lazar knew that the final decision was still to come, or at least he hoped so. He had made little progress on his own. He had overestimated his own position and failed to realize that no one person could have complete control at this time. Malenkov was supported by Beria, and vice versa. Molotov also questioned whether it was wise to shake up Stalin's policies too quickly. He recognized that Georgi was known to the public by being close to Stalin. Such knowledge had happened so smoothly that many in the Politburo, especially Lazar, had not even noticed. Perhaps they would have if they had read the signs along the way.

For one, in December 1948, *Pravda* ran a series of articles by Politburo members in honor of Stalin's seventieth birthday. Malenkov's was the lead article. It was clear who had decided that. Stalin liked Georgi and never feared him. He was not considered a wolf. He was a creation of Stalin's and would rise and fall on that basis. He also had the support of others in the Presidium and Central Committee who supported Stalin right down the line.

"Needn't fret," Molotov had said to Bulganin, Voroshilov, and Lazar. "Keep the country intact. Keep Lavrenti under watch. We will dispense with him soon enough. Georgi will not be able to last for more than a year. I know what I speak. We can do so much at one time.''

"And Nikita?'' Bulganin asked.

"He can be controlled, '' Lazar answered. "I know him too well. I, too, had a creation.''

Khrushchev had just come in the door. He walked over to Malenkov, said a few words, and then stood against the wall of the hallway to see what the locksmith was doing. He didn't even look in Lazar's direction.

There was a noise at the far end of the hall and then a sudden gust of air. The bedroom door had popped open. Everyone headed toward the room except the locksmith, who was now being hurried by a guard in the opposite direction. He would be able to report only on unlocking the door. Nothing more. He had not been permitted to stay there long enough to see what was inside.

Stalin was on the floor, his chest rising and falling in what appeared to be an abnormal sleep. He still had his clothes on, a brown shirt and brown pants. His boots lay to the side of the bed. It was typical of Stalin. He always slept with his clothes on.

The three doctors and Voroshilov lifted him onto the narrow wood-framed bed. His eyelids fluttered. Sometimes the eyes would open, but only for a few seconds. When they did, everyone gathered around closer to his side trying to detect some sign that there was a will to live. The yellowish-brown eyes were no longer reflecting anything. His cheeks were sunken hollows, his hair all white, and his lips were caked dry. Lazar noticed that his pants were wet. He had voided unknowingly.

Most were quiet around the bed. Only Beria seemed unable to restrain himself. Whenever Stalin's eyes closed, Beria began a stream of vile remarks, and insults, calling him every name imaginable, as if that in itself would cleanse him of any part of Stalin's regime. But as soon as the eyes flickered open, Beria's face turned into that of a basset hound demonstrating profound love for its master. "My beloved teacher, my beloved leader,'' he whispered.

At one point, Stalin's eyes remained open much longer than usual.

"He is regaining consciousness,'' said one of the doctors. "*Chai*— 'tea,' '' he called out.

Another doctor put his arm behind Stalin's neck. He raised the head slightly. His dry lips were being patted with a wet towel. Stalin looked around. His eyes seemed to go through everyone in the room as if they weren't even there.

The tea came, and a doctor began to feed him with a small, silver spoon. Stalin at first rejected the attempt, but when he felt the soothing liquid against his lips, his tongue eagerly lapped at the spoon.

The stroke had immobilized his right side. Lazar had not seen Stalin since the stroke. Only Bulganin, Voroshilov, and Malenkov apparently had visited him. He had heard about the paralysis, but now he could see that the right arm lay completely still at his side.

Stalin raised the other arm and pointed to the painting on the wall. It was of a young girl feeding milk to a lamb. His lips tried to smile. They could not. His head fell back on the pillow, and he lay there for another hour, his eyes every now and then opening and closing. The doctors stood by, conferring with one another, but they knew there was little more they could do.

Stalin's face started to gray. He was suffocating. His features became unrecognizable. One doctor put an oxygen mask over Stalin's mouth, but the left hand slapped it away. His yellow eyes were full of hatred and fury. He raised his hand again as though pointing to the ceiling and then brought it down quickly. Finally, there was no more. All movement stopped.

Beria turned on his heels and fled out the door. Lazar could hear his loud voice yelling for his car. He was rushing back to supervise his tanks, no doubt.

Voroshilov and Bulganin were weeping. Malenkov knelt by the bed, staring at the fallen leader. Khrushchev kept to one side of the room, watching the doctors as they continued their frenzied search for vital signs. Molotov was shuffling papers from a briefcase he was carrying. Lazar surveyed the scene as if he were witnessing a theatrical performance. He was there on the inside, yet he felt as though he were an outsider viewing a surrealistic work. He was not sad enough to cry, but he was sad enough to want to.

Malenkov rose and signaled to one of the doctors. He whispered something in his ear. The doctor nodded and went to the other two. They listened to what he had to say and then followed Molotov out the door. Georgi wanted the communiqué drawn then. When it would be released would be something else, but he wanted it in hand. Within a few minutes, Molotov returned and handed Malenkov a piece of paper. It read the way it was supposed to.

During the night between March 1 and 2, Joseph Vissarionovich Stalin was stricken by a hemorrhage in the left cerebral hemisphere, because of high blood pressure and arteriosclerosis, which caused a paralysis of the right side of his body and a loss of consciousness which remained constant.

From the first day of his illness, there were noticeable signs of respiratory difficulties resulting from the disturbance of the functions of the nerve centers. These difficulties increased day to day. They had the character of so-called periodic respiration with long pauses.

During the night between March 2 and 3, the respiratory difficulties assumed a threatening nature. Since the business of the illness, there has also been observed notable changes affecting the cardiovascular system, that is, elevated arterial tension, an acceleration and irregular rhythm of the pulse, a vacillating arrhythmia, and dilation of the heart. In connection with the accentuation of the respiratory and circulatory difficulties, signs of oxygen insufficiency appeared on March 3. From the first days of the illness, his temperature was high and observation was made of a very marked leukocytosis, indicating that centers of inflammation had developed in the lungs.

The last day of illness was marked by a brusque over-all aggravation of his general state and by a repeated increase in heightened cardiovascular insufficiency. An electrocardiogram showed a grave disturbance in the circulation of the blood in the blood vessels of the heart together with the appearance of inflammatory lesions in the cardiac muscle.

During the second half of March 5, the state of the patient worsened with great speed. His respiration became superficial, light, and extremely fast. His pulse went up to 140-50 a minute; the pulse became very weak.

At 2150, the cardiovascular and respiratory insufficiences were accentuated, and Joseph Vissarionovich Stalin passed away.

The communiqué was signed by Tretyakov, minister of health; Kuperin, head of the Kremlin's health service; Professor Lukomsky, head of the therapeutic services of the Ministry of Health; professors Konovalov, Myasnikov, and Tareyev, members of the Academy of Medicine; Professor Filimonov, corresponding member of the Academy of Medicine; professors Glazunov and Tkachev; and lecturer Ivanov-Nezmanov.

It was six in the morning on the following day when it all began. Muscovites turned on their radios to find the airwaves filled with somber music and somber newscasters relating what had happened overnight. The steady stream of information represented medical communiqués from the doctors, including a pathologist's report and the official communiqué from the Central Committee, Council of Ministers, and Presidium. Although the latter was dated March 5, Tass did not begin distributing it until around 4:30 A.M. on March 6.

It was a lengthy document, addressed to all the members of the party and to all the workers of the Soviet Union. It began with the same salutation that Stalin had used at the beginning of the German invasion during World War II, ''Dear Brothers, Sisters, and Friends.'' It was a combination news report and analysis of what Stalin had meant to the people and in which direction the Soviet Union would now head. It was obvious that the hierarchy had sought the best writers in the land to draft the official communiqué which they knew would be distributed worldwide. It was considered a masterpiece for what it was.

''The heart of Joseph Vissarionovich Stalin, Lenin's comrade in arms, and the inspired continuator of his work, wise leader, and teacher of the Communist party and the Soviet people, has stopped beating.''

Lazar marveled at how this one sentence could combine death and inspiration so well. He always viewed with considerable jealousy the putting together of words to form a cohesive and exciting sentence. Lazar had written very little in all these years. He knew how to talk, but that was about all. He was adept at grouping phrases for maximum effectiveness in a speech, but to commit those same words to paper was something else. His secretaries had to do most of the work for him.

The communiqué went on to explain how Stalin's name was ''infinitely dear to our party, to the Soviet people, and to the workers of the entire world.''

It pleaded for unity among the people and, of course, attempted to reaffirm the Communist party. ''The Soviet people continue to have complete confidence in and an ardent love for their beloved Communist party, for they know that the supreme law for all the party's activity is to serve the interests of the people.''

The paper covered all areas, whether domestic or foreign. ''The foreign policy of the Communist party and the government of the Soviet

Union was and remains an unalterable policy for the maintenance and consolidation of peace, the struggle against the preparation and launching of a new war, a policy of international cooperation, and the development of commercial relations with all countries.''

In the middle of the communiqué, it began again with ''Dear Comrades and Friends,'' explaining the task of the government to preserve, ''like the apple of one's eyes, the unity of the party, to train Communists in carrying out active political struggles for the application of the policy and decisions of the party.''

It ended, ''The immortal name of Stalin will always live in the hearts of the Soviet people and the hearts of all progressive humanity. Long live the great, all-powerful doctrine of Marx-Engels, Lenin-Stalin!''

It was broadcast and rebroadcast all day and all night. In between, there was quiet, funereal music. For three days and three nights, this became a never-ending stream, from one end of the Soviet Union to the other.

In the meantime, Stalin's body had been moved from the dacha to Moscow in preparation for the public viewing. Expert embalmers were summoned to make Stalin as attractive as possible. It was decided, without any opposition, that Stalin's funeral would outrank even that of Lenin's. There would be at least three days of public viewing before the body would be laid next to Lenin in the Red Square Mausoleum. The man who had arranged for the preservation of Lenin's body had died, and a scramble began to find someone who knew the technique. No stone would be left unturned. Whatever had been done for Lenin had to be done for Stalin, and even more so.

Already the city was filling with people. Trains and buses kept depositing more and more every hour. The capital had become a mecca. Overnight it had been transformed into one huge funeral. Red flags with black crepe were hung from every lamppost. Large photographs of Stalin appeared on every building. Candles could be seen flickering in every window. It would be the greatest outpouring for an individual, living or dead, in history.

Lazar had returned to his Moscow apartment immediately after the scene at the dacha. He knew that the following days would be long ones, not only with having to stand guard by the bier, as was custom, but in attending the countless meetings to determine the future and fate of the country. It seemed a foregone conclusion that Georgi Malenkov would take over the reins, at least to the outside world. However, all those in the Politburo knew that he would serve only as a titular figure in order to retain continuity for both the government and the party. Behind him, or at least on equal footing with him, would be Beria, Molotov, Bulganin, and himself. In one smaller respect, Khrushchev would be part of that inner group, for Malenkov had given him the job of organizing the funeral arrangements. Lazar was against this appointment, but Nikita had enough "friends" around to secure it. Lazar couldn't understand where these new associates had come from. Khrushchev was not that well liked among the older men, but apparently his support was now coming from the younger elements who were "relieved" that Stalin was gone.

Lazar realized what he had to do. One of the first things was to present the best image possible over the next few days. He agonized about this, rehearsing how he should act and even what he should wear. The first test would be at the watch before the bier. This was important because pictures would be taken and widely distributed. He had to look like a statesman.

By 3:00 P.M. of March 6, Stalin's body was officially on view in the Hall of Columns, in the House of Trade Unions, just a few blocks from Pushkin Square.

Lazar was there as soon as the doors opened along with the other members of the ruling body. They lined up on either side of the bier.

Beria was dressed in a double-breasted suit, while both Molotov and Mikoyan wore well-tailored single-breasted suits with vests. Khrushchev was also in a suit, but it seemed to hang on him like a potato sack. All of them were in dark colors. Bulganin and Voroshilov wore their military uniforms with medals across the chests, and, to Lazar's surprise, Malenkov was in a brown tunic that seemed all wrong for this occasion. Lazar himself wore a single-breasted suit that he thought would deemphasize his already protruding middle and make him look slimmer. He was a shade taller than most of the other members of the Politburo, and he felt it would be beneficial to "tower over one's opponents." All wore armbands of mourning.

Lazar kept looking at Malenkov, who took a position right next to the bier. He resembled a fat, overstuffed pig. Who could take him seriously? A plump man in a tunic?

The Hall of Columns was quiet and beautiful. The crystal chandeliers were decked with black crepe, and a long green carpet surrounded the bier.

The coffin was uncovered, as is traditional in Russia. There were thousands of flowers around it, of many different colors, but arranged in such a manner as to show off Stalin in the very best light. For that matter, Lazar was stunned when he saw the dead leader. It was not what he had expected, and it was quite evident that those who had prepared the body were unrivaled experts.

Stalin looked as he had decades ago. His cheeks were puffy and rosy, and his lips had color. His nostrils were flared as though he were ready to meet any challenge. He no longer resembled a skeleton.

But more than anything, Lazar was amazed at the hair. Days before, it had been stark white. Now it had been darkened, the mustache trimmed and Stalin gave an appearance of someone in his fifties, not seventy-three years of age.

It was extraordinary, and Lazar had to step back from the initial shock. Even Beria squirmed, obviously hoping that Stalin would not suddenly open his eyes and start bellowing orders.

Stalin was dressed in a new, dark-blue uniform with brass hammer-and-sickle insignia serving as buttons on the front of the jacket. Large epaulets decked the shoulders. His hands were draped along his midsection, the fingers loose. There was no question in Lazar's mind that the premier was simply taking a catnap.

The viewing lasted three days. By the third day, the line of people waiting to see their beloved leader stretched for six miles. Beria had ordered additional mounted police from Leningrad and they roamed the streets to keep a semblance of order. Most of the time, they were ineffective, as huge crowds pushed and shoved, overrunning the barricades and trampling anyone in their path in their eagerness to catch a glimpse of their "Father."

Lazar fantasized whether this would also happen for him if he died—"if he died."

The days and nights then were a blur to him. He attended meeting upon meeting, made speeches, met with foreign dignitaries, and generally prepared himself for what would follow. Already, it looked like the country would have three ruling heads, Malenkov, Beria, and Molotov, with Bulganin, Mikoyan, and himself right behind. Everyone was watching everyone else. Khrushchev apparently was also in the thick of it because of his position as secretary of the council. To Lazar, it seemed a temporary jumble, with the final struggle for power and leadership to take place after Stalin was officially put to rest and the foreign representation had gone home.

March 9 was a day of intense cold. Lazar wrapped himself in his warmest black coat with fur collar and fur hat. He would give an appearance of largeness and strength, perhaps overshadowing his colleagues. Besides, he certainly didn't want to shiver himself to death on top of Lenin's mausoleum.

He was surprised that he was not asked to give a speech. Khrushchev had organized that aspect and had selected Malenkov first, Beria second, and Molotov third.

"No, don't make an issue, at least right now," Molotov advised. "It is of no consequence. You are better to keep a low profile anyway; you can show your grief better. Also, you have already been given the initial place behind the cortege. You will walk directly behind Stalin in the lead position. Take that. It will have more meaning in the long run. You don't need the speeches now. I will protect our interests."

Lazar had to trust Molotov. There was too much opposition to his speaking. Distrust ran deep, especially now with Stalin dead.

The funeral procession was slow as it wound its way through the streets of Moscow from the House of Trade Unions to Red Square. Six black horses pulled the coffin, which had been placed on a catafalque on a gun carriage.

True to the word, Lazar marched right behind the coffin with the others to his right and left. There was only one foreign dignitary in that first row, Chou En-lai, who walked between Malenkov and Beria with Khrushchev on the outside. All in the hierarchy wore fur hats except Beria, who decided on a felt brim one. Lavrenti looked out of place, but then Lazar felt that Beria was always out of place. He detested the man more than any other.

The funeral was a long one, as far as Lazar was concerned. It was a cold, gray day, and enough snow remained on the ground to make walking treacherous. At times, he caught himself slipping on the ice.

Red Square was a mass of humanity. Barricades had been strategically placed to protect the visiting heads of state and to separate the military regiments from the general public. Large red banners fluttered everywhere, and behind the mausoleum could be seen enormous likenesses of Marx, Lenin, and Stalin. In fact, Stalin's name was already carved in stone under Lenin's on the tomb.

Khrushchev introduced the speakers and Lazar felt a twinge of resentment. His onetime protégé was climbing fast—too fast.

Malenkov spoke first, promising peace. Beria then promised to protect the rights of all. Lazar winced. By that time, Lazar's mind was wandering, and his eyes were going out of focus. He remembered what it had been like almost three decades ago when Lenin died. At a distance, he recalled seeing men in this same place. He was not one of them, though. Now he was, and as he heard Molotov's high, squeaky voice, he recalled the time he first met Vyacheslav in Stalin's office. He had always liked Molotov. There seemed to be something honorable about the man in spite of what he had done for Stalin.

When the speeches ended, Malenkov, Beria, Molotov, Khrushchev, Voroshilov, Bulganin, Mikoyan, and Lazar, the comrades-in-arms, lifted the coffin to carry Stalin to the tomb below. The coffin was heavy, and twice it almost fell to the ground. Soldiers the size of mountains had to come to the aid of Bulganin. He was having trouble containing his emotions. Lazar was strong and unemotional. He had no problem, although his gloved hands kept slipping on the highly polished brass handles.

As soon as they had put the coffin down, Lazar went over to Bulganin and put his arms around him in a bear hug. Nikolai wept shamelessly. Even one of the guards could not control himself.

It was noon. The Kremlin clock struck twelve times. Cannons roared. Overhead, the red flag that was then at half-mast on top of the tower was hoisted up the pole. The Moscow Regiment, as well as those from the other military academies, moved into position for their final parade before Stalin; their standards dipped.

Throughout the Soviet Union, everything ceased. All work, all transportation from the Gulf of Finland to the Bering Sea came to a sudden stop.

Monday, March 9, 1953, heard the Red Army band of three hundred musicians play Chopin's "Funeral March" for Stalin as he was put to rest in the crypt in Red Square.

An era was over, and a new one was about to begin.

Within an hour following the conclusion of the funeral services, the new leaders were gathered in a conference room on the third floor of the Kremlin. Malenkov presided over an informal meeting. The next few months would be a critical period, and it was imperative that a detailed agenda be prepared of what needed to be discussed and in what order of priority.

281

Everyone who carried Stalin to the crypt was there except Beria, who, it was reported, had dashed to one of Stalin's dachas to supervise the disposal of the furniture and other property. Malenkov, needing Beria's support, was seething.

"That *pizduk*—'bastard.' He couldn't wait? He had to go now? A vulture, he is."

Lazar looked around the table. To say that the group was an interesting one would be an understatement. Each man was an individual in his own right, with his own set of beliefs and ambitions. Lazar realized that it would be strange for them to function without Stalin standing over their heads. Final decisions would now be theirs, and they would be solely responsible for them.

He had waited and planned and schemed for almost all his life to reach a certain position. He was now one of the ruling members of this massive country, with no one in front of him or above him, only a few to the sides, and the rest trailing behind. But he was still uneasy. In earlier years, he was at the pinnacle of power, second to an extraordinarily powerful man. Now he was no longer second. He no longer had that person to contend with, and yet he was still groping. He was wandering through a forest in search of a clearing.

A mentor was not there. He had no one to overtake, to pass. Uncle Levick was gone, Trotsky was gone, Stalin was gone. It was empty in front of him except for the seat of power itself. But the seat was being shared with others, and it seemed as though they were all of equal strength, at least on the surface; yet each one was struggling to break out of the pack.

He surveyed the men seated at the table. Malenkov was Malenkov, looking as fat as usual. He was obviously nervous about his new position, for he constantly nibbled on his fingernails, stopping only when he thought someone was watching him. His pudgy fingers looked even shorter with their nails bitten down.

Next to him was Bulganin, who had already dubbed Malenkov "Big Georgi." Because of his own expanding girth, Bulganin had no right to talk, but the nickname was appropriate. Big Georgi was a buffoon, Lazar felt. A nice man, but a buffoon all the same. Without Beria's support, it would simply be a matter of time before he was thrown out on his fat ass and pudgy fingers.

Bulganin also seemed to offer little in the way of leadership. Nikolai was not a political animal. He liked to be in on the decision making, but he contributed little. He was well liked and commanded some respect, but he was hardly one to be taken seriously and was certainly not in the same category as Molotov.

Now, there was a man you could not underestimate. He had intelligence, cunning, and a knack for staying alive. He had proven that with Stalin, who more than once thought of disposing of his foreign minister. He was indeed a formidable competitor.

Voroshilov and Mikoyan, it seemed, were nonentities, although Anastas did have the brains. His main problem was in communication. He rarely offered his opinion. He was too conservative, never wanting to involve himself in political controversies.

Beria, the only one missing, was someone to be reckoned with. He had more drive than even Molotov, and he was far more ruthless.

Finally, there was Khrushchev, who had taken his place at the table as first secretary of the Central Committee. He really wasn't in Beria's league. He had ambition, that was true, but he had still to show the ability to survive. Up to now, it was Lazar who had kept him alive, who had brought him along to positions of leadership. Stalin would have eliminated him years ago, especially when he was replaced in the Ukraine after the war. Lazar saved him. The question still remained whether or not he could stand on his own feet when necessary.

No, the major problem was Lavrenti, and each one at the table knew that some day the matter would have to be addressed.

The meeting on March 9 was followed by one on March 10 and then on March 11 and so on. It was constant. Within a week, Lazar realized that any kind of collective leadership could not work.

"You can't fart without approval," he said.

They would fix an agenda or select a topic, and then the wrangling would start. Many times it would be on matters that weren't even on the agenda. Everyone had a different idea of what should be done, in what degree and when. Without any single, strong personality controlling the discussions, or at least the outcome, the meetings came full circle on any one issue: Talk was endless, subjects seemed to blend into one another, giving rise to new ones and, accordingly, new discussions. Shouting, name-calling, political jockeying, deals, plots, arrangements were the order of the day. It was so unlike the Stalin years, which had been highly disciplined. This was chaos.

For the first days, the topics centered around what to do with Stalin. Just because he was dead did not mean he was buried. Do his policies continue or not? "If not, then how far do we go in shifting away from the Stalinist road?" Malenkov asked.

These discussions had taken place informally before Stalin's death, but there were never any definitive results.

The consensus at the table was that the Soviet people needed relief. Malenkov, backed by Molotov, Bulganin, and Khrushchev, argued for a "new foot forward," a concerted effort to relieve the people of the hardships and agonies of the past twenty-nine years. Malenkov wanted to concentrate on raising the standard of living. He wanted to reduce the cost of things. One way was to open more foreign trade doors and import a wealth of consumer goods, like washing machines, refrigerators, and even beds. Khrushchev was in favor of the concept of raising the standard of living, but he wasn't so sure washing machines were the answer.

"We need more tractors, more machinery that will produce more than just clean laundry. We have to zero in on agriculture. I like the general idea, but not the specifics." He turned to Lazar. "We can't give Big Georgi everything, can we?" he smiled.

Lazar looked at the sheepish grin, the wide-spaced teeth. He appeared every bit a clown; yet he realized that this fat little man who once listened to his every word, who once licked his boots and took every piece of *gavno*—"shit"—he dished out, was now sitting at this same table with him—almost an equal. The face had not changed in all these years. It was still ugly, and the wart on his nose seemed to be larger.

It was clear where things were heading, and they were changing dramatically now. Were they going to deemphasize completely what was already in place, to obliterate the past, to wean the Russian people onto a new life-style, a new way of thinking, a new way of reacting and behaving?

Lazar was reluctant about deviating too much from Stalin's policies. He felt he understood the Russian mentality better than any of the others. If he was arrogant, then so be it, he thought.

"Russians have always lived under one rule, a strong figure in front. They cannot function without this. They must have meets and bounds. They will be lost if you give them too much freedom. They must be given their limitations. Even Lenin said this."

His efforts were to no avail. Malenkov and Beria were both adamant. They wanted to dissociate themselves from the Stalin reign of terror. They believed the people had had enough of living in a nightmare. Khrushchev also wanted a de-Stalinization program, and he was ready even to vilify Stalin to get it. Molotov tended to side with Lazar but was not as stubborn in holding firm. Self-preservation was still the most important line. He was ready to make concessions if need be.

As a result, *Pravda*, which had reported tirelessly on Stalin's death and the funeral, began to tone down its mention of the past leader. In fact, the name Stalin was becoming harder and harder to find in the paper. Finally, on March 22, the name was no longer seen. On April 7, less than a month after Stalin had been laid to rest, *Pravda* spoke about the "Soviet Constitution," not the previously known and titled "Stalinist Constitution."

Other changes took place. Articles against Jews ceased as did the infamous doctors plot. *Pravda* now said that the so-called conspiracy of the men in white never existed and that the doctors "implicated were therefore completely innocent of these unfound charges." One did not have to mention Stalin directly to slap him.

But the greatest emotional conflict among the hierarchy took place toward the end of March. Malenkov proposed to the Politburo that amnesty be given to those in prison.

"Most are there illegally. They must be released and put back into the labor force where they are desperately needed. Comrades, we cannot afford to keep good workers in prison on charges that may be unreal."

It was almost blasphemy, and Lazar was stunned at what was being proposed. Who was behind this? He had put most of those people there. What would happen if they were released?

He and Molotov argued strenuously against the enactment of such a proposal, but they were outnumbered. Malenkov, Khrushchev, Mikoyan, and Beria were all for it. Beria smirked as the vote was taken. He knew that such an action could only be to his benefit. After all, Kaganovich and Molotov had signed most of the decrees. He had kept his name off the papers, although everyone in the ruling body knew his hands were as stained as the others.

A proclamation was issued:

As a result of the consolidation of the Soviet regime and the rise in the level of prosperity and culture among the population, together with the rise in the level of consciousness of the citizens and their honest attitude toward the execution of their social duties, legality and the Socialist legal order have been strengthened and criminality has notably diminished in our country.

Under these conditions, the Presidium of the Supreme Soviet of the USSR believes it is no longer indispensable to continue to confine in the places where they have been kept persons guilty of crimes that do not represent a great danger to the state.

Lazar was aghast. The beneficiaries of the amnesty would be common criminals as well. They would now be freed in numbers that would be mind-boggling. Lazar could see what would happen. Riots, murders, rapes would fill the country as these prisoners were dumped back into the mainstream of Russian life. This never would have happened in Joseph Vissarionovich's time, he thought to himself. Never!

"The government is trying to be human," he told Molotov, "to swing away from proper control. The Russians cannot handle this. It is impossible. And then, what will happen when they start talking? They should swallow their tongues. *Proglotit' yazyk.*"

But Lazar could not stop it. The rehabilitation of the victims of the purges had begun, and those returning from the prison camps told of the crimes perpetrated on them by Lazar. His name was constantly surfacing. It was wrenching. For decades he had been supreme in his position, unquestioned and unchallenged. Although he was considered a leading Stalinist, Stalin's heirs in the Politburo now began to edge away from him. They did not want to defend and preserve Stalin's myth, at least not in its entirety. Lazar considered making some concessions as long as the Stalinist dictatorship, minus the bloody purges, remained intact. This would be difficult, if not impossible, to do.

These changes were disquieting to him. There were too many, too fast. When he was younger, he had been able to cope with them better. But now he was sixty years of age, and he found himself off-balance, perplexed, and lost, wandering around inside himself. He would still try to keep within the struggle. He would not give up. What he wanted was still attainable. The wolf may be older and slower, he said to himself, but it has become wiser, and it still has teeth.

The one person who unnerved him more than any other was Beria. "The man is insane," he said to Bulganin. "He is basically wicked, the reincarnation of the devil—a *dybbuk.*"

Lazar was especially repulsed by the man's perverse behavior. He knew of his penchant for young girls, but now he had drifted into relationships with ten-year-old boys. It sickened Lazar. Children were off-limits. No Russian could tolerate cruelty or abuse to a child, not even Stalin.

He heard many a tale about a young boy being disfigured because of his refusal to accommodate Beria. One rumor circulated that Lavrenti even had a retarded twelve-year-old castrated so as to "prevent further propagation of this disgusting aberration."

There was only one thing to do. He backed Khrushchev and Malenkov in their plan to eliminate Beria. Things were moving swiftly, and alliances, even those of a temporary nature, were being struck at every turn.

Although Georgi and Lavrenti were friends and each supported the other, it was also clear that Beria was looking for a way to take over the country. He could never have wrested control from Stalin, and he certainly knew he was no match for Lazar when Stalin was standing behind him. But now, with one buried and the other neutralized somewhat by the new policies, especially the amnesty, he would make his play. He had already taken the position of minister of the interior, and coupled with the state security ministry, which was under his wing, he felt it would be relatively easy to turn on his "friend" and grab the wheel of command. He had one fifth of it at present, but that was far from what he really wanted.

The catalyst to the plot to derail Beria was East Berlin. It was also the new collective leadership's first foreign challenge. There was a workers' uprising in the East German capital. The Soviet Union had to be protected at all costs. Another workers' uprising had been seen in 1917, and its effects were now well learned history. No one in the Politburo hesitated in what had to be done. The revolt was quashed with the help of Soviet tanks and troops. A new liberal stance could just go so far. There was no way they would permit foreign, or unfriendly, elements on their frontiers or in the newly established buffer zones.

Beria, to everyone else's delight, was outspoken against the handling of the matter. He roared at the Politburo that the East German government should be sacrificed.

"They are too great a liability."

It was also clear that no matter which way the government moved, Beria would be lying in wait to snipe at every direction. He was obviously going out on his own and threatening Malenkov's own position.

"He is developing a power base," Khrushchev said facetiously. Lazar stared at him. And you're not, you fat *huyisos*—'cocksucker,' he thought to himself. *Ni kruti mne yaitsa*—'don't try to bullshit me.' "

But they were able to reach agreement, at least on Beria. He could not be allowed to succeed. If he did, the results would be ten times worse than under Stalin; besides, each would be guaranteed his own death.

Malenkov, Molotov, Voroshilov, Khrushchev, Bulganin, and Lazar raised their right hands in a secret meeting while Beria was in Leningrad. Only Mikoyan remained with both hands on the table. He would watch and wait. But his reticence to condemn would have its effects later. He would rise just so far, and no more. They would not forget or forgive.

In the middle of June, Lavrenti Pavlovich Beria was arrested and charged with criminal activities against the people of the USSR. Crimes upon crimes were recounted by each of the members of the ruling body but particularly by Khrushchev, who had dug up a mass of information. Lazar was amazed at Nikita's resourcefulness, but he was also wary of it. It could be used for other people as well, he thought.

The charges were levied at a closed hearing before the Supreme Court of the USSR. The five-member panel of judges knew what had to be done. There were still some procedures that would remain part of the country's heritage, with or without Stalin.

When the trial ended, Beria was taken in chains to the basement of the building at 22 Lubyanka Street. Lazar watched him exit. He was stone-faced, his complexion pale, the small wireless glasses perched on the bridge of his nose. He said nothing but stared straight ahead. There was nothing anyone could do. They would all meet the same fate if they sided with him, as did Abakumov, the former minister of state security.

Beria was taken to a cell in the basement followed by the marshals and generals of the military he supposedly controlled, and he was executed.

The children of Russia were now safe. And Stalin's tactics were not completely dead.

Malenkov felt free. They all did. Big Georgi opened more negotiations with the West. This was better, he felt, than uncontrolled competition. Even an armistice in Korea was signed that July. The Politburo could find no fault with this.

But Malenkov was in a no-win situation. Either way, he would eventually lose. With Beria alive, Malenkov had a strong supporter but one who was slowly and surely bent on replacing him. With Beria now out of the way, Malenkov found his star fading. He didn't realize how weak his grip was on the reins of leadership. He was not strong enough to go it alone. He still faced the likes of Molotov, Khrushchev, and Lazar, and they were a handful for any group of people, let alone just him.

As with Stalin and then with Beria, the wolves were closing in again. The chicken coop was open. By January 1955, Malenkov had been devoured. He was relieved of his duties.

And then there were three!

Bulganin replaced Malenkov. It was as simple as that. Actually, Nikolai was the only Politburo member on whom Molotov, Khrushchev, and Lazar could agree. Nonetheless, his appointment would not be a "real" one. Bulganin would be the figurehead of the government, and that was all. He looked the part and played it to the hilt. The country would still be run by the triumvirate behind him. Nobody would be the wiser, nor could anyone even care.

However, Big Georgi was not one of them. Although he remained on the Politburo, he was given little to do. He would simply watch as the new battle lines were drawn. It didn't take very long for that to happen.

On one side was Khrushchev, representing a middle-of-the-road *apparatchiki* faction that was against any continuation of Stalinist policies. The group even resisted an anti-Stalinization program, fearing that party dictatorship and control would suffer. Lazar had originally sided with Molotov, who wanted Stalinist policies to continue, but he quickly saw that he would be caught in a vice that would destroy him if he did not adjust accordingly.

He proposed that the de-Stalinization program should cease. At a Politburo meeting he rose to make the following statement:

"I have in view a boldness which has to do with ideas that are principally theoretical, raising once more the question of the struggle against the cult of personalities. This is not an easy question, but the Central Committee gives a correct Marxist-Leninist answer to it."

The others around the table looked at him, perplexed. Based on what they had heard, apparently Lazar thought the problems were already solved and that there was no need to discuss them anymore. According to Lazar, all discussions should be "principally theoretical," that is, not concrete, not personal, and they should never raise the issue of responsibility or guilt.

Lazar was hoping to stop the most detailed personal attacks on Stalin. At the same time, he even tried to shift the focus to other areas, such as international. He told the Supreme Soviet that Communists would be victorious in their struggle with the free world because "all the advantages are on our side." But he never explained those advantages. It was obvious that he was unsure of them.

He didn't care. He had his own tactic, and it would be to show everyone what he was made of. He wouldn't cave in. He would even tour the country with Malenkov and Khrushchev, addressing conference after conference, speaking to transport workers, industrial workers, and agricultural workers. He would give them all a run for their money.

The problem was that others were beginning to question Lazar's faculties. The Politburo virtually buzzed with questions and comments:

"Is he all right?"

"What was he talking about?"

"He sounds like a mechanical parrot."

"Maybe it's menopause."

"It's senility."

Lazar heard what was being said about him. He had never dealt with this before. Was his age showing? Was his mind slipping? Was he now becoming a senile, old man who would soon no longer be able to curb his tongue, who would slur his speech, dribble his food, urinate without control, whose hands would shake with palsy, and whose memory would be almost nonexistent?

He had become the opposite of a man like Khrushchev who had enormous energy and who was getting things done like never before. Lazar and the others were vacillating, unable to decide the direction in which they would go, while Khrushchev was moving toward a dominant position in the party. On February 24 and 25, 1956, at the Twentieth Party Congress, he found it.

By the time the congress convened, Khrushchev had reached a commanding level. He had successfully maneuvered onto the last rung of the ladder. But he also knew he was being forced into a highly exposed position by his colleagues, who themselves were divided in their aims. Some were concerned that reminding the party Stalin was dead and his successors were firmly in control would smack of another dictatorship. Some reluctantly thought that by forcing Khrushchev to vilify Stalin, he actually might become the first victim of what they saw as a potential backlash against him. Khrushchev, who had opened the congress with his formal general report, felt it would be best not to denounce his late master. So he sat back and watched and waited.

But, things were going slowly, much too slowly for Nikita, and he saw time running out. The congress was wavering. It was turning away from him. He had no choice. He was determined to reverse the direction, and gain credit for the new course that up to now he had not embraced fully. He would have to gamble; it was the only way to drive the issue from the center.

Khrushchev knew that in order to make gains he would have to change his position and damn Stalin completely and unequivocally. He could not continue straddling the fence. He had to go one way or the other.

Lazar saw this coming. It reminded him much of his own past. Nikita, like him, would do what was necessary to advance his own cause, no matter what it was.

Lazar heard about Khrushchev's intentions to expose Stalin's crimes and protested vigorously. He knew that such an exposure would open him up as well, for his own activities would now come to light. The protest was unsuccessful. Khrushchev's speech was, on the surface, intended for the ears of the congress only. It was simplistically termed a "secret speech." It was anything but that. It quickly became public knowledge, as Khrushchev knew it would.

In the speech, he accused Lazar and his associates of trying to defend Stalin because they really agreed with Stalin's policies. In principle, Lazar realized that Khrushchev was not content with just personal attacks. It was something much deeper. There were elements of social democracy to it, what was termed a "typical reformist, right-wing program." Lazar saw where it would lead. More revolutionaries would now come to the front, each with his own set of social reforms that would eventually wreak havoc on the system, and the country. And Khrushchev was the first, for he directly attacked Stalin and everything for which he stood.

"Cut the dragon's head and all fire from the body will cease."

He charged Stalin with ordering the mass deportation of Soviet minorities (meaning Jews) and further accused him of collaborating with the Germans to accomplish this. He even said that he had grown "more capricious, more irritable, and infinitely more brutal" after the war. Stalin, said Khrushchev, was the real cause of all the problems from 1945 on, including the recent rebellion by Tito in Yugoslavia. "He was totally ignorant of the conditions in our country at large."

He claimed that Stalin believed himself to be "the greatest" of all Russian leaders, erecting statues of himself, naming cities, farms, rivers, and even awards for himself.

Of course, Khrushchev requested that his listeners keep this indictment of Stalin to themselves, but Lazar knew this was hardly realistic. He sat and fumed but was powerless to stop it. There would have to be another way.

The secret leaked out, as was intended, and it made an indelible impression on the world in general. A portion of his charges appeared in a June 1956 resolution of the Central Committee entitled "On Overcoming the Cult of the Individual and its Consequences."

Khrushchev's claims contained little that was new; however, just the fact that it came from one of Stalin's "closest comrades-in-arms" carried considerable weight. The indictment was also distortive in a number of other ways. For example, although Khrushchev attributed the purges to Stalin, it was Lenin who had really invented them. Stalin only made them bloodier.

"These traits," he told the congress, "originated in the Leninist organizational principles of the party, with the lack of respect for minority views within its membership and for majority opinion outside it." Khrushchev even ridiculed Stalin's belief in his infallibility but deftly did not mention that such a stance was an inherent part of the Soviet system.

Finally, Khrushchev deplored Stalin's self-glorification, yet he remained silent on the fact that it was he and his associates who developed the art of serving their master in the way they did.

"In essence, they glorified Stalin's name. They were part of the machinery that destroyed so many others in advancing their own fortunes."

Khrushchev's strange and terrible document, which was perhaps without equal in history fully confirmed the immortal truism that "power tends to corrupt and absolute power corrupts absolutely."

Of course, Khrushchev reasoned that if he didn't step forward and tell the congress of all these hateful and despicable things, it would eventually come back to haunt him. His decision was an easy one. He would turn against his own comrades for the sake of advancement, much as Lazar had done against his own people. His mentor had taught him well. Khrushchev had learned how to survive.

Lazar realized that there was nothing else to do but combat Nikita head on. He understood his onetime protégé had grown in power with good support behind him. Therefore, it would probably be best to gather as much backing from as many people as possible for his own cause, even if that meant sharing the seat of leadership. The alternative could be much worse.

Within hours following the close of the Twentieth Party Congress, Lazar met with Molotov. They discussed the options they had open to them. There were none. If they didn't stop Khrushchev now, there would be nothing left for them to do by the time the next congress rolled around. They had to oppose him. Very quickly, Malenkov became the third member and then, with the enrollment of Shepilov, they became informally known as "the Gang of Four."

"We have to band together," said Lazar, "to defeat an enemy that could prove more destructive to ourselves than even Stalin."

They agreed to muster everything they could find about Khrushchev, particularly a listing of all his mistakes in the management of the agriculture ministry in the Ukraine. Lazar was the best source for this because he had firsthand knowledge of what had transpired. After all, Stalin had removed Khrushchev and replaced him with Lazar. Khrushchev had not been able to get the job done.

Stalin claimed he was disorganized, was given little respect by those under him, and had "no brains."

In fact, if push became shove, Lazar could even bring up the fact that Stalin wanted to have Khrushchev "eliminated" because of his inadequacies as a manager. Perhaps he could even explain how, out of the goodness of his heart, he had saved him from a frightful purge. That would definitely show something, he thought. They could even explain how Khrushchev was shaky about all this information when he became first secretary in 1953 and actively tried to rid himself of Lazar. In effect, he was looking to destroy the evidence. There was no question that everyone on the Politburo would be interested in hearing that.

For the next year, the four worked diligently to mount a campaign against Khrushchev. They would have the majority votes. Molotov was sure of it. They had compiled a respectable file on every error Khrushchev had made in his management programs. They would rest their case on those files.

In June 1957, it all came to a head at a meeting of the Presidium, the body that handled legislation between sessions of the Supreme

293

Soviet. It was meeting twice a year then and had thirty-three members. The Politburo of the Central Committee sat on that Presidium. Khrushchev had called for the session to be held in one of the rooms of the Grand Kremlin Palace. The palace stood on top of the highest hill within the Kremlin. It had been built in 1874 and was originally the residence of the czars. Khrushchev thought it would be the perfect place to complete the final stage of his master plan.

In a small paneled room, the thirty-three members sat in upholstered chairs around a rectangular table and listened to what Khrushchev had to say. Lazar was armed with all the material gathered. It would be his last stab for the chair at the head of the table, and he decided to leave nothing unsaid.

Nikita, though, didn't waste any time, nor did he give Lazar the opportunity to present what he had brought. Instead, Khrushchev unveiled thirty-two letters written by Lazar to the NKVD demanding the arrest of many Soviet leaders.

"In fact," he said, "Lazar Moiseyevich Kaganovich here even ordered the arrest of ten executives in his own commissariat simply because their behavior seemed suspicious."

Lazar was stunned. Who had found those papers? They had long since been buried. He was sure of it.

"And here are documents," Khrushchev continued, "which prove that Lazar Moiseyevich Kaganovich, before the conclusion of various court cases, personally edited drafts of the verdicts and arbitrarily introduced any changes he felt like."

"An outrage!" Lazar shouted. "An outrage!"

Nikita turned and smiled. "The congress next year will also think so, too, I am sure."

"I have more documents," Nikita went on, "which prove that Kaganovich introduced any other changes he wanted. For example. that terrorist acts had been planned against his own person. In effect, he demanded arrests simply because he felt people were against him. And those arrests led to deaths. I repeat this."

Khrushchev would not let up. He even called upon Shelepin, his ally, for additional information. They would go over this before the entire congress if need be. Shelepin told the members of certain papers he had in his possession that showed that Molotov and Lazar together sanctioned the arrests and shootings of many prominent leaders, "some of whom were your friends." Shelepin held a paper in the air.

294

"When Yakir had written to Stalin protesting his innocence, Stalin had inscribed the letter, 'A scoundrel and a prostitute.' Voroshilov added, 'A completely precise description.' Molotov signed his name underneath, and Lazar Moiseyevich added, 'For this traitor, this *svoloch*—"bastard"—there is only one punishment—execution.' "

Lazar looked over at Voroshilov. Kliment's eyes dropped. Lazar knew immediately what would happen. Voroshilov had been supporting his position. Now he would go over to Khrushchev's side. That was apparent. And who else would do the same? He turned to Bulganin. Nikolai was fiddling with his pen, capping and uncapping it.

He heard Khrushchev's voice again. More stories were unfolding, one after another.

"Lazar Moiseyevich's cruelty is beyond any form of decency. As soon as he arrived in Ivanovo, he sent a telegram to Stalin: 'FIRST STUDY OF RECORDS SHOWS THAT OBKOM SECRETARY YEPANCHIKOV MUST BE ARRESTED AT ONCE. DIRECTOR OF OBKOM PROPAGANDA DEPARTMENT MIKHAILOV MUST ALSO BE ARRESTED.' Then a second telegram: 'STUDY OF SITUATION SHOWS THAT TROTSKYITE-WRECKING HAS ASSUMED BROAD DIMENSIONS HERE—IN INDUSTRY, AGRICULTURE, SUPPLY, HEALTH CARE, TRADE, EDUCATION, AND POLITICAL WORK. APPARATY OF OBLAST ORGANIZATIONS AND PARTY OBKOM EXCEPTIONALLY INFESTED.' "

Nikita turned to Lazar. There was fire in his eyes.

"Receiving Stalin's sanction, Lazar Moiseyevich decimated the Ivanovo Obkom. His information was all manufactured. And this doesn't even scratch the surface."

He raised a fist in the air.

"When Lazar Moiseyevich became commissar of the means of communication, railway officials began to suffer mass arrests. Comrade Shvernik's speech to the congress evidenced this. Lazar Moiseyevich personally made unfounded charges against innocent people and preached to party activists the omnipresence of disguised enemies, the necessity of intensifying work to unmask them.

"At a meeting of railway activists on March 10, 1937, he said, 'I cannot name a single line, a single road, where there is no Trotskyite-Japanese wrecking. What is more, there's not a single branch of railway transport where such wreckers have not turned up."

Lazar looked over at the stack of papers resting by Khrushchev's left hand. The pile seemed to be growing. He looked around the room at the other members. He thought he had come into the meeting with a clear majority to demote Khrushchev. Bulganin, Malenkov, Molotov, Separov, Probikin, Shepilov, and he held the balance. They could easily convince the others. The votes were levied against Nikita. There was no way out for him. Now what had happened? Khrushchev was still talking, and people were still listening and minute-by-minute, hour-by-hour, he felt something being drained from him. He felt his heart being lifted from his body and all his energies dissipating.

"Under Lazar Moiseyevich Kaganovich, railway officials were arrested according to lists, including all the deputy commissars, almost all the directors of roads, and the heads of the political sections. Lazar Moiseyevich, it is shown, was always ready to make groundless accusations."

His head was whirling. Had he, had they, all underestimated the fat little man? Had time passed them all by? He turned to Molotov. His face was a mask of stoicism. He was too intelligent not to realize what was happening in that room. His gaze fixed now at Malenkov. He was no longer Big Georgi. He had seemed to lose all his hugeness and was slumped in his seat as if he had been pricked by a pin, collapsing in a heap.

Bulganin sat passively. He had no comment. He never had.

He tried to search out his other "friends" in the room. Their eyes avoided his. They had once been all subject to his control, in awe of his power over them, subservient, obsequious in their behavior to him. Now they had clearly turned away from him. Their allegiance was elsewhere, and their actions were in helping their new leader by finding fault with the old one. They, too, knew the measure of survival.

"All power corrupts," he whispered to himself. His ears became almost immune to what they were hearing. The accusations took many different forms. He wasn't sure, but he thought he heard someone say, "It is a pity that such a talent at organization belongs to a man of whose moral qualities there can hardly be two opinions. One cannot rely on his word. He is as facile in making promises as in backing out."

Other comments circulated around the table, some overlapping others: "Lazar Moiseyevich would say, 'We've fought and made the revolution so that both the worker and the peasant would live better than before.' In actuality, he ridiculed party and Soviet workers who were afraid of their own shadows."

"Can we be satisfied with a subpar committee chairman who says that he executes the general line of the party as much as and as best as he can? He cannot commit the slightest shade of doubt, the slightest cleavage between the party and the Soviet organs."

"Lazar Moiseyevich did what had to be done to acquire and keep power and to exercise it in secret. And, like others, he convinced himself that it was all necessary for the good of the republic."

And then.

"Lazar Moiseyevich Kaganovich was responsible for the death of twenty million Russians."

He looked up at Khrushchev. It was incredible what had transpired. He had lifted this sad oaf out of the mud, nurtured him, protected him, taught him. And this is what he gets in return? Perhaps he taught him too much. Perhaps? No, it is true what is said, he thought. "Wash a pig as much as you like, it still goes right back to the mud."

Now a finger pointed at him.

"Your hands are stained with the blood of our party leaders and of innumerable innocent Bolsheviks."

Lazar exploded. He rose from his chair and pounded the table.

"So are yours, you *kurva*, you whore. You were right there with me. You carried out orders and you gave orders. *Pizda tebya rodila* —'you fucking bastard.' Yours are the blood-stained hands, too. Yours are."

Khrushchev half smiled. Another wolf was showing its teeth. He knew it was all over. He waited until Lazar had exhausted himself. The room became still. Lazar was breathing heavily now. He stood, shaking, his face beet red. Molotov tugged at his sleeve. He thought Lazar would have a heart attack if it continued this way. Finally, Lazar stopped. His chest was heaving. They all turned to Khrushchev.

"Yes, my hands are blood-stained too," he answered. "But it is not the same. I was merely carrying out your orders." He emphasized *your*.

"Need I remind you I wasn't in the Politburo then? I am not responsible for those decisions. But . . ."

He didn't bother to look at Lazar. Instead, he surveyed the room. It would be the final nail. And he would drive it home precisely and theatrically.

"But you are!"

* * *

297

For days, Lazar wandered about. To say he was uneasy would be an understatement. He expected guards to arrive at his office at any moment to cart him away in the same manner he remembered seeing others carted away during the 1930s. Khrushchev had hammered the anti-party group to smithereens. The remaining question was whether or not there would be a purge. If this were Stalin, the answer would be obvious. In fact, if this were just a few years earlier, Lazar knew that he would meet the same fate as Beria.

What could he do? He desperately needed someone to talk with, but there was nobody around. Molotov was incommunicado, Malenkov was destroyed emotionally (and physically), and Bulganin and Voroshilov now supported Khrushchev.

Not even Maria could help. She knew nothing. She never did. It was the way of Russia. Wives were not to be included in the machinations of government. They were to stay in the background; thus, they could offer no understanding, not even comfort.

This was something he would have to face alone. His mind recalled Mikhail and the incident in Mikoyan's office. Would he do the same thing? Could he do the same thing? There was only one avenue open.

Early the following morning, he sat in a hard-backed, wooden chair opposite the large desk in the large room on the third floor of the Kremlin. It was Stalin's old office, and his mind flashed back to the time when he first met the man he would eventually come close enough to call Koba. The office had been considerably more Spartan in those days. All it had were a few pieces of furniture, all wood, and a battered beige rug. Now it had a bright-colored Oriental rug in the center, a dark-green leather couch along the far wall, with two brown chairs flanking it, and a round coffee table in front to complete the arrangement. A vase filled with fresh summer flowers added lightness to the solid colors of the chairs.

Paintings were hung from the walls, many of meadows and trees. Gone were the portraits of dour army generals that Stalin liked. Only a black-and-white photograph of Lenin adorned the wall behind the desk.

It seemed strange to Lazar to be on this side. Khrushchev seemed perfectly relaxed. He leaned back in his chair, his stubby fingers interlaced on his stomach. He was so different from Stalin, who liked to stand to survey everything in front of him and whose only appearance of relaxation was when he cupped the bowl of his pipe for warmth.

Lazar found the words difficult in coming. In essence, he was asking his former protégé not to kill him. No, not asking, pleading. It had come down to one simplistic term. They could call it a purge—the only word he knew—or elimination, but the result was the same. He swallowed hard as he called in the last IOU.

Khrushchev ignored the plea at first. He still had some unfinished business. He wanted Lazar to know how good he really was, how firmly he had control of the country.

"You are surprised, I am sure, as to my thoroughness?"

Lazar nodded.

"Then, as old friends, I must share this with you."

He motioned to the stacks of manila folders on his desk. There were four of them, each mound some two feet high. He had obviously retrieved them from the Kremlin vaults for this occasion.

"My work has been done for me by Pospelov, as you know."

Lazar knew quite well, for P. N. Pospelov was one of the party's chief ideologists. He had been editor of *Pravda* from 1940 to 1949 and director of the Marx-Engel-Stalin Institute from 1949 to 1952. He was an expert at digging up old bones. The evidence gathered by Pospelov had proven the most damaging.

Lazar nodded again.

"But, of course," said Khrushchev, "I was able to find information not only about what you did but how you thought. One must be completely sure as to such things. You know that. You were a good teacher. Even Uncle Levick and Morris would have been proud."

Lazar frowned. Khrushchev smiled the wolfish grin. He was more ugly than at any time Lazar could remember.

Nikita leaned back in his chair and tapped a forefinger on one of the folders.

"Oh, yes, Lazar Moiseyevich, we found out all we could about you, and your family. Pospelov did that. He was able to, and he wanted to."

He paused for dramatic effect.

"You see, Lazar Moiseyevich, Pospelov is a Jew—just like you."

Lazar saw the anti-Semitism rising to the surface. Khrushchev was enjoying this to the fullest.

"I had a Jew working against a Jew, just like you did."

He paused again.

"You see, also, Pospelov's real name is Fiegelson."

Lazar's eyes widened. Fiegelson? The same one who knew Uncle Levick in the Bronx, New York? The same one who knew Mikhail and Morris?

Nikita rose from his chair and came around the side of the desk so that he could look down on Lazar.

"I have not forgotten our past, but I have no intention of repeating its mistakes. Our country is tired of it. There will be no problem with you as long as your group does not continue to try and defeat me. It is a simple proposition. You have to understand me, and you have to agree with me."

Lazar looked up into Nikita's face. He saw that the executioner had taken off his black hood, and he would leave it uncovered provided there was compliance.

"You are now sixty-four, Lazar Moiseyevich. You have had a long and fruitful life. We can continue that if you wish."

He turned back to a paper on his desk.

"I have here the managership of the Urals Potash Works in Perm Oblast. I need not remind you that it is the largest of its kind in the Soviet Union. You will take that, no doubt, and be happy."

Lazar struggled out of his chair. Once on his feet, he pushed his shoulders back and stood erect. He stared back at Nikita. Then he turned slowly and headed for the door. He twisted the knob and opened it. He wanted to say something, but there were no words in his mouth. The outside guard snapped to attention. He saluted Lazar. Lazar knew it would be the last time he would see this office.

The trip to Kabany was one of silence. He had taken the Moscow express to Kiev. There, he transferred onto the smaller, local line that went to the sector where the town stood. It made six stops along the way before it reached the place of his birth.

He got off at the railway station which was now much larger, and looked at the name on the wooden plate swinging under the mail-sack pole. His name was clearly spelled out. People walking by pointed to him and whispered quietly. They knew who he was and what he meant. They would keep their distance. Too close an association could lead to problems with state security.

He began to walk along the main thoroughfare. He wanted to be alone, but the man behind him was still there. He had spotted him on the train to Kiev and watched as he transferred to this one. He knew exactly who he was and who sent him. It was no secret. In fact, he even nodded to him at one point. Khrushchev had taken pains to make sure that state security knew where Lazar was at all times. The man was young, perhaps no more than twenty-five. He had a massive build and wore a wide-brimmed hat. Lazar remembered when he, too, had been that age and had that stature. It reminded him of himself some forty years ago.

Lazar walked up one street and down another. Nothing was the same. There were even traffic lights. There were also all new buildings, quadruple the number when he was last here. Factories involved in manufacturing various armament parts seemed to occupy most of the town: a barrel factory on one street, trigger housings on another. What was once a sleepy village was now a vital area to the country and its defense. That part felt good. It was a place worthy of his name.

He headed up the hill toward the house where he was born, but there were no longer houses at the top. Instead, he saw one large building that had a small sign affixed to its side. It was a factory for making cinder blocks. A truck leaking oil stood in the very spot where Sasha had had her garden.

The building extended through the area where Uncle Levick had lived. He saw two men standing in what had once been Morris's bedroom reading papers. One smoked a cigarette and the other scratched his balls.

Uncle Levick, Morris. His mind drifted back to those days in Kabany when the most important activity was finding enough to eat, especially after the Cossacks rode through. He recalled, too, the dirt coffins that hid Sasha and Rosa, protecting them from what would have been instant rape or death.

He searched for the tree where he and Morris used to etch the figure of the czar and then throw stones at it to demolish the features. The area was now cleared of trees and occupied by another building: a small red brick one that was the regional headquarters of the Communist party. A portrait of Lenin hung from the facade where the tree had once stood. Lenin in place of the czar. But no one would dare to throw a stone now.

He could not help but think of Morris. For years, he had been meaning to write him. He knew where he was. State security had done the job he had asked of it. The report had come in years ago. They had tracked Morris to an area of Philadelphia. He was a tailor—a *schneider*—on a street appropriately called Taylor Street, eking out a living with his wife, Hannah. They had produced four children, one of whom had died. The three surviving ones had all married and had kids of their own. Morris was a grandfather. He wondered whether he would ever see the light of day with a grandchild; Maya was still unmarried.

Perhaps he should have written. Perhaps he should have contacted him. It wasn't too late. Now, more than ever. It is never too late. Oh, how he would like to talk to Morris now. He would speak with any of them if he could: Morris, Uncle Levick, Mikhail, Yuri, Rosa, Sasha . . . even Moisev.

He looked around at the buildings. The heavy-set youth leaned against one of them. There would be little to his report. He nodded to him.

"Come," Lazar said, loud enough for him to hear. "We return."

He walked back to the train station, the youth closer behind than before. He stood waiting for the train and watched the sign under the mail post swinging gently in the breeze. He knew it would soon be gone.

July 4, 1957, *The New York Times*:

LAZAR MOISEYEVICH KAGANOVICH DISMISSED
AS FIRST DEPUTY PREMIER

Lazar Moiseyevich Kaganovich is a man of driving force. Perhaps his drive and ability were the reasons that he was able to survive as the last Jew in the Soviet Union to wield any real power. Many of the leaders of the Soviet Union were his protégés including Nikita S. Khrushchev and Nikolai A. Bulganin themselves.

Mr. Kaganovich had been very close to Stalin. In the early 1930s when Stalin brought him to Moscow from the Ukraine, Mr. Kaganovich reached the height of his power. He was often ranked as number two to Stalin and was considered a possible successor to the dictator.

302

October 7, 1957, *The New York Times*:

The town of Kabany, once known as Kaganovich, is now officially known as Novokashirsk. Lazar Moiseyevich Kaganovich had eight towns and villages named in his honor. All have had their former names restored. The Kaganovich Subway is now known as the Lenin Subway.

Epilogue

It was now dark. I squinted and reached for the lamp on the end table. My head seemed like it had begun to separate from my shoulders and was floating away from my body. My eyes burned. I tried to focus. It was difficult, and I could feel a pain beginning at the temples.

In front of me were the remnants of what we had consumed over the past ten hours: There was the soft center of some black bread (we liked the crust), the dried-out end of a kielbasa, the skin of a sturgeon, crumbs from the raisin pound cake, and yellowed cups from the endless parade of *chai*. The tea was strong, and I could feel my bowels churning. I had not been to the bathroom since I came in, and I could now feel the rumblings and urgings.

I rose from my slumping position, and the bones in my neck cracked. I stretched my legs, and it felt as though the joints had solidified. I badly needed a warm shower to soften the muscles and to put my blood back into circulation.

The man opposite me didn't even blink. He continued rocking in his padded wicker chair which looked like it belonged on a front porch somewhere, perhaps in Indiana, and smiled at my discomfort.

"You're much too young," he said. "Strength will come with age."

305

"Sure." I shrugged. "You have room to talk. You're double my age. You're a spring chick at almost ninety, and I'm an old fart at forty-six, right?"

"Huh?" he frowned. Obviously, he did not understand my cynical colloquialisms.

I walked around the room, shaking the kinks out of my legs. I could now study the apartment for the first time. When I had originally arrived, I couldn't take my eyes off him. His appearance and his voice had me riveted. Who had time or even the inclination to scrutinize the surroundings?

And when he began talking, I had no choice but to listen carefully in order to remember everything he said. There was so much, too much. I would have to find other sources to corroborate. He would not permit notes to be taken, or even photographs. And, of course, no recording devices of any kind. In fact, he made sure I emptied my pockets before he would say anything. Perhaps he was looking for something more destructive than a tape recorder.

It seemed so silly and so strange. He knew why I was there. Did he think it was simply to make small talk about the family? He had to realize where the conversation was going. Yet, he continued talking as if he were unafraid. It was true what was said: The source of Russian logic is illogic.

"What happens now?" I asked.

"What happens? Nothing happens. Do you think I will telephone Andropov as soon as you leave?"

"I don't know."

"Then I do know. Of course not. It is not the KGB's business. But I will call Leonid. It is his business, and I am under an obligation to do so."

I froze. I could feel the blood being drained from my face. I probably turned white as a sheet. It had come down to this. All my efforts would result in my father and myself being carted off to Siberia, never to be heard from again. A number of people had warned us not to come here. We had ignored them. Instead, we had lied on our visa application by saying we had no relatives in the Soviet Union and that our name was Kahan with no connection whatsoever to any politico in Russia. Now we would be caught. How stupid could we be?

Lazar saw my eyes twitching. He smiled.

"No need to worry, my young friend. Leonid is also from the Ukraine and is one of my protégés. He will protect your interests."

"Sure, like Khrushchev protected yours?"

Lazar winced. It was so many years ago, but it was still a sensitive spot.

"I'm sorry," I said. "I didn't mean to—"

He waved a hand in the air.

"No, not to be sorry. It's my problem, not yours. It always was. At least, Nikita's dead, a good place for him to be. But me, I'm still alive—and kicking."

He lifted his heel slightly and then quickly changed the subject.

"Do you know I am the dominoes champion in this neighborhood? Perhaps in all of Moscow, eh? And do you see those electric lights in the yard outside?"

He pointed to the one window in the room. I glanced at it.

"I was able to get electric lights installed right down there so that I and other men of this area could play well into the night. This was just about a year ago I did this. Heh!"

He laughed heartily. "I still have my power, eh?"

I was wandering around the apartment now, my fingers gently gliding over the furniture. It was a small place, and I imagined that some of what he had had in his large apartment on the Kutuzovzky Prospekt was jammed into these two rooms. In fact, his wicker rocking chair obviously came from the dacha that was also no longer his.

I looked again at the photograph of the woman on the mantle. He understood and nodded his head. "Maria died many years ago. Cancer." He looked away from me.

"Morris is not here either," I said.

"I know."

"He died two years ago. I didn't know if you knew, or wanted to."

Lazar continued rocking, more quickly now.

"I did. I made a point of it."

"I am sorry you never got to talk since—"

"Is that what he said?" Lazar looked annoyed.

"No, not at all. I spoke to him at length over the years. We spoke a lot about you, and the family. He never mentioned whether or not he ever heard from you."

"He never approved of what I did, correct?" There was a hostile edge to his voice.

I paused to make sure I would say the right thing.

"Yes, that is correct. He never approved. 'A Jew doesn't turn against a Jew,' he said. 'We are landsmen; the Torah says it is so.' "

There was silence. Minutes ticked by. They seemed like hours.

"I have everything I need here," he said as he watched me settle back down again. "I am given one hundred and twenty rubles a month as a 'pension personale.' I have put enough aside anyway to live comfortably although one must continue to try and get things for free. Why? I enjoy *hondeling* with the grocer on the next street. Anything that causes confusion and problems, eh? Where do you think the term *red tape* comes from? I created it."

He laughed again, trying to show he had a sense of humor. I was beginning to doubt it. I could easily imagine him some fifty years ago. He must have been impossible. He must have been a horror. No wonder he stayed in power for as long as he did.

"Maria used to say to me, 'Lazar Moiseyevich, you make an opera out of everything.' Perhaps so. I like to make things difficult, eh?"

I noticed a photograph of Trotsky on the end table. Lazar saw me studying it.

"You know what Trotsky used to say, don't you? He said that life was beautiful. 'Let the future generations cleanse it of all evil, oppression, and violence, and enjoy it to the full.' "

"Do you think they are doing that?" I asked.

He shook his head. I leaned forward.

"Uncle Lazar, did you ever read Yevtushenko?"

The face was stoic.

"Read him. 'The younger generation does not have any sources for learning the tragic truth about Stalin's rule, because they can't read about it in books. The truth is replaced by silence, and silence is a lie.' "

"Then why don't you write something?" he said.

"How about you?" I asked.

"I can't write, but why should I? You can do it for me. I have fought long enough and hard enough. Besides, it will make no difference. You can't talk about things happening or ever will. They don't happen until they do. You have to wait for that. You can do nothing about it."

I chuckled.

"The future is his who knows how to wait, right?"

Lazar's face registered disgust. He rose from his chair and walked over to me. The steps were heavy, decisive.

"Are we to spend the rest of the time in cliches? You still don't understand, do you? There's no good answer to a stupid question. Let us discuss what is the essence. Look at from where you come. Materially, your country, the United States, remains far more advanced than we. You have a high standard of living, I admit that. We admit that. And, as the strongest economic power in the world, it is thus the foremost enemy of socialism. We consider that to be true. And it will always be true until your capitalism is destroyed and you and your people are brought into our socialist camp.''

I started to say something, but he put up a hand. His chest swelled. I could feel power oozing out of him. He looked down at me.

''History decrees this. You can do nothing about it. And remember, Lenin believed that it can best be achieved through whatever means are necessary to do so. *We* have those means.''

He looked at the book titles in his library.

''I have seen it written, by some in your America, that you people have still to understand the morality of socialist behavior. An example was drawn that you must think of humanity as one great body, but one that requires constant surgery. Need I remind you that surgery cannot be performed without cutting membranes, without destroying tissues, without the spilling of blood?

''Thus, we must destroy whatever is superfluous. These are unpleasant acts, granted, but we do not find any of this immoral. You see, all acts that further history and socialism are moral acts. It is so written.''

He turned from me and walked to the window. I rose from my chair and followed him.

''You believe that? You really believe it?''

Lazar Moiseyevich Kaganovich stood at the window. He saw the formation of the dominoes game. His partners were waiting for him. The electric lights had been turned on. He pointed outside.

''Here in Russia, my dear nephew, we all believe it. I assure you, we all believe it!''

Author's Note

I returned to the United States and began writing to Uncle Lazar. I wanted to continue the contact, a combination of using him for my own means and to continue the last strand of the Kaganovich line back to the old country.

A year later, I decided to return to the Soviet Union, and I spoke with the Soviet consulate in New York about arrangements for another visit. I especially wanted to go to Kiev and then to Kabany; of course, I wanted to spend more time with Uncle Lazar.

When responses to my letters from Uncle Lazar failed to come, I wrote to Leonid Brezhnev and asked him to intercede to find out what the difficulty was. I even contacted the Moscow bureau chief of *The New York Times* for information. Finally, Mr. Brezhnev stepped in, and arrangements for my return were made. I hadn't heard anything further from Uncle Lazar, but I found out he was still alive.

The trip was set: I would fly to Paris, where I would be picked up by Aeroflot, the Soviet airline, and escorted to Kiev. My travel agent, well experienced for over fifty years, issued the tickets. I completed a new visa application, and this time I told the truth about my identity. What choice was there?

311

Family and friends tried to dissuade me from going. They said I was looking for trouble and that I would be sucked in and then arrested. Articles in a number of newspapers had appeared about my identity and my relationship with Lazar Moiseyevich Kaganovich.

The logically minded people said that were I enticed back to the Soviet Union I would never be seen or heard from again. After all, I would be considered a "threat" to the interests of the Soviet Union.

I ignored all these pleas, as I am wont to do.

However, four days prior to my scheduled departure, I was advised that the plug had been pulled. I was listed as persona non grata.

I knew immediately what had happened. It took no genius to figure this out. The original approval for my return had come from Brezhnev. But now that order had been countermanded. It meant one thing. Brezhnev would either be ousted or dead within a few months. And it was also clear who would succeed him.

And that's precisely what happened. Communication between Moscow and me had been severed.

I hope somehow, somewhere, this can be reconnected. Uncle Lazar, as of this writing, is still alive and ninety-three years old. I would like to see him again.

Interviews

Ash, Ehiel (New York, Moscow Institute)
Bergman, Stanley (Yivo Institute, New York)
Dobroszycki, Lucjan (Yivo Institute, New York)
Kaganovich, Lazar Moiseyevich (Moscow)
Kaganovich, Morris Levick (New York, Philadelphia, Cape May)
Massell, Gregory (New York)
Polk, Grace D. (Washington, D.C., U.S. Department of State)
"Undisclosed," L. (Komitet Gosudarstvennoy Bezopasnosti, Leningrad)
"Undisclosed," L. (Komitet Gosudarstvennoy Bezopasnosti, Moscow)
Vishniac, Roman, M.D. (New York)
Weisner, Sara Kaganovich (Miramar, Florida)
Gerbi, Claudio, M.D. (Rome, New York)

Additional Information

Eydman, Galina I., Dr. (Plymouth Meeting, Pennsylvania)
Kaganov, Etta H. (New York)
Turnoff, Howard, M.D. (Miami, Florida)

Bibliography

Alliluyeva, Svetlana. *Only One Year*. New York: Harper, 1969.

Ausubel, Nathan. *Pictorial History Of the Jewish People*. New York: Crown, 1972.

Beria, Lavrenti. *Memorandum*. Moscow: 1953.

Biagi, Enzo. *Svetlana: An Intimate Portrait*. New York: Funk & Wagnall's, 1971.

Bialer, Seweryn. *Stalin and His Generals*. New York: Pegasus, 1969.

Bolshaya Sovetskaya Entsiklopediya. 1935 and 1953.

Bolsheviks of Ukraine. 1932. Moscow Library Archives.

Bortoli, Georges. *The Death of Stalin*. Paris: Praeger, 1973.

Broder, Gloria Kurian, and Broder, Bill. *Remember This Time*. New York: Newmarket, 1983.

Christian Science Monitor: "Soviet Memoranda," May 1982.

Clarkson, Jesse D. *A History of Russia*. New York: Random House, 1961.

Crankshaw, Edward. *Khrushchev: A Career*. New York: Viking, 1966.

Current Biography Yearbook. Moscow: 1955.

Fainsod, Merle. *How Russia Is Ruled*. Cambridge, Mass.: Harvard University Press, 1963.

BIBLIOGRAPHY

Fisher, John. *Why They Behave Like Russians*. New York: Harper, 1946.

Frankland, Mark. *Khrushchev*. New York: Stein & Day, 1967.

Gilbert, Martin. *Atlas of Russian History*. London: Dorset, 1972.

Goldston, Robert. *The Russian Revolution*. New York: Bobbs-Merrill, 1977.

Gregory, James S. *Russian Land, Soviet People*. New York: Pegasus, 1968.

Hingley, Ronald. *Joseph Stalin: Man and Legend*. New York: McGraw-Hill, 1974.

Hirschfeld, Burt. *Khrushchev*. New York: Hawthorn, 1968.

Hutton, Bernard J. *Stalin: The Miraculous Georgian*. London: Spearman, 1961.

Izvestia: December 2, 1952.

Kaganovich, Lazar M. *Istoria Metro*. Moscow: Moscow Press, 1935.

———. *Stalin Leads Us to Victory*. Moscow: Moscow Press, 1946.

Kaiser, Robert G. *Russia: The People and the Power*. New York: Atheneum, 1976.

Khrushchev, Nikita. *Secret Report to the Twentieth Party Congress*. Moscow: 1957.

Kochan, Lionel. *Jews in Soviet Russia*. London: Oxford University Press, 1978.

Kopelev, Lev. *The Education of a True Believer*. New York: Harper & Row, 1981.

Lauterbach, Richard E. *These Are The Russians*. New York: Harper, 1944.

Life magazine: January 1, 1945; June 3, 1946; August 9, 1948; May 15, 1950.

Louis, Victor, and Louis, Jennifer. *The Complete Guide to the Soviet Union*. New York: St. Martin's, 1977.

Masaryk, Thomas. *The Spirit of Russia*. Moscow: Novosti Press, 1955.

Medvedev, Roy A. *On Stalin and Stalinism*. London: Oxford University Press, 1979.

———, and Zhores A. *Khrushchev: The Years in Power*. New York: Columbia University Press, 1976.

Millar, James R. *The Soviet Rural Community*. Champaign, Ill.: University of Illinois Press, 1971.

Miller, Francis Trevelyan. *History of World War II*. London: Universal, 1945.

Nerhood, Harry W. *To Russia and Return*. Columbus, Ohio: Ohio State University Press, 1969.

Paloczi-Horvath, George. *Khrushchev: The Making of a Dictator*. Boston: Little, Brown, 1960.

Pistrak, Lazar. *The Grand Tactician*. New York: Praeger, 1961.

Pravda: February 7, 1952; July 14, 1952; October 8, 1952; December 1, 1952; March 5, 1953; April 9, 1953; April 16, 1953; July 10, 1953; December 30, 1980.

Reed, John. *Ten Days That Shook the World*. New York: Random House, 1960.

Salisbury, Charlotte Y. *Russian Diary*. New York: Walker, 1974.

Salisbury, Harrison E. *A Journey for Our Times*. New York: Harper & Row, 1983.

Shipler, David K. *Russia: Broken Idols, Solemn Dreams*. New York: Times Books, 1983.

Simmonds, George W. *Soviet Leaders*. New York: Crowell, 1967.

Smith, Hedrick. *The Russians*. New York: Quadrangle, 1976.

Smolensk Archives (USSR), May 6, 1933.

Souvarine, Boris. *Stalin*. New York: Octagon, 1972.

Soviet Life Magazine: December 1982; April 1983.

Taaffe, Robert N. *An Atlas of Soviet Affairs*. New York: Praeger, 1982.

Talbott, Strove. *Khrushchev Remembers*. Boston: Little, Brown, 1974.

Tucker, Robert C. *Stalin as Revolutionary*. New York: W. W. Norton, 1973.

Vitukhin, Igor. *Soviet Generals Recall World War II*. Moscow: Sphinx Press, 1981.

Warth, Robert D. *Joseph Stalin*. New York: Twayne, 1969.

"World Epochs." U.S. Flag Association: Washington, D.C., 1936.

Zhukov, Georgi. *Reminiscences and Reflections*. Moscow: Novosti Press, 1969.

STUART KAHAN
20 WATERSIDE PLAZA/8H
NEW YORK, N. Y. 10010
—
(212) 689-3021

ПРЕДСЕДАТЕЛЮ ПРЕЗИДИУМА ВЕРХОВНОГО СОВЕТА СССР
ГЕНЕРАЛЬНОМУ СЕКРЕТАРЮ ЦК КПСС
ЛЕОНИДУ ИЛЬИЧУ БРЕЖНЕВУ

Многоуважаемый Господин Президент!

В ответ на мои письма и телеграммы я получил от Посольства СССР в Вашингтоне любезное приглашение приехать в СССР

Посольство СССР в Вашингтоне направило меня в Интурист, где я встретил полное понимание и содействие. В настоящее время мой агент предпринимает необходимые усилия для организации моего вылета в начале второй недели октября с.г.

Как я уже сообщал, я намерен провести несколько дней в Киеве и посетить место рождения моих родителей - село Кабаны. Затем я проведу примерно четыре дня в Москве с тем, чтобы повидать моего дядю Лазаря Моисеевича Кагановича и преподнести ему подарки от наших родственников живущих в США.

Я очень надеюсь, что получу возможность повидать Вас лично и поздравить вас - с опережением на два месяца - с днем рождения.

Примите, Господин Президент, мои самые наилучшие пожелания.

Искренне уважающий Вас

Стюарт Каган   (Каганович)

03 сентября 1982 года.

This is a copy of my letter to Leonid Brezhnev regarding my return to the Soviet Union. Brezhnev and Lazar were good friends.

TRANSLATION

Mr. Leonid Il'ich Brezhnev
Chairman, Presidium, USSR Supreme Soviet
Central Committee of the Communist Party
Staraya Place, 4
Moscow, USSR

My dear Mr. Chairman:

Further to my letters and cables, I have now received advice
from the Embassy for my return to the Soviet Union. I have
been referred to Intourist here in New York by Mr. Dobrynin's
office in Washington, and I am most pleased with the courtesy
and cooperation I have received.

I am now having my travel agent make the appropriate arrangements to commence the second week in October. My intention
is, as previously advised, to spend a few days in Kiev with
a side trip to see the family birthplace at Kabany. Then, I
will spend approximately four days in Moscow to see Uncle
Lazar and to bring with me birthday presents from the family
here.

I do hope it will also be possible to see you and to wish
you a happy birthday, although it will be two months in advance.

My customary good wishes to you.

Sincerely,

Stuart Kahan (Kaganovich)

*This is a translation of my letter to Brezhnev regarding my return to
the Soviet Union.*

Humbert Travel Agency, Inc.
400 Madison Avenue
New York, New York 10017

Tel: (212) 688-3700

September 30, 1982

Mr. Stuart Kahan
20 Waterside Plaza
New York, New York 10010

Dear Stuart;

I have been advised by General Tours, an official Intourist Agency, that your visa application for your trip to Russia has been denied.

Mr. Bill Porter from General Tours stated that the Russian Government does not give reasons but merely a yea or nay.

I am truly sorry that your arrangements have to be aborted.

Yours truly,

Ilene Levine

50 years of experience and service

This is a copy of the letter I received from the travel agency advising me that my visa had been denied just three days prior to my depar-ture. I knew then that Brezhnev was on his way out and that Andropov would come into power because only the KGB had the power to deny visas.

STUART KAHAN
20 WATERSIDE PLAZA/8H
NEW YORK, N. Y. 10010
—
(212) 689-3021

October 4, 1982

Mr. N. Antipov
Consular General
Embassy of the USSR
1706 18th Street, NW
Washington, D.C. 20009

Dear Mr. Antipov:

You will recall that you telephoned me a few months ago regarding my forthcoming visit to the Soviet Union and assured
me that there was no problem with a visa clearance. Accordingly, I made arrangements for such a return scheduled to
commence this Friday, October 8th.

I have just received word from the booking agent that my visa
has been turned down. Apparently, I am "persona non grata."

I cannot understand this complete turnaround. Although born
in the United States, I am Russian in heritage and have been
deeply interested in knowing more about the country of my an-
cestors, many of whom, as you well know, have been prominent
in the Great Revolution and thereafter. My visit last year
was simply an appetizer and I was genuinely looking forward
to many visits to the Soviet Union.

I would appreciate your channeling this letter to the proper
parties and advising me as to why I should now be placed in
such a negative category.

Thank you for your courtesy and cooperation.

Sincerely,

Stuart Kahan

/s

*A copy of my letter to the Soviet embassy complaining about the visa
matter. I am still listed as* persona non grata.

Index